TRAVELER'S

MALAYSIA & SINGAPORE COMPANION

The 1998–1999 Traveler's Companions

ARGENTINA • AUSTRALIA • BALI • CALIFORNIA • CANADA • CHINA • COSTA RICA • CUBA • EASTERN CANADA • ECUADOR • FLORIDA • HAWAII • HONG KONG • INDIA • INDONESIA • JAPAN • KENYA • MALAYSIA & SINGAPORE • MEDITERRANEAN FRANCE • MEXICO • NEPAL • NEW ENGLAND • NEW ZEALAND • PERU • PHILIPPINES • PORTUGAL • RUSSIA • SPAIN • THAILAND • TURKEY • VENEZUELA • VIETNAM, LAOS AND CAMBODIA • WESTERN CANADA

Traveler's MALAYSIA AND SINGAPORE Companion
First Published 1998

World Leisure Marketing Limited
9 Downing Road, West Meadows Industrial Estate
Derby, DE21 6HA, England
Web Site: http://www.map-world.co.uk
Published by arrangement with Kümmerly+Frey AG, Switzerland

ISBN: 1 84006 063 8

© 1998 Kümmerly+Frey AG, Switzerland

Created, edited and produced by
Allan Amsel Publishing, 53 rue Beaudouin
27700 Les Andelys, France. E-mail: aamsel@aol.com
Editor in Chief: Allan Amsel
Editor: Fiona Nichols
Original design concept: Hon Bing-wah
Picture editor and designer: David Henry

Printed by Samhwa Printing Company Limited, Seoul, Korea

TRAVELER'S
MALAYSIA
& SINGAPORE
COMPANION

by Sean Sheehan and Wendy Hutton
Photographed by Alain Evrard

Kümmerly+Frey

Contents

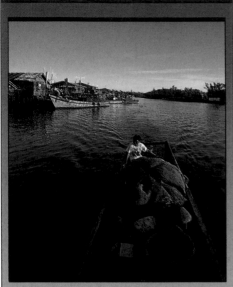

TOP SPOTS

Stay in a Longhouse

IF YOU'RE ACCUSTOMED TO CONDOMINIUM LIVING IN THE WEST, YOU'LL FIND THE TRADITIONAL BORNEO EQUIVALENT A REAL EYE-OPENER. Despite increasingly modern lifestyles, many Sarawakians still live in longhouses, which are practically a village under one roof. Each family has its own sleeping and cooking quarters adjoining a communal area where children play, dogs sleep or scuffle, old men mend fishing nets, and women weave mats, baskets or stunning *ikat* fabric at backstrap looms.

Visitors to Sarawak will find it easy to visit a longhouse, either through a tour operator or by striking out alone. Unlike neighboring Sabah where few navigable rivers exist and the remaining Rungus longhouses are located inland, Sarawak longhouses are almost invariably built along a river bank.

Don't go expecting skulls hanging in the rafters and men sitting around in loincloths. The people of Sarawak are very much part of the modern world and most of the longhouses have been modernized (I must confess that I find a cement-floored communal verandah a sad substitute for the old wooden planks raised high on stilts, old buildings where the breezes kept things cool and where one always had a view of the river). Large longhouse communities usually have a government-provided generator and, in others, many families run their own generator at nights for television. You may even see a washing machine not far from the traditional wood cooking fire.

Some tour operators have, at the request of the longhouse people themselves, built separate (and more comfortable) accommodation for visitors, complete with basic toilet facilities. This gives both parties more privacy and the welcome you are shown during your time in the longhouse is in no way diminished. If you go with a tour operator, you'll probably be given a special welcome ceremony and dances as well as dinner. Most longhouse people, particularly the fun-loving Iban, enjoy the chance to party on with guests, but will still be up at dawn to work in their rice fields or vegetable gardens.

OPPOSITE: Increasingly worldly, children in many longhouses now have radios and even televisions. ABOVE: A traditional Orang Asli longhouse, Sarawak.

Going with a tour operator usually enriches your experience, as you can ask questions more easily. (For some recommended tour operators and costs, see VISITING LONGHOUSES, page 180). Whether you go with a tour operator or decide to strike out on your own, always take some gifts for the headman's family: sarongs, cigarettes, comics and magazines in Bahasa Malaysia for the children, and a bottle of cheap whisky if it's not a "dry" community are all appreciated. If you're traveling independently, you should pay for your food — around $8 to $10 (RM20 to RM25) per day is the current standard. It's also a good idea to bring a few tins of meat or sardines, instant noodles, biscuits and fruit as a gift. Carry photos or postcards from home so the cultural exchange will be two way; the longhouse folk invariably want to know all about you, your family and country.

Alfresco Feasts

SOME OF THE GREATEST FEASTS IN THE EAST CAN BE ENJOYED AT THE OPEN-AIR FOOD STALLS FOUND ALL OVER MALAYSIA AND IN SINGAPORE. Some groups of food stalls are referred to as hawker centers, because they were set up to house many of the mobile hawkers who once carried their offerings along the streets, selling to householders who would come out with their own bowls for a helping of noodles or sticks of freshly grilled satay.

In Singapore, Kuala Lumpur and other big Malaysian towns, the same traditional favorites sold at open-air stalls can be found in more upmarket surroundings in air-conditioned food centers, tucked away inside glossy modern shopping complexes. But there's nothing like eating in the open-air at night at one of the thousands of food stalls which set up around sunset.

One of the most striking aspects of food stalls in both countries is the enormous variety, with several styles of Chinese cuisine, Indian food, Malay favorites and even local interpretations of Western fast food, all available in the one spot. You can eat your way around Asia, mix and match to suit your whim and, at the end of it all, have a fantastic ice-based dessert or a slice of succulent tropical fruit. And all this (provided you don't order beer, which costs more than the food) for as little as $2 to $3 per person.

The technique is to wander around to see what's on offer. Prices are normally clearly displayed and even though the name of the dish mightn't mean anything to you, if it looks good, order it. One tip is that if there's a line in front of a particular stall, the food is probably exceptional. It's best to select your table first so you can tell the stall holder where to bring the food when it is cooked. The normal practice is to pay for the food when it arrives. Hot and cold drinks are sold at a drinks stall (almost invariably run by Indian Muslims), and freshly squeezed juice is usually available from the fruit sellers.

One of the best places for stall food in all of Malaysia is **Penang's Gurney Drive**, where the stalls are set up under the casuarina trees along the waterfront just outside of Georgetown, on the road going towards the resorts of Batu Ferringhi. Open only at night, this

OPPOSITE TOP: The glories of a Malay buffet, Kuala Lumpur. OPPOSITE BOTTOM: Peranakan Place, Singapore, where open-air dining, music, and drink go hand in hand. ABOVE: The morning market or *pasar* is a colorful part of life in each village or town.

collection of stalls is particularly good for Penang specialties such as *rujak* and *laksa*. It has a big selection of Malay food, seafood and some of the best soya bean milk you'll find in the country.

A visit to Langkawi's cluster of stalls along the bay in front of the town of Kuah is as good for tuning in to the laid-back lifestyle of the locals as for sampling the simple Malay food; try the local *pasembor* salad, which has a sweetish dressing thickened with mashed sweet potato. The Medan Selera stalls on the town side of the bridge along the waterfront specialize in Thai-style food, including seafood.

At Johor Bahru's **Tepian Tebrau** food center, on Jalan Abu Bakar, the wafting sea breezes from the Straits of Johor accentuate the aromas of the food. These stalls are crowded with Singaporeans as well as locals; the most popular dishes include spicy marinated fish grilled in a banana leaf, a seafood fondue or steamboats, and the Indian *nasi biryani*, a spicy combination of rice with meat or chicken curry.

Across on the East Coast of the Malay peninsula, Kota Bharu offers some food you won't find elsewhere, including *ayam percik*, seasoned barbecued chicken, and *nasi kerabu*, a healthy mixture of rice with herbs, coconut and fish. These and other delights are to be found at night at the street stalls opposite the Central Market. Many of the most popular open-air food stalls in Kuala Lumpur have disappeared with modernization, including those all-time favorites that once clustered next to the Hilton.

Singapore most popular open-air stalls are favored by visitors as much for their convenient location (not more than one stop on the MRT from Orchard Road), as for their food. Newton Circus has a fantastic variety of Chinese, Indian Muslim and Malay dishes, fresh fruits and juices (you can sample durian in season), and (overpriced) seafood. Some personal favorites here include *or chien*, an omelet stuffed with tiny sweet oysters, Hokkien *popiah* (fresh spring roll), Singapore *laksa lemak* (a creamy, spicy

chicken noodle soup) and Hokkien *mee* (fried noodles). Basically, you can find just about anything you want, from Malay satay to Indian *murtabak*, Chinese fish ball soup to shaved ice topped off with sweet syrup, dried fruits, silver fungus and *ch'eng tng*, lotus nuts.

For other recommendations on where to find the other food stalls, check under the WHERE TO EAT section of each region.

Take a Trishaw

THE PERFECT WAY TO SEE THE SIGHTS WHILE RELAXING IN THE SHADE AND LETTING SOMEONE ELSE DO THE WORK IS TO TAKE A TRISHAW RIDE. The trishaw — a three-wheeled pedicab with a large umbrella or canopy shading the passenger — was once the main method of traveling short distances around Malaysian towns and the old suburbs of Singapore. Today, the ubiquitous motor car, diesel-belching taxis and public buses which crowd the cities and major towns, have made taking a trishaw unpleasant, if not downright dangerous, in the most areas. However, a perfect place to enjoy the delights of a trishaw is in Penang's Georgetown.

The streets of Georgetown are a fascinating mix of traditional Chinese shophouses, British colonial administration buildings and churches, Indian mosques and Hindu temples, Chinese temples and ornate clan association buildings. To see the constantly changing architectural delights of the town without wearing out your shoe leather and perspiring in the tropical sun, just hail the nearest trishaw. More likely, the driver will hail you, as they tend to wait outside the hotels in search of customers. Most drivers speak enough English to understand where you want to go and when you want to stop. Expect to pay around $8 (RM20) an hour and make it clear to the driver whenever you want to stop to take a photograph or to go inside a temple or mosque. Provided you don't pay the driver until your tour is over, you can be sure he'll still be waiting for you when you emerge.

If you set off early in the morning, you'll see plenty of trishaws around Lebuh Pasar and Lebuh Chulia. This is the time of day when groups of children are ferried off to school, housewives head back from the market with the trishaw laden with vegetables and fish, or small traders arrive at their stores with sheets of glass or cardboard cartons. Arm yourself with a map so you're familiar with the location of the main places of interest, but keep an eye open for the unexpected as you go from one important landmark to another. For example, as you're pedaled up Jalan Masjid Kapitan Kling, from the India mosque towards the lovely old Kuan Yin temple further up the same road, you'll pass a stall crowded with brilliant fresh flowers and perhaps catch sight of a garlanded Ganesh, the Hindu elephant god.

OPPOSITE: A fabulous eclectic mix of religious architecture can be found in Georgetown, Penang, including Wat Chayamangkalaram, a Thai temple. BELOW: All of Georgetown can be easily visited by trishaw.

The most interesting streets are between Lebuh Pantai on the east and Jalan Penang on the west, going from the cross street of Lebuh Melayu right up to Fort Cornwallis, and including the Clock Tower, the High Court, St. George's Church and the Museum towards the seafront. Don't forget to travel along Lebuh Leith, where you'll see the magnificent Cheong Fat Sze mansion, and to make a stop at the Khoo Kongsi clan house in Lebuh Cannon. You can probably rely on your trishaw driver to know all the sights. After all, judging by the average age of the drivers, they've been taking visitors there for many, many years.

Just a word about the way the trishaw drivers blithely ignore one-way signs and pull out in the face of traffic. There's no point in white knuckling it the whole time, or worrying about accidents. As the drivers will tell you, all Penang motorists are accustomed to their rather cavalier style of navigation and know from past experience to give all trishaws a wide berth. So just sit back and relax, and enjoy the passing parade of Georgetown.

Experience Thaipusam

THE AWESOME THAIPUSAM PROCESSION IS ONE OF THE MOST DRAMATIC FESTIVALS IN THE WORLD. Sometimes called a festival of penitence, **Thaipusam** is celebrated annually by southern Indian Hindus in both Malaysia and Singapore at the end of January or beginning of February. It is, however, not only an occasion for those who consider they have sinned to make atonement, but often a matter of devotees, who asked a favor from the gods in the past, keeping their part of the bargain by taking part in the Thaipusam procession.

Male devotees, who have fasted and abstained from sex for several days, pray themselves into a trance and have their bodies pierced with dozens of hooks, some holding dangling limes. Other hooks are attached to awesome metal chariots or *kavadi*, decorated with

peacock feathers, which the devotees support on their shoulders. Some devotees even place a massive long skewer right through their cheeks or pierce their tongues. The women and children taking part get off lightly in comparison, carrying pots filled with milk on their heads. The procession sounds gruesome (and is definitely not for the squeamish), but it is also a very moving demonstration of religious faith and the power of the mind over the body.

The **Batu Caves**, just outside Kuala Lumpur, attract around 100,000 pilgrims to the festival each year, the penitents climbing the steps up to the temple located within a 100-m (328-ft)-high cave.

Another place in Malaysia where Thaipusam is celebrated is in Penang, along the road leading up to the Botanic Gardens. In Singapore, the Thaipusam procession winds its way from the Veeramaknaliamman Temple in Serangoon Road to the Tank Road

OPPOSITE and ABOVE: Devotees at the Tamil festival of Thaipusam enter a trance-like state then pierce themselves with skewers and needles in preparation for the spectacular annual procession.

temple, friends and family accompanying the penitents chanting and singing all the way. In a heady blend of incense and the perfume of jasmine garlands, with the noise of drumming and chanting, coconuts are dashed to the ground to signify the accomplishment of vows.

Check with the local tourist board to see if Thaipusam will be celebrated during your visit: Kuala Lumpur ((03) 264-1149, 264-3929; Penang ((04) 262-0066; Singapore ((65) 736-6622, 334-1336.

Go on Safari

TO EXPERIENCE THE DELIGHTS OF GOING ON SAFARI WITHOUT HAVING TO MOUNT A MAJOR EXPEDITION, JUST VISIT SINGAPORE'S MOST POPULAR TOURIST ATTRACTION. You have far more chance of coming face-to-face with a rare Asian rhinoceros or of seeing fishing cats trying to scoop their evening meal out of a pond at the **Night Safari** ((65) 269-3411) than in any national park in Malaysia. Adjacent to the **Singapore Zoo**, the Night Safari (the only place of its

kind in the world) established itself as Singapore's number one tourist attraction within six months of opening. No matter how good a tropical zoo might be, animals are just as affected by the sweltering heat of day as humans. Once the sun sets, however, they come alive and you can view tigers, tiny mouse deer, Madagascan lemurs and the large-eyed slow loris as never before. Most of the animals are separated from visitors by natural barriers such as moats, vertical earth walls or special ramps set across the train tracks, enhancing the feeling of being in a totally wild environment.

Clever lighting at the Night Safari enables you to see the animals but does not disturb them, making it possible to watch them feeding, playing, prowling and even mating. To discover some of the 1,200 animals here, take the walking trails and also ride on the special tram which traverses a region where you can came face-to-face with the one-horned rhino or wild mountain goats. If you have time to visit only one spot in Singapore, this should be it.

For directions on how to get to the Night Safari, please refer to Singapore Zoological Gardens and Night Safari, Singapore (page 227).

Cultural Potpourri

MELAKA IS THE ORIGINAL HOME OF A DISTINCTIVE CULTURAL GROUP WHICH EMERGED IN THE STRAITS SETTLEMENTS OF PENANG, MELAKA AND SINGAPORE. Known as **Peranakan** or **Straits Chinese**, many of the Melaka Peranakans are the descendants of early Chinese traders who settled in Melaka and took local brides, mostly of Achinese or Buginese origin. The men were referred to as Babas and the women, Nyonyas (also spelled Nonya), and their culture evolved into a unique blend of Chinese and Malay. In Penang, some of the Chinese who took local brides had come from Burma or Thailand, adding another cultural element, while many Singapore Peranakan moved to the island from Melaka or Penang, or even came from Java.

Many of the Straits Chinese became very wealthy, and also adopted some of the fashions of the colonial British. Nyonya ladies seldom ventured outside their homes, where they were expected to master the household arts, including beadwork, embroidery and, above all, cuisine. The Nyonyas traditionally dressed in a batik sarong with a lacy embroidered *kebaya*, the fitted blouse held together with *kerongsang*, ornate gold pins, and their cuisine evolved into a similar fusion of Malay and Chinese elements.

Many of the wealthy Peranakan families of Melaka built two-story houses on the edge of what is now referred to as Chinatown, particularly along Jonkers Street (Jalan Hang Jebat) and Heeren Street (Jalan Tun Tan Cheng Lock). A slow stroll along these streets will reveal the incredible blend of architectural styles

Despite its highly urban profile, Singapore is actually a fine place to see Southeast Asian wildlife either in its excellent zoo OPPOSITE or ABOVE in the Jurong Bird Park.

typical of Peranakan homes — European tiles, carved Chinese wooden screens covered with gilding, European-style shutters and plaster embellishments. Recently, developers have been buying and restoring many of these magnificent houses, transforming them into antique shops, restaurants and small hotels.

One wealthy Chinese family has preserved its heritage in the most imaginative and generous way, creating the **Baba Nyonya Heritage Museum** ((06) 283-1273 which everyone interested in this unique culture should visit. For further details on location and opening hours, refer to WHAT TO SEE, Melaka, page 153.

You can experience the flavors of Peranakan cuisine in a number of restaurants in Melaka. **Jonkers** ((06) 283-5578 is the prettiest of all, and has one or two Nyonya favorites as well as a range of other local and Western dishes. The **Old China Café** ((06) 283-2180 has very good Nyonya cuisine, while the **Peranakan Town House** (283-5578, not only offers authentic food but serves it in typical surroundings, not "prettified" or "reinterpreted" Nyonya but a genuine, eclectic and slightly faded mixture of furnishings and decoration.

You may find the beautiful (but expensive) porcelain created especially for wealthy Straits Chinese families in some of Melaka's antique shops, with

the typical soft pink, pale greens and turquoise motifs which makes it instantly recognizable. Look also for finely beaded slippers and other Nyonya embroidery.

Time Out for Turtles

MARINE TURTLES HAVE LAID THEIR EGGS ALONG CERTAIN STRETCHES OF MALAYSIA'S BEACHES SINCE TIME IMMEMORIAL. By some mechanism which scientist still do not understand, female turtles always return to the beach where they themselves were hatched to lay their eggs. It takes about 20 years before a turtle matures sufficiently to start laying, and

obviously any interruption to their breeding cycle will have far-reaching consequences.

Turtle eggs (which are actually quite tasteless) are considered a delicacy by many locals, who wait for the turtles to lumber ashore during the laying season, dig a pit and deposit around one hundred eggs. The human predators then scoop up the unhatched eggs to eat or to sell. Noticing a decline in the number of nesting turtles, the Malaysian authorities reserved certain areas for conservation, including **Rantau Abang** near Kuala Dungun in Terengganu, and the **Turtle Islands Marine Park**, off Sandakan on Sabah's East Coast.

It is now illegal to gather the turtle eggs, and rangers collect the eggs and re-bury them in a protected area to allow them to hatch undisturbed. The tiny hatchlings are then returned to the sea, yet it is estimated that only three percent of these will survive long enough to eventually return to breed. Parts of Rantau Abang beach are closed to the public, and other areas open to visitors for a fee. Careful monitoring now prevents thoughtless individuals from attempting to ride the giant Leatherbacks, bans the playing transistor radios and the use of

Turtles are today protected in sanctuaries such as this LEFT on Redang island or around Sipadan, ABOVE, a world-class dive site off the coast of Borneo.

flashlights, all of which can disturb a turtle so that it will return to the sea without laying. The peak laying time in Rantau Abang is August, but turtles come ashore from May to September. Leatherback turtles are a highly endangered species which have only a few locations worldwide where they choose to lay their eggs.

If you are visiting Sabah you will have an opportunity to view Green turtles, which are more common there than the Leatherbacks; on rare occasions, you might even spot a Hawksbill. The Turtle Islands Marine Park, made up of three small islands and their surrounding waters, is visited every night of the year by turtles coming ashore to lay their eggs, so that you are virtually guaranteed a sighting. Park staff live on the islands and each night they are engaged in the task of tagging new arrivals, collecting their eggs and transplanting them to the protected hatcheries where they are safe from human and animal predators.

Visitors staying at the Sabah Park's accommodation on Pulau Selingan will be told when the turtles have arrived, and a warden will escort them to the beach to observe the egg-laying at close quarters. Before this, around the time of sunset, you can help the wardens collect the newborn turtles that are emerging in the hatchery. Often, some of them will find a way through the wire netting and you'll have to scamper off trying to catch them. When the buckets are full of hundreds of little turtles, you return to the beach where they are tumbled onto the sand. They then begin their mad headlong dash for the water, and watching them, you can only hope they will return in a couple of decades time to continue the cycle.

For further information on Rantau Abang, contact the **Visitors Centre** at ((09) 844-1533 while in Sabah, contact **Sabah Parks East Coast Division** ((089) 273-3454.

In northern Borneo there are some vast caves OPPOSITE in the Gunung Mulu National Park. Here visitors are dwarfed by the vastness of Fairy Cave.

Going Underground

SOME OF THE WORLD'S MOST IMPRESSIVE CAVES ARE FOUND WITHIN THE DENSE TROPICAL RAINFOREST OF SARAWAK'S GUNUNG MULU NATIONAL PARK. A total of four "show" caves are open to the public, with carefully constructed boardwalks and lighting which is switched on for a limited period of time to ensure minimal damage to the environment.

The **Deer Cave**, one of the most spectacular caves open to visitors, is easily accessible via a three kilometer boardwalk (just under two miles) raised above the forest floor. Although the walk itself is impressive, with peat swamp forest all around, the caves themselves leave the most lasting impression, and leave you searching for superlatives. The cavern of Deer Cave, for example, is so vast that it could hold London's St. Paul's Cathedral five times over. Wandering through the cave is an awe-inspiring experience; so, too, is watching the stream of bats funneling out of the cave mouth at dusk. For about 20 minutes the bats keep on coming, and as they pass overhead, you can hear the deafening wingbeats of hundreds of thousands of bats setting off for their nightly forage in the forest.

Not normally open to visitors, the **Sarawak Chamber** has earned a place in the *Guinness Book of Records* as the world's largest cave chamber. It's reckoned to be capable of holding 40 Boeing 747s or 16 football fields. Impressive, to say the least.

Clearwater Cave, which has a river running through it, is the longest cave in Southeast Asia, although most visitors explore only the entrance of its 75-km (47-mile) length. Adventure cavers, however, can pass underground from the Wind Cave to Clearwater Cave, traveling along and constantly crossing the surprisingly cold underground river for the final hour of the passage.

A number of other caves are open only to experienced cavers, but the average

visitor can view the beautiful **Lang Cave** with its stalagmites and stalactites, and **Wind Cave**, where a strong breeze can be felt at a strategic position.

For further information, contact a tour operator or the Sarawak Tourism Board Information Centre ((082) 410944; the National Parks and Wildlife Office in Kuching ((082) 442180, or the new Tourist Information Centre in Miri ((085) 434181.

Close Encounters

SABAH'S ORANGUTAN REHABILITATION CENTRE OFFERS A RARE CHANCE TO WITNESS CONSERVATION IN ACTION, AND TO COME FACE-TO-FACE WITH NATURE. Seeing animals in the wild is a totally different experience to observing them in a zoo, no matter how well maintained and designed that zoo might be. **Sepilok** is a sort of half-way house, a place where injured or captured adult **orangutan** are brought for treatment, and where baby orangutan are nurtured and taught how to fend for themselves until they are ready to be released into the surrounding rainforest.

Once the orangutan are deemed capable of surviving in the wild, they are released but, initially, they voluntarily return twice a day to feed on milk and bananas. Eventually, they decide that life in the wild is more appetizing than the repetitive diet at the center, and disappear into the surrounding forest sanctuary. It is a remarkable experience to watch these apes (especially the adorable babies) slowly grasping branches or lianas as they swing their way cautiously to the feeding platform. Independent adults will return only occasionally, generally feeding and departing in haste, while many of the females who once spent time at Sepilok return from the forest when they are about to give birth.

The orangutan, found only in Borneo and in Sumatra, is a large, gentle red ape, a solitary creature that has the distinctive habit of making a nest of branches high in a forest tree before it goes to sleep each

night. Endangered primarily because of loss to its habitat, the orangutan is being given a chance for survival in places like Sepilok, and every visitor to Sabah should take the opportunity of coming face-to-face with this magnificent orangutan, the "man of the forest", as its Malay name translates into English.

For further information on Sepilok, please refer to SEPILOK ORANG-UTAN REHABILITATION CENTRE, Sandakan, page 212.

Silk for a Sultan

EXQUISITE FABRIC THREADED WITH GOLD AND SILVER, ONCE WORN ONLY AT MALAY WEDDINGS AND ON OTHER SPECIAL CEREMONIAL OCCASIONS, IS STILL HANDWOVEN IN KELANTAN AND TERENGGANU. Regarded by many as the epitome of the weaver's art, shimmering lengths of silken *kain songket* are created at wooden looms in many simple villages and workshops along the northeast coast of Peninsular Malaysia. It is sometimes possible to see this craft demonstrated at cultural

displays, such as the Malaysia Fest in Kuala Lumpur each September, and at the **Handicraft Centre** in Langkawi, but if you're visiting the most traditional area of Peninsular Malaysia, it's an ideal opportunity to see *kain songket* being created on home ground.

The background fabric for the *kain*, usually made in a standard sarong length of two meters (a little over six feet), is silk, often in strong clear colors such as emerald, deep blue, cerise or maroon. This is fastened onto a simple frame with treadle-operated heddles for the threads which provide the pattern. Hand-thrown shuttles are used to create a floating weft of either gold or silver thread, shaped in traditional motifs such as chevrons, stars, lozenges and the triangular *tumpel*.

An experienced weaver can create a relatively simple length of *kain songket* in about one month. Naturally, the combination of silk thread and painstaking workmanship results in an expensive piece of fabric; it is not uncommon to pay $200 to $300 for a good example.

At **Chendering**, a village six kilometers (four miles) southeast of Kuala Terengganu, the **Malaysian Handicraft Centre** offers the opportunity of seeing *kain songket* being created, and of buying small items made of the fabric if the prospect of buying a whole length is daunting. You can also see items made of *kain songket* at Desa Craft, a handicraft center set up by the state government close to the jetty in Kuala Terengganu, and lengths of *kain songket* can also be found in the central market or Pasar Payang.

In Kelantan, about four kilometers (two and a half miles) outside Kota Bharu on the way to Pantai Cinta Berahi, a *songket* weaving factory be visited at **Kampung Penambang**.

Two sanctuaries for orangutan are open to visitors. OPPOSITE: An appealing young ape in Sarawak and ABOVE a feeding platform in Sabah.

YOUR CHOICE

The Great Outdoors

Malaysia's prime attraction for many visitors is its tropical rainforests, remarkable wildlife, glorious beaches, coral islands, caves and mountains. Being a highly urbanized island, Singapore is not worth considering in this area, the one exception being its appeal for bird watchers, who will find a surprising number of species in its different habitats.

Those used to temperate climates will find that hiking is a far more challenging sport in the humid tropics. There are, however, some cooler hilly regions (most notably Kinabalu Park in Sabah and the Bareo Highlands in northeastern Sarawak) where hiking is a pleasure

rather than a sweaty endurance test. Dedicated camping grounds are almost nonexistent, except in some of the national parks. However, there's nothing to stop you pitching your tent just about anywhere you choose. But be prepared for curious bystanders if you're in a remote area. I once pitched a tent on the banks of the Rejang river, in Sarawak, in the tiny outpost of Belaga during a festival, and the tent attracted far more attention than the wrestling matches between Penan newly emerged from the jungle, or the races held between war canoes manned by 50 Dyaks!

PENINSULA MALAYSIA

There is a total of 30 parks in all of Malaysia, the largest being **Taman Negara** (literally "National Park") which sprawls across three states roughly in the center of the Malay peninsula. Access to the park is by boat, and all transport within either on foot or by boat. It is possible to go jungle hiking, climbing, observe wildlife from a hide, rafting and camping, to explore a couple of modest caves and to fish within the park, which has a range of accommodation to suit all pockets. If you are visiting Peninsular Malaysia only and are interested in the natural environment, then this place is an absolute must.

Morning mists OPPOSITE lend an air of mystery to early morning departures in the Sarawak jungle. Sunset ABOVE over the South China Sea.

Two accommodation options are available with the Park, the more upmarket **Taman Negara Resort**, which can be booked at ((03) 245-5585 FAX (03) 261-0615 and the less pricey **Nusa Camp**, which is further upriver ((03) 262-7682 FAX (03) 262-7682. For further information on Taman Negara, see page 171.

SARAWAK

Gunung Mulu National Park, Sarawak's pride and joy, offers plenty of adventure options, including worldclass caving. If your idea of bliss is spending hours underground getting covered with mud and bat excrement, fumbling in the dark to re-light the carbide lamp in your helmet, flattening your body through a "squeeze" leading to another cave passage, and wading waist-deep in an icy river in the depths of a vast cavern, you'll adore adventure caving in Mulu.

Climbing to the dramatic kaarst formations known as the **Pinnacles**, on the side of Gunung Api, is an arduous but ultimately rewarding exercise which should be attempted only by the fit. Serious climbers could try the three-day hike to the summit of Gunung Mulu (2,326 m or 7,630 ft). For a good mixture of river travel, hiking along jungle trails and a night in an Iban longhouse, the so-called **Headhunter's Trail** in or out of Gunung Mulu is ideal (but best done through a tour operator). This begins (or ends) in the town of Limbang in northern Sarawak, where a half-hour bus ride to Medamit is followed by a longboat ride up the Medalam river to an Iban longhouse, Rumah Bala Lasong, where you spend the night. A second longboat ride up the Sungei Terikan takes you near the spot where head-hunting Kayan tribes had to haul their canoes through the forest for three kilometers. At Kuala Terikan, it's time to put on your hiking boots and start the four-hour trek into Gunung Mulu's Camp 5, where you spend the night. On the next day,

Pristine rainforest is still one of the greatest magnets for making a trip to Sabah or Sarawak.

there's an 11-km (seven-mile) trek into the Park Headquarters (and a very welcome shower).

To book accommodation and obtain permits, contact the Sarawak Tourism Board Information Centre next to the Sarawak Museum, or the information office in the Waterfront Park, Kuching. Alternatively, book at the National Parks and Wildlife Office in Kuching ((082) 442180 or Miri (for Niah and Gunung Mulu) ((085) 434184. For further information on Gunung Mulu National Park, see page 195.

SABAH

The highest mountain between the Himalayas and New Guinea is the centerpiece of Sabah's **Kinabalu Park**, and attracts thousands of climbers who scale the 4,101-m (13,455-ft) summit of Mount Kinabalu each year. No special expertise is needed, but you should be reasonably fit to attempt this two-day trip. Provided the weather is good, climbers enjoy stunning views as well as the changing vegetation and birdlife as they hike up to Panar Laban, just below the summit plateau. The weather can be bitterly cold from here on up to the summit. Experienced rock climbers who bring their own gear will find the dozen peaks of the summit plateau offer endless challenges.

Bookings for accommodation at Kinabalu Park should be made in advance at Sabah Parks ((088) 211881, Jalan Tun Fuad Stephens. Advance reservations are strongly recommended in February, April, July, August and December. Write to PO Box 10626, 88806 Kota Kinabalu, Sabah, Malaysia. For further information on Kinabalu Park, please refer to page 208.

One unusual aspect of **wildlife watching** can be enjoyed in a couple of locations, at Rantau Abang in Terengganu, Peninsular Malaysia, and the Turtle Islands Park off Sandakan on Sabah's East Coast. Giant marine turtles haul themselves ashore at night to dig a pit in the sand and lay around 100 eggs (see TOP SPOTS).

Sabah is the best place in Malaysia for seeing the often-elusive wildlife of the rainforest, including elephants, a range of monkeys, deer and many other mammals, and brilliantly-colored birds. The unique proboscis monkey is easily spotted along the banks of the Kinabatangan river and some of its tributaries, especially the Menanggol (refer to SUKAU, page 213). The Sepilok Orang-Utan Rehabilitation Centre (see CLOSE ENCOUNTERS, SABAH in TOP SPOTS, page 212), are justifiably famous and give visitors a chance to see conservation in action as these gentle apes are trained to return to the wild. The whole gamut of Borneo's wildlife exists within Sabah's huge Danum Valley Conservation Area, and serious naturalists should not miss spending a few days at the Borneo Rainforest Lodge within this area (see DANUM VALLEY, page 214). Plant lovers will find Sabah offers the chance to come face-to-face with some rare specimens, including the giant, foul-smelling Rafflesia (the world's biggest bloom), which can be seen in the Rafflesia Forest Reserve at Sinsuron (see page 207).

A host of carnivorous pitcher plants can also be seen in Sarawak's Bako National Park (see page 186) and Kinabalu Park's Mountain Garden (see page 208). The best place for hundreds of species of native orchid is the Agricultural Park at Tenom; some blooms typical of lower montane forest can also be seen at Kinabalu Park's Mountain Garden.

Sporting Spree

As you might expect in view of the glorious year-round summer temperatures, water sports of all kinds are very popular in both Malaysia and Singapore. **Water-skiing** is available at many resorts in Malaysia, particularly on Langkawi and Penang. In Singapore, the Ponggol Water Ski Centre ((65) 386-3891 rents ski boats and equipment. Resorts often rent out **windsurfers**, although the winds are often disappointing except during the northeast monsoon season.

SAILING

Sailing is generally available through the various sailing or yacht clubs in both countries, and resorts often rent out small sailing dinghies or Hobie cats. Once again, wait until the wind picks up (generally around mid-day between December and March) before you go to the trouble of hiring. In Singapore, try the Changi Sailing Club ((65) 545 2876 to see if someone is happy to have extra crew on board a private yacht. The Kinabalu Yacht Club in Kota Kinabalu welcomes visitors ((088) 253008.

The islands off Peninsular Malaysia's East Coast (particularly Pulau Tioman, Pulau Aur, Pulau Perhentian, Pulau Redang and Pulau Tenggol) are excellent for the increasingly popular sport of SCUBA **diving**, while the island of Sipadan, off the East Coast of Sabah, is

The carnivorous pitcher plant OPPOSITE is one of the more unusual plants in Sabah. Penang BELOW may offer some pristine forests, but it is the beach at Batu Ferringhi which seduces most visitors.

world renowned for its 600-m (2,000-ft) wall dive and amazing marine life. Some Malaysian resorts in areas worth diving have qualified divemasters and rental equipment. In Singapore, the **Great Blue Dive Shop** ((65) 467-0767 organizes dive trips to islands off Malaysia, as does **Asia Aquatic** ((65) 536-8116. Pulau Sipadan, off the southeast coast of Sabah, is one of the world's top dive spots; contact **Borneo Divers** ((088) 222226 FAX (088) 221550 for a complete dive package.

WHITE WATER

White-water rafting is available along some of the rivers in Peninsular Malaysia; contact **Asian Overland** ((03) 452-9100 FAX (03) 452-9800, or **Tracks**

Outdoor ((03) 777-8363 FAX (03) 777-8363. For more challenging rafting along the Padas River not far from Kota Kinabalu, Sabah; contact **Borneo Expeditions** ((088) 222948 FAX (088) 222720.

Jet skis (also known as water scooters) are very popular in some areas of Malaysia, although a great annoyance to others seeking a little tranquillity along the beaches or lakes. They can be hired from many resorts, some of which also offer **parasailing**.

GOLF

One of the most popular sports in the region is **golf**. Malaysia has over 170 courses throughout the country, with an average of five to six new courses being constructed annually. Because it is perceived locally as a prestige sport, the club houses at the various golf clubs are usually surprisingly opulent. There are golf courses in the highland areas (such as Genting Highlands, Fraser's Hill and Mount Kinabalu), on islands (Tioman, Langkawi and Redang) and just about everywhere in lowland areas. Many resorts have their own golf courses, or are located adjacent to a course. One of the premier clubs is Melaka's A'Famosa Golf Resort, near Alor Gajah just outside Melaka. Another often voted as the country's "most memorable golf course" is the Saujana Golf and Country Club.

Top hotels in Singapore will usually arrange for visitors to play golf at one of the prestigious clubs. One course open to the public, except for weekends, is the Sentosa Golf Club on Sentosa island ((65) 275 0022.

WHEELS

Most resort hotels have **tennis courts**, and some also offer **squash**. **Mountain biking** is gaining in popularity and bikes can be hired through some tour operators in Sabah such as **Borneo Endeavour** ((088) 249950 FAX (088) 249946, or **Borneo Expeditions** ((088) 222948 FAX (088) 222720, and in Sarawak, contact **Borneo Adventure** ((082) 410569 FAX (088) 422626.

Four-wheel drive safaris can be organized in Sabah, where the rugged terrain offers plenty of challenges. Contact **North Borneo Explorer** ((088) 436223 FAX (088) 435223.

The most popular spectator sport in both countries is undoubtedly soccer. Even more interesting for the visitor is the game of *sepak takraw*, played with a woven rattan ball which is kicked or butted with the head over a net. You may catch sight of a game being played in the local villages.

ROYAL SPORT

Polo is played in Singapore, Pekan (the royal town in Pahang state), Johore and Kuala Lumpur, except during the Muslim fasting month. The best place to be sure of catching a game is at the **Singapore Polo Club** ((65) 256-4530; matches are held late on Saturday and Sunday afternoons, with practice games on Tuesday and Thursday.

The Open Road

With a few exceptions, driving a car in Malaysia is not a relaxing experience.

Although the roads are generally in adequate condition and therefore technically safe, most Malaysian drivers are not and the accident rate, especially during peak holiday seasons, is horrific.

LANGKAWI

An ideal place to rent a car is **Langkawi**, where roads are new and in good shape, with tourist attractions well marked, and where the traffic is generally sparse. The one caveat is wandering water buffalo, especially at night. As Langkawi's manufactured attractions (like the Taman Legenda, Underwater World, Handicraft Centre and Galleri Perdana) tend to be spread about the island, a rented car is the most practical way of seeing these. You also get to enjoy the changing rural scenery and Malay villages on the way. The beaches along the west and north coasts are worth exploring, and the rainforest near Datai Bay is magnificent. On the East Coast of the island you can see the marble quarries, while in the south, the main town of Kuah is worth

Langkawi OPPOSITE TOP offers tourists not only beautiful scenery but excellent hotel facilities.Polo, ABOVE is still popular in Singapore and Malaysia but is losing ground to golf OPPOSITE BOTTOM.

visiting if you want to visit Taman Legenda or have a drink and a bite at Langkawi Yacht Club. A tour of Langkawi can easily be done in a day; most rental agencies deliver vehicles and rates start as low as $28 for 24 hours.

PENANG

While more congested than Langkawi, **Penang** is another good place to hire a car for a day or so. On the north of the island, the beach at Batu Ferringhi is lined with resorts. Driving west, you come to Teluk Bahang, which has one super-deluxe resort and an excellent seafood restaurant. Just south of Teluk Bahang, there's the Penang Butterfly Farm and the Pinang Cultural Centre. Close to the Butterfly Farm, the Recreational Forest (Rimba Rekreasi) has an interesting Forestry Museum and some good walking trails. Continuing south, the road climbs up through old rubber plantations and durian orchards. Just off the road at Titi Kerawang, you can cool off under the deliciously cool waterfall. The view from the road up here looks down over vast coconut plantations on the flat land below, and toward the mangrove swamps fringing

the west coast. The road continues through spice gardens, where nutmeg and clove plantations line the roads, and goes past the turnoff to Pantai Aceh (renowned for its pungent dried shrimp paste or *belacan*) to Balik Pulau, "durian capital" of Penang. To avoid the heavy traffic in the southeast corner of Penang island, drive east from Balik Pulau and then take Jalan Paya Terubong towards Air Hitam, with its famous Kek Lok Si temple and access to Penang Hill's funicular railway nearby. You can then return either to Georgetown or keep heading back up to Batu Ferringhi. Car hire is in the region of $40 to $45 a day.

MALAKA

To see some of the gorgeous traditional wooden Malay houses in Melaka state, and to catch a glimpse of a rural backwater on the west coast of the Malay peninsula, it's worth hiring a car in **Melaka** and taking the old coastal road via Muar down to Johor Bahru, or doing a circle via Air Hitam back to Melaka. It's surprising, given the recent spate of modernization around Melaka, how many beautiful old wooden houses remain in the *kampungs*. Take the Muar road south

through Kampung Umbai (where there are lots of delightful traditional houses) and head for Serkam. Continue on through Merlimau (23 km or 14 miles) from Melaka, where you will find the Penghulu's house, sometimes described as the prettiest traditional house in Malaysia. Built in 1894, the house has wonderful art nouveau tiles and carved wood panels.

There are dozens of lovely old houses and traditional mosques along the road as you continue heading south to Muar, a riverine town with a fine mosque and the handsome Sultan Abu Bakar building, constructed in the neoclassical style favored by the colonial British. The food at the stalls along the river here is worth sampling, especially the pungent salad, *rojak petis*, available at Tanjung Park towards the river mouth. Continuing south towards Batu Pahat, the road passes through countless orchards renowned for their rambutan, durian and *duku*. This region hasn't changed much in the past few decades, although there are motor cycles or even Protons (the national car) instead of old push bikes outside the wooden Malay houses and the few traditional Chinese homes. In recent years, the town of Batu Pahat has lost most

of its charm — and its racy night-time reputation for *kupuk kupuk malam*, literally butterflies of the night. The drive south along the coast towards Pontain crosses a flat plain with dozens of *parit*, small canals, where colorful boats often moor. At Pontian Kecil, you could enjoy the Malay food at the stalls along the coast, or keep heading south for another 19 km (12 miles) to the stilt village of Kukup, justifiably renowned for its seafood restaurants. From Kukup, back-track to Pontian then take the highway to Johor Bahru. Alternatively, forget Pontian and Kukup and instead head east from Batu Pahat through Air Hitam (known for its local potteries) and take the expressway back to Melaka. Car hire in Melaka is in the region of $45 per day; you could hire a chauffeur-driven limousine for not much more than that by contacting Raman at ((06) 232-1642.

SARAWAK
Across in Malaysian Borneo, the roads are seldom conducive to self-driving,

OPPOSITE: Tropical seas and balmy weather make Penang a year-round destination. ABOVE: Malaka still has some delightful, traditional wooden homes.

especially in Sarawak, where highways are replaced by navigable rivers through the jungle. However, you could hire a car in **Kuching** and head down through the old gold mining town of Bau, pausing before this at Siniawan Bazaar to see the cleaning of edible birds' nests carried out in the back of some of the marvelous old wooden shophouses. There are some pleasant caves worth exploring around Bau. The road heading northwest from here towards Sematan was once notorious, but has finally been sealed and one can do the trip from Kuching to just beyond Sematan, where the road ends, in not much more than two hours. But why rush? Admire the scenery en route and then pause for a *kopi* at the charming town of Lundu, where many old buildings remain and the atmosphere is pleasantly laid back. You could pause at Gunung Gading National Park nearby, where you may be lucky enough to see a Rafflesia in full bloom. There are lovely cool waterfalls here and you could even stop overnight in one of the park's chalets. Not far away is the pleasant beach of Pandan, where jelly fish are gathered for drying on the beaches in May and June. Sematan, 27 km (17 miles)

from Lundu, is a friendly little town where watching the action from the jetty near the river mouth is never dull. On the hills behind Sematan, at *Kampung* Pueh, is a 200 hectare mulberry plantation where silk worms chomp their way through tons of leaves to produce silken cocoons. You can learn a lot about sericulture by visiting this farm. Car hire in Kuching is in the region of $60 a day.

SABAH

One of the most interesting routes you could drive while in **Sabah** is to head north from Kota Kinabalu to the Kudat district. You could stop en route to Tuaran at the potteries lining the main road at Telipok. From Tuaran, head north across the bridge until you see the sign for the road which crosses the hills towards Kota Belud. Massive road works are in progress on the road crossing the Crocker Range south of Kota Belud, but the road should be in a better condition by 1998. Kota Belud is interesting primarily for its mixture of Bajau and Illanun Muslims and Kadazan/Dusun Christians, with fascinating faces and costumes to be seen here. If you're driving through on a Sunday, don't miss the big weekly market or *tamu*. The road then crosses the Tempasuk Plains, where — weather permitting — you'll get stunning views across endless paddy fields to the western flank of Mount Kinabalu. The swampy land on either side of this road is actually a bird sanctuary, and you will often spot interesting species here, especially during the northern winter. The road passes through forests of softwood trees and then, near Kota Marudu, endless oil palm plantations.

Take the road towards Kudat, and then follow the directions (see page 208) to reach the interesting Rungus longhouse at Kampung Bavanggazo. You could stay overnight here and the next day head further north to explore some of the beautiful beaches such as the one at Terongkongan, or further north, Pantai Kelambu. This gorgeous double bay is accessible by following Jalan Tamalang, to the left off the highway 14.5 km (nine miles) before Kudat, and taking to dirt road all the way to the coast. For a change of scenery coming back to Kota Kinabalu, take the Ranau Bypass Road at Kota Belud. This follows beautiful scenery along the river (it resembles New Zealand with paddy fields) and then climbs up the Crocker Range through some wonderful forest to eventually link up with the main road between Kinabalu Park and Kota Kinabalu. Take a right turn here and follow the road back to Kota Kinabalu.

Backpacking

Although camping grounds and youth hostels are not a feature of Malaysia — and certainly not in highly urbanized Singapore — it is still possible to travel relatively cheaply by using public transport and by staying in the many inexpensive hotels found throughout Malaysia. If you're on a budget, you won't want to spend much time in Singapore where everything from food to buses to "cheap" accommodation is considerably more expensive than the Malaysian equivalent.

Almost every town in Malaysia has its Chinese-run hotels, often above a shop in one of the busy streets of town, usually within walking distance of the bus station. These vary in price depending on the location and facilities, but you can usually get an air-conditioned room with attached bathroom, television and telephone for around $15 a night. In some popular tourist destinations, such as around Cherating and Marang on the East Coast of Peninsular Malaysia, and around Batu Ferringhi in Penang, there are a number of very cheap "homestays" where a bed, shared bathroom and all meals can cost as little as $8 a day. The Malaysian government is trying to encourage homestays as a way for local people to earn a little extra money, and although there has been talk of some listing system, at the moment it's just best to go to the area you want to stay and

start looking. It's also worthwhile picking up the brochure on Budget Accommodation from any Tourism Malaysia information center or at the airport on arrival.

National Parks in Peninsular Malaysia, Sabah and Sarawak have a variety of accommodation, including perfectly adequate hostels offering dormitories, a kitchen for self catering and a communal room, an excellent deal at around $4 per night. Some parks offer a student discount so be sure to have your student card with you.

Buses are an excellent and inexpensive way to travel in Peninsular Malaysia and Sabah; in Sarawak, express boats are sometimes the only option. Express buses are usually air-conditioned, reasonably comfortable and more than reasonably priced. It costs, for example, $2 to go from Kuala Lumpur to Melaka, and you can go all the way from Singapore up to Kota Bharu near the Thai border for only $18.

OPPOSITE: Into the heart of Borneo via the Rejang River. The proliferation of flora and fauna in Taman Negara ABOVE provides a chance to hike amid virgin rainforest habitat.

You can eat very well for amazingly low prices by frequenting food stalls or coffeeshops. Here a bowl of noodles or *nasi campur*, a mixture of spicy Malay meat and vegetable dishes plus rice, costs around $1.50. Unfortunately, due to exorbitant taxes, the local beer is expensive (at least $2 a small can) except in duty-free Langkawi.

Living It Up

Both Malaysia and Singapore offer an almost indecent number of luxurious hotels and sumptuous restaurants. As most of the top hotels have been built recently, they have the benefit of modern technology with the added advantage of staff with traditional attitudes towards service. Unlike many of Europe's top hotels, the finest establishments in the cities of Malaysia and Singapore include what would be considered resort facilities elsewhere, such as pools, fitness centers, saunas, tennis and squash courts. Despite their unashamed luxury, most of these top hotels cost less than similar establishments in Europe and the United States.

EXCEPTIONAL HOTELS

Although most of the top hotels are modern, there are a couple of exceptions. The most romantic, elegant and luxurious historic hotel is, without doubt, the exclusive **Carcosa Seri Negara** ((03) 282-1888 FAX (03) 282-7888. In 1896, the first resident-general of the Federation of Malay States — the dashing, polo-playing Sir Frank Swettenham — began the construction of his official home on the jungled hills overlooking the Lake Gardens, not far from the heart of Kuala Lumpur. Carcosa remained the residence of the highest British representative until 1941, when it became the Japanese Senior Officers' Army Mess. Together with the Seri Negara or King's House which was built on an adjacent hill in 1904, this two-story mansion was renovated in 1989 and opened as an exclusive hotel for such illustrious guests as HRH Queen

Elizabeth II, the Emperor and Empress of Japan, the Sultan of Brunei, South African President Nelson Mandela and President Ramos of the Philippines.

Exclusivity and discreet, personalized service make guests staying in the six-suite Carcosa, or seven-suite Seri Negara, feel they are private guests in a wealthy home. The size and comfort of even the smallest suite is quite remarkable, and each suite is individually furnished with different fabrics, paintings, sofas, armchairs and wicker *chaises longues*. Surrounded by luxuriant gardens with wild jungle fowl and kingfishers, the air perfumed by fragrant cempaka trees near Carcosa's tennis courts and swimming pool, it is hard to believe you are minutes from the center of Malaysia's capital city. Leisurely afternoon tea on the verandah, Sunday curry tiffin or a gourmet dinner in the elegant Mahsuri restaurant all contribute to an atmosphere redolent of a more gracious past. Naturally, such excellence is not inexpensive, but if you decided to be self indulgent just once during your visit, make it at Carcosa Seri Negara.

The other top historic hotel in the region is Singapore's **Raffles** ((65) 337-1866 FAX (65) 339-7650, the almost legendary hostelry that summed up, for writer Somerset Maugham, Noel Coward and a host of other luminaries, "all the fables of the exotic East". Established in 1887, Raffles Hotel was designated a national monument exactly one hundred years later. The hotel underwent major restoration and reopened its doors in 1991 with just 104 suites. To protect the privacy of the hotel's guests, access to the enclosed courtyards and other areas of the hotel occupied by guests is not permitted to the crowds of sightseers who flock to the Raffles to dine in its gracious Tiffin Room, to have a Singapore Sling at the Long Bar or to browse in the exclusive shops in the extensive Raffles Hotel Arcade.

The standard guest suite at the Raffles is furnished in a style marrying that of an English colonial home and an English country residence, exuding comfort and good taste. There is a small sitting/dining room leading on to the bedroom, dressing room and bathroom. While nowhere near as large as the suites at some of the modern hotels (or, indeed, the luxurious Carcosa Seri Negara), they also have a table and couple of chairs on the wide verandahs overlooking the lushly planted courtyards with their famous traveler's palms. If you're looking for historic charm in Singapore, then Raffles Hotel must be your choice.

Singapore has any number of luxurious modern hotels, but the current favorite with visitors to whom money is no object is the **Ritz-Carlton Millennia** ((65) 337-8888 FAX (65) 338-0001, which all the taxi drivers refer to as the "six-star hotel". Located down in the Marina Centre, this stark 32-story building has a stunning view of Marina Bay or the Singapore skyline. Modernity is the keynote in the entrance lobby, including a floating sculpture by a famed New York artist which you'll either love or hate.

Exclusive comfort, OPPOSITE, at the Carcosa Seri Negara, Kuala Lumpur. Doorman BELOW at Raffles, Singapore, opens up the world of colonial style.

But it is the guest rooms and suites that set the 610-room Ritz-Carlton in a class of its own. For a start, they're about 25 percent larger than the average five-star hotel. Another unique touch is having the bathrooms positioned on the outside wall, so you can literally loll in a bubble bath while enjoying an unobstructed view of Singapore. The rooms are furnished in a style that manages to be both sumptuous yet understated, with only the very finest fabrics used. Judging by the number of repeat guests, the Ritz-Carlton Millennia, which opened in 1996, is likely to maintain its position as one of Singapore's most popular luxury hotels.

Malaysia has literally dozens of resorts, but everyone (including hoteliers themselves) agrees that the finest of all is **The Datai** ((04) 959-2500 FAX (04) 959-2600 set in lush rainforest on a private beach on the northwest coast of Langkawi. Billed as "Malaysia's first grand deluxe resort", The Datai has a deceptive simplicity and serenity that seems to merit some other description than "resort", with its implications of tour groups. The Datai is nothing if not exclusive (the restaurants and other facilities are for the use of the

hotel's guests only), with only 54 deluxe rooms, 14 suites and 40 private villas literally surrounded by rainforest (guests are encouraged not to leave food around in case the monkeys come inside their villas!).

The natural timbers, wooden tiles and open concept design of the public areas of the Datai enable the buildings to merge into the surrounding environment. Guests can discover more about this environment by trekking in the forest with a naturalist. There are mountain bicycles, a magnificent golf course nearby and a couple of pools — not forgetting the beach and non-motorized water sports. If you want the ultimate holiday in an environment that encapsulates some of the best of what Malaysia has to offer, with its beaches and rainforests, then The Datai is the obvious choice. And for honeymooners, what could be better than their own private villa tucked away in the rainforest, with a private beach for moonlight strolls nearby?

EXCEPTIONAL RESTAURANTS

If your idea of living it up is to dine in style, you'll feel right at home in Malaysia and Singapore, where food is

taken seriously and money often considered irrelevant where fine dining is concerned. The Chinese, in particular, love a lavish banquet. The **Hai Tien Lo** restaurants, located in the Pan Pacific hotels in both Singapore ((65) 336-8111 and Kuala Lumpur ((03) 442-5555, are among the finest Cantonese restaurants you'll find anywhere. The cuisine, decor and service are all supremely elegant, and only the finest quality ingredients are used, including for their lunchtime *dim sum*, which is very popular.

For the most romantic surroundings in Kuala Lumpur, dine out at Carcosa Seri Negara's beautiful **Mahsuri** ((03) 282-1888 (for reservations), a restaurant specializing in Continental cuisine with a fresh modern touch. The ambiance, service, wine list and food make this one of the capital's top restaurants.

Bon Ton ((03) 241-3614, set in an old colonial house in Kuala Lumpur, is not as expensive as the surroundings and quality of the food might suggest. However, if you wanted to splurge, you could not only eat your way through the imaginative East-West menu but indulge in one of their excellent, super-rich cakes for dessert.

Singapore has many lavish restaurants serving fine food, including the exquisite **Nadaman** ((65) 737-3644 in the Shangri-La hotel, where a Japanese *kaiseki* meal is the ultimate dining experience. Or you could try the same hotel's fine Continental restaurant, **Latour**. For Northern Indian food in truly lovely surroundings, complete with classical Indian music, the **Tandoor** ((65) 733-8333, in the Holiday Inn Park View, is the place to go. Refined Thai palace cuisine can be expensive, especially the seafood, but every morsel justifies the cost at the **Thanying** restaurants, in the Amara Hotel and also on Clarke Quay in Singapore ((65) 222-4688 and (65) 336-1821. Innovative Cantonese cuisine as well as classical dishes are featured at the elegant yet restrained **Li Bai** ((65)737-6888, in the Sheraton Towers in Singapore, regarded by gourmets as one of the best restaurants in town.

For more detailed information on these and other restaurants, see the WHERE TO EAT sections for Kuala Lumpur and Singapore.

Scores of luxury hotels offer the best of Asian hospitality and Western comforts. Holiday Inn Damai Beach OPPOSITE, Sarawak and ABOVE *chaises longues* relaxation at Penang's Rasa Sayang.

Family Fun

Traveling with children in Singapore and Malaysia can be a real pleasure for the entire family and is helped by the fact that the locals genuinely like children (particularly those with blond hair). **Beach holidays** are generally a great hit with children, and places like Penang, Langkawi, Cherating, some of the resorts in Terengganu, Damai Beach in Sarawak and resorts around Kota Kinabalu in Sabah have plenty of water sports. The kids can ride an inflatable banana, learn to sail a dinghy, try a kayak or simply frolic in the water.

There are lots of little things that will interest children as you travel about.

They could learn to fly a traditional kite in Terengganu or Kelantan, try their hand at doing batik in the same region, ride in a trishaw in Penang or Melaka or take the quaint funicular railway up **Penang Hill**. The zoo at Kuala Lumpur, or the bird park and deer park within the Lake Gardens are an introduction to Malaysia's wildlife. Even better would be to take the children to see turtles laying their eggs on the beach at **Rantau Abang** or in Sabah's Turtle Islands. A visit to the **Sepilok Orang-Utan Rehabilitation Centre** is certain to be a memorable experience for the children (as well as their parents).

THEMED FUN
Peninsular Malaysia has a number of theme parks where the children can have a whale of a time. One of the newest is **Mines Wonderland**, south of Kuala Lumpur, 60 hectares (150 acres) of derelict tin-mining land transformed in a family playground. There's a Snow House (which may not appeal if you've come from the cold north), water taxis to ferry visitors along the canals and onto the lake, a water screen laser show which is really spectacular, and a musical fountain which dances and changes color to the beat of music. Go in the late afternoon or early evening. Another theme park near Kuala Lumpur is the **Sunway Lagoon**, with a wild west section and a water theme park.

Discovering the world under the sea is no long restricted to scuba divers. The family can come face-to-face with a shark and other denizens of the deep by visiting Langkawi's **Underwater World**, or the Underwater World on Singapore's Sentosa island.

WILD SINGAPORE
Singapore can be an even better place for a family holiday than Malaysia, especially if the children are still relatively young. All the attractions are within easy reach by comfortable, air-conditioned public transport (the MRT train or bus) or by taxi, so the children don't get tired by long traveling times.

The **Jurong Bird Park** is perfect for a half-day visit, and with bird shows four times a day, you're sure to be in time for at least one of them. The **Singapore Zoo** is excellent, especially the Children's Zoo where they can interact with some of the animals or have breakfast with an orangutan. Plenty of shows here, too. An absolute must for the whole family is the **Night Safari**, where the magic of seeing the animals close up as they go about their normal activities in natural surroundings is the highlight of any visit to Singapore.

SINGAPORE'S FUN ISLAND

Sentosa island has enough to occupy the whole family for a couple of days; in fact, a stay at one of the two resorts here is not such a bad idea. Apart from water sports, roller skating and bicycles for hire, there's a butterfly park, coralarium, **Volcano Land**, **Underwater World** and the enormously popular **Fantasy Island**, with its fabulous water rides. The whole family (provided you don't have children under five) will be thrilled by their experience of virtual reality in **Cinemania**, the republic's largest interactive simulation theater. Even

riding the cable car across to get to Sentosa from the top of Mount Faber is an exciting experience for all.

While in Singapore, the children could also have their fortune card selected by a parrot in Little India, indulge in eating with their hands at a Southern Indian restaurant, watch stilt walkers at Clarke Quay (another good spot for family fun) or take a bum boat ride on Singapore river.

DON'T SPOIL THE FUN

One important thing to remember, if your children aren't accustomed to a tropical climate, is that dragging them around in the heat of the day is likely to lead to tears or temper tantrums. Try to do your sight-seeing in the cooler hours of the early morning or later in the afternoon. Be sure to watch out for sunburn, especially on the beaches, and make sure the children wear a sun hat. If the kids do get headachy and cranky,

OPPOSITE and ABOVE: Safe waters, warm seas and sandy beaches provide perfect beach holidays for families. Singapore's Jurong Bird Park LEFT is a fine place to meet the colorful inmates.

it could well be because of dehydration. Make sure they (and you) drink plenty of water; it's a good idea to carry a large bottle of water, or buy mineral water instead of sweet carbonated drinks each time you stop.

Cultural Kicks

Like most other countries in Southeast Asia, Malaysia and Singapore have been racing headlong into the future for the past two or three decades at such a rate that all traces of the past were in danger of being obliterated. Singapore pulled back from the brink of destroying some magnificent architectural treasures and has designated a number of areas such as Chinatown and Little India for preservation. Malaysia's attitude towards saving its architectural heritage seems to vary, depending upon the location. The Penang state authorities are attempting to gazette a heritage area which will preserve parts of Georgetown, (colonial buildings, Chinese temples, Indian mosques and shophouses), while Kuching's

architectural treasures seem safe. Many of Kuala Lumpur's finest buildings seem certain of preservation, being occupied as government offices, although the future of Melaka's historical houses in Chinatown seems to be in the hands of private individuals. While none of the buildings in the region is really old by European standards, they bear witness to the remarkable mixture of peoples and cultures which has created the Malaysia and Singapore of today.

THE ARCHITECTURAL LEGACY
Some of old buildings in the towns and cities of Malaysia and Singapore are a unique blending of Chinese and European neoclassical architecture, with touches of Malay wooden fretwork often thrown in. This style, sometimes known as Chinese Baroque, is seen in many of the houses and shophouses (buildings combining the business area or shop downstairs, with living quarters above) of Penang's Georgetown, in the Chinatown area of Melaka, in Kuching and in Singapore, especially in Emerald Hill, Tanjong Pagar and Chinatown.

While each building has its own peculiarities, certain elements are common; the roof style is normally Chinese, with terra cotta or green tiles while Malay timber fretwork decorates the area above the windows or forms ventilation panels. The painted wooden scrolls above the windows and doors are Chinese, yet the Doric and Corinthian columns and louvered timber shutters are very much European. Melaka's Peranakan or Straits Chinese architecture is unique, with the very narrow, long houses containing two or even three open courtyards for light and ventilation.

While Chinese Baroque is generally confined to domestic or trading buildings, the administration offices, churches, banks, town halls and court houses built during the colonial era have a style all their own. This varies from the Moorish fantasies of the Kuala Lumpur Railway Station and the Sultan Abdul Samad Building (opposite the Padang, also known as Dataran Merdeka) to the many fine colonial buildings of Georgetown and Singapore (St. Joseph's Institution in Bras Basah Road now housing the Singapore Art Museum and Raffles Hotel, in Beach Road, being just

a couple of examples in the latter). Kuching has a number of fine colonial-era buildings in excellent state of preservation, particularly the Court House (opposite the Waterfront Park), the old wing of the Sarawak Museum (which has French elements thrown in for good measure), the Post Office, Fort Margherita and the Astana where the White Rajas once resided. The last two are both across the Sarawak River and reached by ferry.

MUSEUMS

The museums and art galleries of the region are uneven in quality, having not been a matter of priority in the past. Singapore is setting what culture vultures hope will become a trend in the area, seriously upgrading its museums and encouraging the arts. The **Singapore Art Museum** (see page 226) houses the sculpture and paintings of local and other Southeast Asian artists, and is a joy to explore. The first **Asian Civilisations**

The Thai Wat Chayamangkalaram, Penang, OPPOSITE houses one of Asia's longest reclining Buddhas. Sarawak Museum ABOVE is a rich showcase of ethnic and natural history exhibits.

Museum, devoted to Chinese civilization, opened in 1997 and is truly excellent, while the second, concentrating on Indian and Southeast Asian civilizations, is due to open in 2000 (see page 224).

Singapore's Art Galleries Association publishes a free map and guide to around a member dozen galleries; you can pick this up from one of the tourism information centers. You could try looking on the second level of Raffles Hotel Arcade, where there are several rather pricey but good galleries, including **Plum Blossoms**, which focuses on Chinese art, and **Artfolio**. **Tzen Gallery** in the basement of Tanglin Shopping Centre is another gallery of repute.

The **Sarawak Museum** in Kuching, the oldest museum in the region (founded in 1891 by the second White Raja), houses interesting ethnographic material in its new wing, with a mixture of natural history and ethnography in the old wing. The museum, like Kuching itself, has an idiosyncratic charm. It lacks the state-of-the-art displays of Singapore's museums and galleries, but the contents themselves are enough to keep the visitor fascinated to half a day (see page 184).

MUSEUMS

Still in Sarawak, the **Sarawak Cultural Village** at Damai Beach (see page 185) is billed as a "living museum". This award-winning center has a collection of traditional houses representing the major ethnic groups of Sarawak, and showcases their lifestyles, handicrafts, music and cultural dances.

The privately run **Baba Nyonya Heritage Museum** in Melaka (see page 153) gives a glimpse inside the home of a wealthy Peranakan family, allowing visitors to see the magnificent carved wooden screens, tiled floors, ornate furniture, clothing and everyday household items. This museum is definitely worth a visit. The museum inside Melaka's old town hall or Stadthuys is more interesting for the building in which it is housed rather than the contents, but the **Melaka Sultanate Palace**, reconstructed to resemble the fifteenth-century Malay palace of Sultan Mansur Shah, is good for an insight into the city's past.

The **National Museum** in Kuala Lumpur is disappointing, although if Penang's Museum, due to reopen late 1997, retains most of its original collection it should be on every visitor's list (see page 138). The **National Art Gallery** in Kuala Lumpur should be able to display more of its interesting collection of paintings once it moves to larger premises. Lovers of fine art might like to check whether Kuala Lumpur's **Galeri Petronas (** (03) 275-3061 is holding an art exhibition. To see an interesting collection of paintings and sculpture by Malaysian and other Southeast Asian artists, be sure to visit **Valentine Willie Fine Art (** 284-2348, an excellently managed gallery on the first floor, 17 Jalan Telawi 3, Bangsar Baru, Kuala Lumpur. Special exhibitions are held here on a regular basis, covering themes as diverse as Sarawak tribal textiles to the work of top Filipino artists.

Shop Till You Drop

Malaysia produces some beautiful batik and basketware, mostly on the east coast of Peninsular Malaysia, in Terengganu and Kelantan. Brightly-colored paper kites make suitable small gifts and come ready packed. Filigree silver and pewterware are other good buys, found mostly in craft shops in Kuala Lumpur. In the state of Johore, locally produced pottery, as well as a tremendous amount of imports from China, is on sale in the town of Air Hitam, just off the highway between Singapore and Kuala Lumpur.

In Sarawak, baskets and mats made from rattan, bamboo and pandanus are a good value; there is also attractive, locally produced pottery characterized by geometric black and white designs, sold in Kuching. In both Sabah and Sarawak, one finds wood carvings and other locally made artifacts, as well as items imported from Kalimantan. The craft shops in Sarawak's capital are far superior to those in Kota Kinabalu, the capital of Sabah, particularly those along Kuching's Main Bazaar. In Sabah, the best place to look for handicrafts is in the shops inside Wisma Merdeka and

Centrepoint, and also at Nabaulu Market en route for Kinabalu Park.

DUTY-FREE SINGAPORE

Singapore offers just about everything that every other Asian country produces, at tourist prices. So if you are traveling around Thailand or Bali and you don't want to carry around that gigantic wooden green frog holding a hibiscus that you've taken a liking to, rest assured there are lots of them in Singapore. What Singapore can also offer are good deals in electrical goods and computers. Many tourist shops in Singapore will be able to arrange packing and delivery overseas. Using a credit card is often a good idea for this kind of purchase because it offers some redress if the goods fail to appear, though generally speaking this is not likely to happen.

BARGAINING

Shops where bargaining is out of the question are few and far between. I once

OPPOSITE: Distinctive Sarawaki designs, here in the museum, can be bought in the local shops. ABOVE Traditional shopping arcade in Kuala Lumpur.

received a pleasant surprise when considering some antique Chinese furniture on sale in a large department store in Chinatown in Singapore. Without particularly thinking I might be successful, I inquired if there was any discount for paying by cash (always a good opening move) and was promptly told that 20 percent could be knocked off the marked price.

More information on shopping appears in the SHOPPING section of each region and under SHOPPING, page 255.

Short Breaks

If you're looking for somewhere to go for a long weekend or a holiday of less than a week, you'd be advised to choose just one area of Malaysia, or to spend all your time in Singapore, rather than trying to fit too much in.

Should you decide on **Singapore**, you should think of the joys of an urban holiday: great restaurants and shops, museums and a good art gallery, perhaps a visit to the theater or a concert, and a night at a jazz bar, fun pub or disco. If you stay in a hotel with a swimming pool (and even three-star hotels often offer these), you can get in a bit of relaxation as well. For a taste of nature, don't forget the Zoo or the Night Safari. And for a touch of the exotic, make a trip down to Little India and to Chinatown.

Malaysia has so many options that you need to decide what you want (and bear in mind the season you're visiting) before narrowing it down to the actual destination. For a historical weekend with a bit of antique hunting thrown in, **Melaka** is ideal. Or you could consider

Penang, which has so much to offer that anything less than three days would be really frustrating. There's fabulous food, plenty of history in Georgetown, a diverse landscape as you drive around the island, Penang Hill and the resorts long the north coast at Batu Ferringhi. If you're looking a resort holiday and don't have any expectations of an interesting cultural atmosphere, you could consider Langkawi, or perhaps Pulau Pangkor. With Langkawi's convenient air connections, however, you're likely to spend less time traveling.

If you want to explore the rainforest and have at least five days (you'll spend the better part of a day both getting in and out), plan a visit to Peninsular Malaysia's **Taman Negara**. Remember that this park is closed during the height of the northeast monsoon, in December and January.

Any of the islands along Peninsular Malaysia's **East Coast** (Pulau Perhentian, Redang, Tioman and Sibu, to name just a few) are perfect for a beach holiday, especially if you love scuba diving or snorkeling. Don't go between November and March, when the monsoon has a bad effects on visibility and makes the sea unpleasantly rough. Of all these islands, **Tioman** is perhaps the quickest to reach, having an airport with flights from Singapore plus a direct ferry service from the republic.

Kota Kinabalu, the capital of Sabah, offers beautiful islands and beaches right on its doorstep, with Kinabalu Park an easy and rewarding day trip, and the options of going white-water rafting or making a day trip across to the famous Sepilok Oran-Utan Rehabilitation Centre in Sandakan.

Kuching or nearby **Damai Beach**, with its resorts and the nearby Sarawak Cultural Village, is a lovely place to spend a few days. It would be a good idea to be based at Damai Beach, and make day trips into the city (less than an hour away) to explore its historic buildings, excellent museum and its irresistible handicraft and antique shops along Main Bazaar.

Festive Flings

The multiculturalism of Malaysia and Singapore leads to a bewildering array of holidays and festivals. Some are common to both countries, while others are only celebrated in either Malaysia, Singapore or only in a particular state. Many holidays are calculated from a lunar calendar and change every year. This is true of Ramadan, the major event in the Muslim year, and also Chinese New Year.

Call the tourism information center in the relevant city to check if any festivals are taking place during your visit:
Kuala Lumpur ((03) 264-1149, 264-3929
Penang ((04) 262-0066
Melaka ((06) 283-6538
Kuching ((082) 410944
Kota Kinabalu ((088) 219310
Singapore ((65) 736-6622, 334-1336

JANUARY/ FEBRUARY
The **Thaipusam festival** is celebrated with great drama in both Singapore and Kuala Lumpur by Hindus towards the end of January. The region's most spectacular festival. (See TOP SPOTS).

Chinese New Year is celebrated either in January or February, depending on the

Georgetown OPPOSITE TOP retains much of its Chinese historic roots. Pristine waters OPPOSITE BOTTOM off Pulau Perhentian. Festivals ABOVE are an intrinsic part of the Asian calendar.

Hari Raya Aidilfitri, which marks the end of the Muslim fasting month, Ramadan, moves back each year. In 1999 it will be held in early January. Muslims dress in their finest clothes (great for photography) and after praying at mosques, visit friends and relatives for feasts of curries and cakes.

MARCH/ APRIL

Good Friday is a holiday and in Melaka a candlelit procession is held at St. Peter's Church. In Singapore, there is a similar event at St. Joseph's Church in Victoria Street.

The **Birthday of the Monkey God**, in February or March, is celebrated in Singapore at the Monkey God temple in Seng Poh Road. Chinese spirit mediums, said to be possessed by the naughty Monkey God, slash themselves with blades.

Vesak Day is a public holiday commemorating the birth, enlightenment and entry into the perfect state of existence of Buddha. In both countries, Buddhist temples have candlelit processions at night after the daytime practice of freeing of caged birds which symbolizes the liberation of captive souls.

lunar cycle. In many respects like Christmas in the West, it is a time for family reunions and general good cheer. Traditionally it was also a time for letting off fireworks, although these are now strictly banned in both countries. To compensate for the lack of noise and excitement, Singapore holds the Chingay Procession towards the end of the two-week New Year festivities, with stilt walkers, acrobats and floats. Check local newspapers or with the Tourist Board for details of the procession route. In both countries teams of lion dancers are seen traveling in open-backed lorries and performing publicly, being rewarded with *hong bao*, red packets containing money, for the luck they bring businesses and householders.

MAY/JUNE

Sabah Fest & Harvest Festival The Sabah Fest is a week-long celebration of local arts and culture, leading up to the official celebrations in Kota Kinabalu of the Kadazan/Dusun harvest festival or Pesta Ka'amatan on May 30 and 31.

The indigenous peoples of Sarawak celebrate the harvest festivals in their longhouses late May or early June. The official celebrations of the **Gawai** Dyak are held on June 1 and 2 in Kuching.

Some time in June, the **Pesta San Pedro** is held by Portuguese-Eurasians of Melaka in honor of St. Peter, the patron saint of fishermen. Boat decorating competitions and folk dancing are the highlights.

The **Dragon Boat Festival** in June is the time for dragon boat races in Singapore, Kota Kinabalu and Penang, with long wooden boats bearing a dragon's head

being powered through the water by rowers urged on by a drummer.

JULY/AUGUST

Singapore's National Day on August 9 is a public holiday that includes firework displays, processions and other festivities.

Malaysia's National Day Malaysia on August 31 is a public holiday with celebrations and a procession in Kuala Lumpur.

During August or September, the **Festival of the Hungry Ghosts** is the time when the gates of hell are symbolically opened and spirits are free to roam the earth. Friendly ghosts make house calls to relatives but destitute spirits need appeasing with offerings in the form of burning gifts, including "hell money" (fake currency notes) and mock passports for wandering souls. Stalls with food offerings and giant incense sticks are set up all over Singapore and wherever there are sizable Chinese communities in Malaysia.

SEPTEMBER/OCTOBER

Lanterns are lit on the night of the year when the moon is believed to be at its brightest. During the Chinese **Moon Festival**, lantern processions and special lion and dragon dances are held, especially in Singapore. Rich moon cakes, said to once carry secret messages during a revolt, are eaten in abundance.

The spectacular **Thimithi** is a fire-walking ceremony when Hindus walk across a pit of burning embers in honor of Draupadi. In Malaysia, this takes place at the Gajah Berang Temple in Melaka and in Singapore, at the Sri Mariamman temple in South Bridge Road.

NOVEMBER/DECEMBER

One of the prettiest festivals of the year is **Deepavali**, the Hindu celebration of the victory of light over dark. It is a public holiday when Indian homes and temples are decorated with lamps and garlands. The specially illuminated Little India district of Singapore is full of activity in the time prior to the festival.

OPPOSITE TOP: Iban dances are part of a longhouse experience. Parades, often spectacular and always colorful, can take place at night such as Chingay in Singapore ABOVE and OPPOSITE BOTTOM.

Galloping Gourmets

Malaysians and Singaporeans are passionate about their food, and the visitor quickly discovers why. There are few places in the world offering such an enormous range of cuisines at such reasonable prices, served in such a wide variety of surroundings. Although there are supremely elegant restaurants (particularly in the five-star hotels), the general rule is informality and there is a complete absence of the snobbery that is sometimes found in restaurants in Europe and America.

The ethnic diversity of both Malaysia and Singapore is evident in the cuisine as much as in the faces, so you find not only the food of the Malays and the indigenous peoples of Sarawak and Sabah, but dishes from many different Chinese provinces, food from both the south and north of the Indian subcontinent, Indonesian cuisine and a number of styles and dishes which have evolved as a result of different ethnic groups living side by side and adopting methods and ingredients from each other.

You should have no difficulty in obtaining Western cuisine if this is what you fancy, but do yourself a favor and try as many of the local cuisines as possible and you could find yourself becoming as passionate about the food as the locals.

FOOD STALLS

One of the most popular and least expensive places to eat is at the food stalls, sometimes referred to as hawker centers (see ALFRESCO FEASTS, page 13). These were traditionally in the open-air, perhaps clustering down a lane, at the edge of a river or under a huge tree. The "kitchen" was a pushcart or temporary table shaded from the mid-day sun by a tarpaulin, and open to the stars at night, with a few simple tables and stools set around. You'll still find the old-style food stalls in the smaller towns, but in the cities they're often relocated in air-conditioned shopping centers (actually more comfortable during the heat of the day). You can pick and chose from several different stalls — say a dozen sticks of satay (skewers of seasoned meat or poultry grilled over charcoal and served with spicy peanut sauce) from a Malay stall, *murtabak*, a flaky Indian bread stuffed with minced mutton from another stall, an oyster omelet from a Chinese cook, a freshly squeezed watermelon juice from the fruit vendor — the options are almost endless (see TOP SPOTS, page 13).

COFFEE SHOPS

Another local institution is the coffeeshop (*kedai kopi*), as much a place for socializing as for having a drink and a light meal. The coffeeshop is invariably open-sided and fan-cooled, with the anchor tenant serving hot and cold drinks and various other stall holders within dispensing their speciality such as chicken rice, noodles fried or in soup, or a range of ready cooked dishes to be served with rice. A meal in a coffeeshop is always inexpensive and informal. Most of them serve a popular breakfast of toasted white bread slathered with *kaya*, a rich jam of coconut milk, egg yolks and sugar.

An inexpensive and varied meal based on rice can be enjoyed by ordering *nasi campur*, literally "mixed rice". For around $1.50, you get a mound of steaming white rice and then just point to the cooked vegetables, meat, eggs, poultry and fish on display and a dollop of each will be added to your plate.

In Malaysia, you'll find the coffeeshops in the commercial areas of every town, for this is where most local people eat their breakfast and lunch. There are almost always coffeeshops near the more modestly price inner city hotels, near long-distance bus depots and in suburban shopping complexes, including Singapore's Housing & Development Board "new towns" (commonly referred to as HDBs).

Birds are frequently kept as pets on housing estates and taken out for air and competitive song in cafés.

LOCAL RESTAURANTS

Moving up from the coffeeshop, you get an enormous range of air-conditioned restaurants selling every kind of local cuisine, plus other Asian food (Thai and Japanese are very popular) and international favorites, particularly in the major cities. The craze for Western fast food has caught on in Malaysia and Singapore, as much a statement of the Westernization of today's youth as genuine appreciation of the ubiquitous hamburger, fried chicken or pizza.

Recommendations of certain local specialties, such as the excellent Penang *laksa* and *rojak*, the delightful Nyonya cuisine of Melaka, Penang and Singapore, and *nasi kerabu*, the interesting herbal rice or *nasi ulam* of Kelantan, and where to sample these, are given under WHERE TO EAT in the relevant travel sections of this book.

FRUITS

Apart from the cooked food, be sure to take advantage of the excellent tropical fruits available. Papaya, pineapple, mangoes, refreshing starfruit and bananas of all sizes are year-round favorites, but watch out for seasonal delights generally available in July and August: the furry red rambutan, the spiky and evil-smelling (yet utterly divine) durian, the small beige-skinned *langsat* and *duku* which both hint of grapefruit. Ready-cut fruits are sold at stalls inside many coffeeshops or outside the markets; avoid these if you have a delicate constitution (except in Singapore, where hygiene standards are rigorously enforced), and buy whole fruits at the markets.

SEAFOOD

If you love seafood, you'll be in seventh heaven in Malaysia and Singapore. A huge range of fish, prawns, crabs, lobsters, squid and shellfish is available throughout the year and cooked in a variety of ways. The Chinese often steam seafood, although many dishes such as the famous chilli crab involve tossing it around the wok with pounded chillies and other seasonings. One of the most popular ways of cooking prawns at the moment (and culinary fashions change quite quickly here) is the so-called butter prawns, developed by a Chinese chef and combining Chinese, Indian and Malay ingredients and cooking techniques.

Although live seafood plucked straight from the restaurant's tank can be quite expensive, seafood in Singapore and particularly in Malaysia is generally very much cheaper than in Europe, North America and North Asia. Naturally, seafood is best found in coastal restaurants and resorts, and since few of Malaysia's major areas of interest are located inland, this means just about everywhere. Penang is regarded as one of the best places in terms of quality and price in all of Malaysia; Kota Kinabalu in Sabah, and Kuching and Miri in Sarawak, are less known but equally good. In Singapore, seafood tends to be pricey compared with Malaysia, but you cannot leave without trying the famous chilli crab and the fish-head curry.

Finding food is never going a problem, except in some rural parts of Malaysia during the month of Ramadan when Muslims are forbidden to eat between sunrise and sunset. In traditional Malay areas like Kelantan, Terengganu or Kedah, this may cause occasional snags during the day, but you can usually find a Chinese coffeeshop somewhere.

DRINKS

Unfortunately, owing to high taxes, wine and beer are ridiculously expensive in both Singapore and Malaysia, though in duty-free Langkawi and Labuan (an island off southwest Sabah) they are reasonably priced. Local beverages such as young coconut water, soya bean milk, barley water and sugar cane juice are, however, very moderately priced. In longhouses in Sarawak and Sabah, you'll probably be offered *lihing*, *tapai*, or *tuak*, the local rice wine, which can often be very palatable. Since it's made without any chemical additives, the locals insist it never leaves you with a hangover, a claim I would challenge based on personal experience.

Seafood dining, alfresco OPPOSITE is very popular throughout the region, often in pretty gardens. Intricate beadwork ABOVE from Sarawak tempts connoisseurs and collectors.

Special Interests

Unfortunately, despite the enormous potential for special interest tours, very few tour operators in Malaysia or Singapore arrange these trips so in most cases you'll have to go it alone. Specialized tour operators overseas often arrange for their own tour leader to bring groups to pursue such diverse interests as orchids, cuisine, tropical fruits and birdwatching, so you would do well to check the options before leaving home.

BIRDWATCHING

One exception to the above is **birdwatching**. Somewhat surprisingly, Singapore is remarkably good for seeing birds in a diversity of environments — mangrove forest, freshwater swamp, grasslands, secondary forest — with close to 300 species, both resident and migratory. A day spent with a specialized guide is a most rewarding experience. Contact **Subaraj** ((65) 787-4733 and FAX (65) 787-7048. The acknowledged specialist in Peninsular Malaysia is Dennis Yong of **Kingfisher Tours** ((03) 242-1454 FAX (03) 242-9827.

BOTANIC GARDENS

If you're interested in **tropical gardens**, don't miss the well maintained **Singapore Botanic Gardens**, corner of Napier Road and Cluny Road the best in the region with some magnificent palms and an excellent orchid house. Apart from the ornamental trees, shrubs and flowers, there are specimens of various crop plants, including rubber which Henry Ridley experimented with here before pleading with planters in Malaya to plant the seedlings. The **Penang Botanic Gardens** are pleasant although a little run down, but worth a visit if you're already in Penang. They were, like the Singapore gardens, begun during the Victorian period and in one area, have a surprisingly English walkway fringed by tropical plants. The **Shah Alma Agricultural Park**, just outside Kuala Lumpur, has interesting features on plants of commercial importance, including rice, but at the time of writing, parts of the Park were rather poorly maintained. If you're visiting Sabah, don't miss the Mountain Garden within Kinabalu Park, where dozens of the rare plants found of the mountain are grouped together, including a number of pitcher plants, orchids and rhododendrons. Still in Sabah, the basis of the **Sabah Agricultural Park**, due to be fully opened by late 1998 or early 1999, is already well established. This includes an outstanding collection of native Borneo orchids and a fascinating crop museum.

CRAFTWORK

Educational opportunities — such as the chance to study Malay or Chinese, or to learn various handicrafts — are still largely restricted to the locals. Formal courses are not readily available for visitors, although if you wanted to learn the basics of **batik**, the art of producing designs on fabric by using the wax-resist technique, you could try around Beserah, north of Kuantan, on the East Coast of Peninsular Malaysia. There's a batik workshop over the bridge just south of the town; they may give you lessons or arrange for someone else to do so. The **Handicraft Centre** or **Gelanggan Seni** in Kota Bharu, Kelantan, can arrange for a homestay with a batik maker, an ideal chance to get thoroughly immersed in the art. Contact the **Kota Bharu Tourist Information Centre** ((07) 748-5534, for further information.

CUISINE

Despite the excellence of the **local cuisine**, few places are geared up for giving cooking lessons to visitors. One exception is the **Raffles Culinary Academy** ((03) 331-1747, attached to the famous Singapore hotel. They offer half-day courses from Monday to Friday, starting at 9:30 AM and finishing at midday; booking in advance is recommended. The Monday class features Chinese cuisine (S$95), Tuesday is for Malay and Nonya cuisine (S$85) and Wednesday is Indian (S$75). International cuisine and Raffles' signature recipes are featured on Thursday and Friday. Naturally, with such a short period of time devoted to demonstrating the cooking and actually serving the food, the lessons are, of necessity, only an introduction to these complex cuisines.

Tea OPPOSITE TOP swathes parts of highland Malaysia like a rich velvet carpet. Traditional basket work BOTTOM forms one of the main basics of the Sabahan and Sarawaki handicrafts industry.

Welcome
to
Malaysia
and
Singapore

STRUNGOUT over vast areas of land and ocean, Malaysia and Singapore are unique countries in which no two visits need ever be the same. They are lands of stunning cultural and geographical differences with food to suit every palate, accommodation ranging from the sublime to the bizarre, and activities for all ages, from white-water rafting to ballroom dancing, and from jungle trekking to cut throat bargaining in the myriad shopping complexes. The many histories of these once disparate communities could have come straight from a historical romance as settlers battled it out for domination over indigenous populations time and time again.

This book selects the most rewarding and delightful aspects of each country for the short stay visitor or for those with time to visit the more remote, but no less fascinating, places and communities. It sets out to offer a perspective on the sometimes wild and violent history of the region, the cultural diversity of its peoples, makes suggestions for accommodation for all budgets and tastes, and offers guidance to the stunning variety of cuisines on offer. Most importantly of all, it offers a considered opinion on the attractiveness of the many resorts, parks, cities, historical sites and means of travel available. Places to visit, where to eat and stay, and how to reach the various towns, resorts and attractions are set out for Peninsular Malaysia, Sarawak and Sabah on the island of Borneo, and Singapore.

If you are wondering what a holiday in Malaysia and Singapore has to offer you, let us go on a brief journey around these lands. Beginning, as many people do, in the tiny island state of Singapore, the first time visitor will be stunned by its modernity and apparent Westernization. As you enter the city, you will pass the architecturally diverse hotel complexes, the late twentieth century's answer to the beautiful cathedrals of earlier times. From your luxury hotel or from one of the many budget Chinese hotels you can venture out braving the tropical heat to countless shopping centers offering all the ethnic goodies of Asia. Or if history is more to your liking, Singapore's beautifully restored riverfront, many older buildings and relics of a past empire will tell their own tale. In the safe streets old Chinatown at night you can sample the nightly array of food to suit all budgets. Suitably fed, watered, and rested in Singapore, you can move on to the delights of the much larger and more nature oriented West Malaysia.

Just across the causeway to Johor Bahru, the traveler will notice a change in pace and atmosphere. JB, as the locals affectionately call it, is a more raunchy, colorful city which comes into its own at night when Singaporeans scurry across the causeway to sample the delights of its nightlife, shopping

and restaurants. A shopper's paradise in its own right, Johor Bahru simply buzzes at night with all the excitement and chaos of a bigger Asian city. Further up the west coast, Melaka (known to the British as Malacca) offers evidence of its maritime history and quaint antique shops. Further north again, Penang is one of the most fascinating places in Malaysia for its culture and food (plus a few fairly ordinary beaches) while Langkawi has lots of beautiful empty beaches and luxurious resorts where one can get away from it all.

OPPOSITE: The sleek lines of Kuala Lumpur's tower blocks define the curving grace of the Jame Mosque. ABOVE: The calm beauty of a young Malay girl.

But it is along Peninsular Malaysia's East Coast where the traveler will really discover some of the true glories of Malaysia. Its pristine beaches stretch endlessly into the distance and tiny unspoiled islands offer unparalleled snorkeling, fishing, windsurfing and sailing opportunities. At night one can sample homely Malay dishes from hawker centers or opt for the most elegant cuisines of Europe in the big resorts. In Kota Bharu the visitor will notice the distinctive dress, manners and lifestyle and the practice of ancient crafts such as batik work, silver and brass beating, kite-making, dance and music. Also to be found here is some intriguingly different cuisine.

For some the most enticing reason to visit Malaysia is to see its magnificent rainforests. Taman Negara, Malaysia's largest National Park, contains a range of wildlife from monitor lizards, which will try to take your lunch, to elephants and even the occasional tiger. It offers luxury accommodation or just a tent hidden away in the jungle, and you can watch from a perch in the tree tops for the jungle's inhabitants or take exhilarating river trips down rapids to picnic spots deep in the heart of the forest.

Peninsular Malaysia isn't the only place to offer tropical beauty. Sabah and Sarawak also have their special places where a little effort will allow the visitor to see unique insectivorous plants, mangrove, orangutan communities and the giant turtles which have laid their eggs for centuries on the islands off Sandakan. In Malaysian Borneo you can climb to the summit of Mount Kinabalu, come face-to-face with Borneo's unique proboscis monkey, stay in a longhouse and observe the customs and lifestyle of the once head-hunting Iban and explore some of the world's most dramatic caves at Gunung Mulu National Park, in the heart of the Borneo rainforest.

After all this, Kuala Lumpur may seem to be an anticlimax but it too has its qualities. At first seeming chaotic and noisy, it has its unique pace and atmosphere as well as a history reflected in the colonial architecture and excellent museums.

There are so many festivals that you will be bound to come across some celebration of a kind. The people of these countries have

a special way of welcoming visitors and children are especially welcome in Singapore and Malaysia. In Malaysia children are held in particular esteem. Don't be surprised if local people ask if they can photograph your children, especially if they are blonde or scantily clad by Malay standards.

The safety of Singapore's streets is apparent to anyone streetwise in New York or London and the cleanliness and efficiency of the city is a minor marvel.

For some, the sheer variety of food and culinary diversity provides a reason in itself to visit the region and the styles can seem bewildering at first. Cantonese, Teochew (Chiu Chow), Hokkien, Sichuan, Foochow, Malay, Nyonya, North Indian, South Indian, all introduced by immigrants to Singapore

and Malaysia, delight the palate. And this is before one even starts on the huge variety of cuisines from Indonesia, Thailand, Japan, Mexico and Europe. If you are a food buff, the cities of Singapore and Kuala Lumpur will be difficult to escape from. Restaurants abound and good food can cost anything from two or three to hundreds of dollars.

Malaysia and Singapore also serve as a good base to visit other countries in the region, and from Singapore's Changi Airport, one of the world's most comfortable, direct flights are available to many regional destinations as well as to Europe and the United States. Boats travel from Singapore to many Indonesian islands while trains go north into Thailand. From Penang or Kota Bharu a trip to Thailand can be easily arranged, while

Sabah lies close to the southernmost islands of the Philippines.

Whether you choose a beach resort, a city hotel, a longhouse in the jungle; whether your ideal day trip is a trek in the rainforest or another around the consumer delights of Orchard Road in Singapore; whether you enjoy mountaineering, sunbathing, eating or partying or just a bit of everything, the following sections will provide the information and advice to help make your visit to Singapore and Malaysia both memorable and enjoyable.

The Sarawak River near Kuching, Borneo.

The Countries and Their People

HISTORICAL BACKGROUND

BEFORE THE EUROPEANS

The location of the Malay peninsula at the meeting point of sea routes between India and China contributed tremendously to the development of its cultures and traditions. Valuable natural resources also shaped the country's future, as they still do today. Not only were tin and gold available, but also camphor, exotic feathers, rattan, damar resin and hornbill casques from the forests.

The Malays, who came down to the beaches and traded with the Arab, Indian and Chinese merchants, were not the first inhabitants of the Malay peninsula. That distinction belongs to the 20 or so tribes making up the *Orang Asli* (literally Original People), who retreated into the interior when the forefathers of the Malays began arriving from Taiwan some 4,000 years ago. The indigenous, non-Malay element in Malaysia is even more apparent in Sabah and Sarawak — part of the large island of Borneo now shared by Indonesia, Brunei and Malaysia. Sarawak and Sabah are peopled by around 50 different tribes who have little ethnic connection to the Malays.

By the end of the seventh century, a powerful Indian-influenced maritime empire grew up in Sumatra, based near the port of Palembang. Known as Srivijaya, this Buddhist empire spread across through Java and reached its height by 1000 AD. It was then attacked by the Hindu Chola kingdom of southern India and never fully recovered. Palembang was subsequently dominated by the Javanese, and in the thirteenth century some colonists from Palembang founded a settlement on a tiny island which they bestowed with the honorific Sanskrit title of *Singapura*.

Towards the end of the fourteenth century, a refugee from Palembang's nobility fled to a small fishing village on the west coast of the Malay peninsula. The village became known as Melaka and within a hundred years had developed into a cosmopolitan trading port. It was the town of Melaka that became the focus for the international trade between India and China and the legendary spice trade which connected the East with Europe.

It was also through Melaka that Islam, brought by merchants from western India, became firmly entrenched.

While the northern part of the peninsula remained undisturbed under the sovereignty of Siam (Thailand), the spice trade put the Malay peninsula on the map and quickly attracted the attention of European powers.

SPICE TRADERS AND COLONIZERS

The Portuguese were the first to relish the idea of seizing Melaka because they badly

wanted to wrest control of the spice trade from the Muslim Arabs. Following on from the rounding of the southern tip of Africa by explorer Vasco da Gama in 1498, they saw a chance to bypass the formerly inescapable journey through Arab lands. A secure base in Southeast Asia was essential and by the year 1511, Western influence had arrived in Southeast Asia. A contemporary Portuguese account of Melaka — "Goods from all over the East are found here; goods from all over the West are sold here. It is at the end of the monsoon, where you find what you want, and sometimes more than what you are looking for" — reflects the strange mixture of commercial greed and genuine adventurism that drove those men to a then unknown land.

Little more than a century later, in 1641, the city of Melaka fell into the hands of another colonial power which was to dominate the region for four centuries, the Dutch.

OPPOSITE: Ethnic dress of Sabah, East Malaysia. ABOVE: The Sarawak River, life blood of the thriving city of Kuching.

Subsequently, the Anglo-Dutch treaty of 1824 gave all lands west of the Melaka Straits to the Dutch, and everything to the east, including Melaka, to the British.

THE ARRIVAL OF THE BRITISH

The British wanted their own base for the China run, where they sold opium and cotton, and to establish a foothold in the rich lands of the East Indies to counter the influence of the Dutch in what is now Indonesia. At first the northeast of Borneo attracted their

attention. Pirates here proved to be a big problem and so they looked elsewhere. A small island off the west coast of Malaya, Penang, attracted their attention. In 1786 Francis Light, a trader, took formal possession of Penang but despite its attractive position close to the tin-mining areas, Penang was too far north to serve as a trading center.

Enter Stamford Raffles, a freewheeling Englishman who became convinced that rivalry with the Dutch necessitated a new entrepôt that, unlike Penang, would be on the major trade routes. He settled for the small, almost uninhabited, island of Singapore and made it a free port. As Dutch economic power waned England's rose and Singapore has never looked back.

SARAWAK AND SABAH

An Englishman, James Brooke, arrived in Borneo in 1839 and helped the local ruler of Brunei to quash a rebellion, receiving in return a large measure of land which became his personal kingdom of Sarawak. He went on to establish a dynasty that lasted until the Second World War. In his kingdom, ethnicity dictated occupation. The Malays were to help administer the country, the Chinese were to be brought in as laborers, and the native Ibans were to act as military backup.

England's interest in northern Borneo, now the state of Sabah, was partly a strategic one: limiting the spread of Spanish influence from the nearby Philippines. However, it was a trading company which gained control of what was then named British North Borneo, which did not become a crown colony until after the Second World War.

The sole dynamic to England's interest in the Malay peninsula, Sarawak and Sabah was trade and commerce. Europe wanted antimony from Sarawak, tin (and later rubber) from the peninsula and gutta percha. This gum of the gutta percha tree provided a resin that was remarkably pliable and capable of protecting undersea telegraph cables. In an ominous nod to the future fare of the rainforests, the greedy entrepreneurs cut down the gutta percha trees in the thousands until none was left. The Chinese continued in a trade that had been going on for over one thousand years, exporting such Borneo exotica as camphor, canes from the rattan palm, pearls from the Sulu Sea and edible birds' nests.

THE GROWTH OF SINGAPORE AND MALAYSIA

The tiny island of Singapore served as the natural center for all this trade, and the duty-free port grew and prospered out of all proportion to its size. It received an enormous boost when new steamships made it through the even newer Suez canal, cutting 90 days off the London-Singapore trip, making Singa-

ABOVE: Prized hardwoods, especially in Borneo, form an important part of the Malaysian economy. OPPOSITE: No longer prime minister, but still a force for stability in Singapore — Lee Kuan Yew.

pore the final coaling station for the last hop to the Far East. Singapore became what Melaka had been in the fifteenth century. Immigration was unrestricted and taxes exempt (except for the lucrative vices of opium, alcohol and gambling).

Tin and rubber production were alien activities to the indigenous Malay farmers or the forest-dwelling natives of Borneo. Tin mining was especially dangerous and only the needy and desperate would work for low wages in such a risky occupation. So the British turned elsewhere and set about encouraging thou-

Chinese feel to it. Singapore contains all three cultures, but as more than 75 percent are Chinese, it seems a Chinese city through and through.

For the first three decades of the twentieth century the unchallenged British rule kept such a racial mix under control. The Second World War changed all that.

WORLD WAR II AND ITS AFTERMATH

The Japanese started their invasion at Kota Bharu, in the northeast of Malaya, in De-

sands of Chinese and Indians to come to the newly created Straits Settlements, as the colonies of Penang, Melaka and Singapore were known since their combination in 1826.

This policy, more than anything else perhaps, has shaped the nature of these modern nations. Although many emigrants probably intended to return to India and China, most never did. They stayed, married, had children — and the foundations for a future multiracial and multi-cultural Malaysia and Singapore were created. The East Coast of the Malay peninsula, where tin did not exist and little rubber was planted, is still a predominantly Malay part of the country and here the Muslim influence is strongest. The west coast, by comparison, has a distinctly

cember 1941 and began their blistering campaign that led to the humiliating surrender of the English in Singapore only three months later. The British were lined up in public on the *Padang* in Singapore on the morning of February 17, 1942, kept waiting in the heat for hours, then ignominiously marched off to jail at Changi Prison, and the myth of white superiority went with them.

Thousands of Chinese were murdered while the Malays were encouraged to col-

ABOVE: The Boh tea plantation in Malaysia where tea is still hand picked, dried, graded and packaged. OPPOSITE: Commerce is the *raison d'être* of Singapore and is carried out with fervor and determinatión.

laborate with the Japanese invaders, who cynically fostered and fed ethnic Malay-Chinese rivalry. Much of the Chinese population fled into the jungles and took shelter in Maoist communism, an ideology that sustained their opposition to the British long after the Japanese armies had been expelled in 1945. A guerrilla war lasted through the early 1950s and although what was termed the Emergency came to an end by the early 1960s, it was only in 1989 that the legendary communist leader, Chin Peng, finally emerged from the jungle.

MODERN MALAYSIA AND SINGAPORE

Independence came to the Federated Malay States in 1957 after protracted discussions about what to do with a land which the Malays felt was theirs, even though economic power rested securely with the Chinese. Largely because the Malays did not have a clear numerical supremacy, Sarawak and Sabah, with their large non-Chinese populations, were urged to join the new Federation of Malaysia, which was to include Chinese-dominated Singapore, in 1963. The Chinese power bloc in Singapore continued to cause problems, however. Lee Kuan Yew, the leader of Singapore, was not happy with the ethnic preference given to Malays within Malaysia and wanted a more egalitarian system not based on race. This was unacceptable to Kuala Lumpur and in 1965 Singapore was ejected from the coalition. Tension erupted in 1969 when racial riots broke out in Kuala Lumpur as a reaction by the Malays to a perceived Chinese threat caused by a Chinese victory in a by-election.

Today, Malaysia and Singapore are at peace, despite occasional bickering. Economic prosperity in both countries has proved to be the key to civic order and racial harmony. In Sabah, ironically, the prosperous natural resources, timber and oil, have caused some dissent. Some politicians in Sabah have been unhappy that too much of Sabah's wealth is siphoned off to Peninsular Malaysia, and for nine years, a Christian-dominated government led the state. The ruling coalition party of Malaysia, Barisan Nasional, gained control in 1994, and the dissent seems to have gone underground for the moment. Neighboring Sarawak, far wealthier in terms of natural resources than Sabah, has kept the political reins firmly in local hands since the formation of Malaysia and enjoys a more amicable relationship with the Federal government.

The Government and the Economy
Both countries follow a parliamentary democratic system modeled on that of the British, though both have managed to adopt this in a rather authoritarian manner. In Malaysia, power is firmly in the hands of UMNO (United Malays National Organization), one of the components of the ruling Barisan National, whose intention it is to try to reverse the economic advantages held by the Chinese population. A Muslim fundamentalist thrust comes from PAS (Parti Islam), which holds power in the eastern state of Kelantan, but it is most unlikely to ever wield national power. At the time of writing, the prime minister, Dr. Mahathir, balances the various ethnic and political forces with some success, though in 1987 a repressive Internal Security Act was used to imprison a variety of opponents including active environmentalists who were drawing attention to the destruction of the rainforests in Sarawak and Sabah. The press is still effectively muzzled.

The economy of Malaysia is amazingly strong in terms of natural resources. Timber, palm oil and rubber have been large earners, though now petroleum is one the nation's most lucrative assets. In Southeast Asia, Malaysia's economy is only outshone — for the moment — by that of its southern neighbor, Singapore.

The island of Singapore might be small, but economically it continues to thrive, despite lower growth rates since 1995. To appreciate the stature of this achievement one should keep in mind that Singapore has no natural resources, unless you count its surrounding waters which it has managed to turn into the world's busiest port serving massive petroleum refineries. The promotion of English as the medium of educational instruction (Malaysia abandoned English in favor of the Malay language, a move which made more political than economic sense)

GEOGRAPHY

The geography of Malaysia is remarkable when you consider that the country consists of Peninsular Malaysia, occupying what used to be known as Malaya, and Sabah and Sarawak on the island of Borneo, some 650 km (400 miles) east across the south China Sea. Sabah and Sarawak are lands where diminishing tracts of rainforest remain unlogged. Mount Kinabalu, 4,101 m (13,455 ft) dominates the Kinabalu Park and is a beacon to

has helped to create a business environment that continues to grow and prosper.

Unfortunately this economic success has been accompanied by a sorry state of political life. The ruler since independence in 1965 until 1990, Lee Kuan Yew, ruthlessly crushed any signs of dissent. It was only in 1989 that a political prisoner was released after 23 years in jail. A very strange and sad event was the arrest in 1987 of a score of church and social workers and members of the opposition. Trial was by television and their crime was an alleged Marxist plot to overthrow the government. The current prime minister, Goh Chok Tong, has a more tolerant image, but Lee's influence may well prove to have been permanent.

air travelers crossing the country. Peninsular Malaysia too has large tracts of relatively unexplored mountainous forest, although none of its peaks reach the majesty of Kinabalu. A flight over Malaysia reveals the enormous inroads being made into the forests, the old tin workings looking like a huge moonscape and vast areas of oil palm plantation intersected by brown access roads and the occasional small town.

Singapore's chief geographical feature is its enormous natural harbor, now considerably extended by several land reclamation

OPPOSITE: Police parade at the Merdeka Day celebration in Kuala Lumpur. ABOVE: Cloud formations can be appreciated from an amazing proximity and intensity on Mount Kinabalu.

projects. It is almost uniformly flat and was once marshy, although you would be hard put to find any marsh nowadays. Its two hills are fairly uninspiring. Bukit Timah Hill has a small nature reserve with wild macaques and a number of interesting birds in its patch of virgin rainforest, while Mount Faber blended into the urban landscape long ago.

CLIMATE

The climate can come as a surprise. Everyone speaks of a wet season from November to the end of February but the term is somewhat misleading. Generally, it means you get heavier rain than at other times of year, although rain showers are usually brief and arrive during the afternoon. The heavy rains of the northeast monsoon can certainly spoil beach holidays on the East Coast of Peninsular Malaysia; indeed, many of the big resorts here close down completely and other places have reduced rates. Taman Negara, the large national park in Peninsular Malaysia, also closes down for two months and it will probably be equally wet around Kuching and on the East Coast of Sabah. You could easily spend one of these months in Singapore or Kuala Lumpur and be more aware of the heat than the rain. This is mainly because of the constantly high humidity rate that rarely falls below 90 percent. Night-time temperatures seldom drop below 23°C, except in the hill stations, and during the day it will usually be around 30°C.

A CULTURAL MIX

Although the government of Malaysia is dominated by the Malays (who make up close to 50 percent of the population) and Islam, their religion, is the official faith of the country, Malaysia is a truly multiracial country. Chinese make up more than one-third of the total population, with Indians and a host of different ethnic groups in Sabah and Sarawak adding further racial variety.

Singapore, like Malaysia, is multi-cultural: over 75 percent Chinese, 14 percent Malay, less than seven percent Indian plus Eurasians and other minorities. The cultural diversity of both Malaysia and Singapore is reflected in the many festivals that are celebrated in the traditions of the many ethnic groupings (see FESTIVE FLINGS, page 49). Most of the Chinese in both Singapore and Malaysia are descendants of poverty-stricken peasants who left southern China in search of a better life. The majority of them came from southern China and although they still speak their own dialect (such as Cantonese, Hokkien, Teochew, Hakka, Hainanese and Foochow), Singapore actively promotes Mandarin, the official language of China, as a standard means of communication. In Malaysia, Malay is the official national language. It is

the mother tongue of Malays and has for centuries been the *lingua franca* in this part of the world. However, like the Chinese, who form close to 30 percent of Malaysia's population, ethnic groups in Sarawak and Sabah speak their own language. In Sarawak, this may be Iban (they form about 30 percent of the population), Bidayuh, Melanau, Kayan, Kenyah, Kelabit, Murut, Lun Dayeh, Penan, Punan or another minority language. The Kadazan/Dusun group of languages are spoken by about 20 percent of Sabah's population, while the Bajau, Bisayan, Suluk, Illanun and other groups have their own distinct languages, culture and customs.

OPPOSITE: Inside the Sultan Mosque in Singapore.
ABOVE: Fortune telling on the streets of Melaka.

Kuala Lumpur
Malaysia's Capital

BACKGROUND

In 1857, a group of Chinese tin prospectors led by an agent of the ruler of Klang, Raja Abdullah, discovered rich open seams of tin in the state of Selangor. A small trading post was established at the confluence of two rivers where the shallow waters upstream made further navigation difficult, and was aptly named Kuala Lumpur (Muddy River Mouth). Fortunes were made and squandered as miners and merchants struggled for survival; at

one stage a gang boss was even offering cash rewards for the delivery of his enemies' heads. Malay princes squabbled over rights to the tin, and soon the British saw the value of establishing order in the interests of peaceful trade. By the turn of the century, the shanty town was a proper town, with a railway line and tin millionaires aping the colonialists by building European-style mansions.

By the early twentieth century, the rubber plantations added new sources of wealth, and Indians came in the thousands to tap the trees. Dunlop established a big office here, and the British owners set up their clubs and drank their gin until the Japanese cycled in and established a new order in 1942. Three years later they were gone, but Britain's colo-nial stranglehold was loosened, and in 1957 the city was freed by the declaration of independence.

GENERAL INFORMATION

The headquarters of the Tourist Development Corporation are at the top of the Putra World Trade Centre ((03) 293-5188, but general information and maps are available at any of the Tourist Information Centres. The best place to try is the Malaysian Tourist Information Complex (MATIC) in a restored colonial house, 109 Jalan Ampang ((03) 264-3929 FAX (03) 262-1149. There is an information booth at Terminal 1 of **International Airport** ((03)746-5707, while the Kuala Lumpur **Tourist Visitors Centre** ((03) 238-1832, is at 3 Jalan Hishamuddin. There is yet another information center in the railway station at Jalan Hishamuddin ((03) 274-6063, and at Lot 1, Plaza Putra, Dataran Merdekan, Jalan Raja (opposite the Padang). The Tourist Police Unit can be contacted at ((03) 241-5522.

The *Visitor's Guide to Kuala Lumpur* is a useful free brochure that is updated every month; you could also look for the Kuala Lumpur edition of *Malaysia Now.* Other telephone numbers that might prove useful: **Subang International Airport** ((03)834-1002. **Kuala Lumpur Railway Station** (Reservations: North) ((03) 274-7434. (Reservations: South) ((03) 274-7443 Complaints/Hotline ((03) 249-6590. **Malaysia Airlines** ((03) 261-0555. The headquarters is in the MAS Building, Jalan Sultan Ismail, just opposite the Hilton Hotel. The 24-hour reservation number is ((03) 774-7000. **24-Hour Call Cabs** ((03) 293-6211, 733-0507, 221-1011.

GETTING AROUND

Taxis are highly recommended because they are cheap; any trip around town should cost around $2 to $4 (RM5 to RM8), provided you don't get stuck in a traffic jam. Taxis are metered and although the drivers had a bad reputation for refusing to take taking passengers unless they agreed to pay a higher fare than that shown on the meter, things have

The glittering night skyline of Kuala Lumpur.

changed. An increase in prices in 1996 seems to have mollified the drivers and for the moment, most use their meter without being asked to. Around town there are many designated taxi stops and although you can hail one anywhere, the stops are best during peak times. Waiting times can sometimes be infuriatingly long. For longer distances there are special cab ranks and these "out station" cabs have no meters. Ask at your hotel how much these cabs should cost.

Stops for minibuses are often close to the taxi stops and they're handy for straight runs. Be forewarned, however, that they don't give change. If you are not sure where the minibus is going, or even where you're going, ask someone for help.

The first phase of a light rail transport system (LRT), running between Ampang and Jalan Sultan Ismail, was introduced in 1996 in an effort to cut down on the grid-lock traffic jams which make Kuala Lumpur more and more like Bangkok every day. This, however, is not of much use to a visitor yet, although other lines are opening progressively and the new airport at Sepang will be on the LRT system eventually.

The *Visitor's Guide to Kuala Lumpur*, available from the tourist offices, has a useful map showing the various bus stations for out of town travel.

Car rental is readily available from Avis ((03) 242-3500, Hertz TOLL FREE 800-3086, or Thrifty ((03) 230-2591. Check the Yellow Pages for more.

WHAT TO SEE

The town sights are conveniently packed into a small area, and if you are short of time I would suggest the following itinerary that takes in most of them on foot, starting at the railway station and ending in Chinatown. Because of Kuala Lumpur's worsening traffic jams, walking is often the quickest way to get anywhere reasonably close in the city. In some areas, unfortunately, the road planners have forgotten the pedestrian and it can be impossible to walk from one building to another further along the same road because there's nothing but expressway in front of you. An example of this is trying to get from the National Museum to the National Gallery opposite the Railway Station.

Whether you arrive by train or not, the **Railway Station** should not be missed. No one term can represent an eclectic architectural style that successfully combines the Islamic, Mogul, Moorish, Gothic and Greek, and the surprising result is a visual treat. An excellent viewpoint can be had from the first floor of the similarly styled Railway Administration building directly across the road. Incidentally, the architect of both these buildings was a man of little experience. Before designing these places he had done nothing more than work on alterations to site plans!

Dawn at Kuala Lumpur's eclectically styled railway station.

NATIONAL ART GALLERY AND MUSEUM

Opposite the station and next door to the Railway Administration is the **National Art Gallery** and three blocks west of that, the **National Museum** (both open at 10 AM). Despite its interesting collection of works by local and regional artists, the Art Gallery is perhaps still more famous for what it once was — the number one colonial hotel, the Majestic, used during the Second World War by the Japanese as their headquarters. One

point of interest is that the interior of the former hotel has not been gutted; the domed exhibition area was the hotel's dining hall and ballroom and canvases now adorn the walls of what were once bedrooms. The art gallery is due to be relocated and the Majestic turned back into a hotel. Check with the tourism information center to make sure of its new location.

The National Museum is a disappointment to those who have seen the excellent displays in Singapore's museums, or enjoyed the charming Sarawak Museum in Kuching. As it is crowded for space, most of the collection is not on view and the situation seems unlikely to improve for the moment. However, the upstairs' galleries, especially the one devoted to the various cultural groups in Malaysia, are worth looking at if you're in the area.

On top of the hill opposite the National Museum is the **Planetarium Negara**, open Tuesday to Sunday. Inside the planetarium is a Space Theatre where two different shows are presented, as well as a space science

exhibition, viewing gallery and ancient observatory park. This is an excellent place to take children.

About six blocks north of the railway station is the 32-sided **Dayabumi**, a striking Islamic-influenced edifice that easily stands out from the majority of Kuala Lumpur's mundane skyscrapers.

Continuing north brings you to an open green on the left, with Tudor style houses behind it, and on your right there are huge palace-like stone buildings. This was once the very nucleus of colonial Malaya, and the history of this patch of green marks many of the significant stages in the evolution of modern Malaysia. The green *Padang* used to be the playground for colonial sportsmen, and the mock-Tudor buildings housed their **Royal Selangor Club**. This was where the expatriate tin and rubber merchants came to relax with a drink and watch cricket or play bridge. The club was first constructed in 1884 on top of what had been swamp land. The green was drained for a police training ground before being turned into a sporting green. It is here that football (soccer), now a popular sport among young Malaysians, was first introduced to the country. When the Japanese arrived in 1942 they reconverted the ground to agriculture, and banana plants and tapioca grew there for a brief while. The English converted it back to a sporting ground and play was resumed until 1957. On August 31, 1963 the Malaysian flag was raised for the first time and continues to hang from the 100-m (328-ft) flagpole that now decks **Dataran Merdeka** or Independence Square.

The first stone building opposite the green is so similar in style to the one next to it that they are often confused or taken to be one. Both were designed by A.C. Norman in 1896. The first stone building, once the General Post Office, is the **Infokraf**, a craft center that displays and sells traditional items. The second building, the one spouting lacquered copper domes, now houses the Supreme Court and is known as the **Sultan Abdul Samad Building**.

ABOVE: A busy street in Kuala Lumpur's Chinatown. OPPOSITE TOP and BOTTOM: The elegantly serene national mosque in Kuala Lumpur marks the spot where the first settlers landed.

Kuala Lumpur: Malaysia's Capital

Turn into Lebuh Pasar Besar, the road that runs between these two stone buildings, and you'll soon come to a small girdered bridge. Look over to your left and you will have a view of **Masjid Jame** on Jalan Tun Perak. This is an elegant mosque, open to the public and significant for its location as much as its aesthetic appeal because it was on this very spot, at the muddy confluence of the two rivers, that the trading post for the pioneering tin miners was established.

CENTRAL MARKET

Another short walk south will bring you to the **Central Market**. The Central Market was once just what the name indicates, but now it has been imaginatively transformed into a shopping mall with an emphasis on arts and crafts. The original slabs, used by the butchers and fishmongers to cut and display their produce, now host a variety of inexpensive consumer artifacts, and this is one of the best places for browsing for souvenirs and presents. The artistic atmosphere continues to be enhanced by an active policy of encouraging street artists and entertainers to perform on the pedestrian streets outside, and a stroll around here in the early evening can be very entertaining.

Seen as emblematic of the tremendous growth in Malaysia and of the government's desire to flaunt the nation's achievements, the 88-story twin towers of the national petroleum company, Petronas, thrust up into the smog with their gleaming glass and stainless steel fingers. Among the tallest buildings in the world, the **Petronas Twin Towers** are linked at the 44th floor by a pedestrian skybridge. The land where they are located was once the Kuala Lumpur race course.

For a dramatic view out over the ever-expanding capital city, take the lift to the top of **Kuala Lumpur Tower** (Menara Kuala Lumpur), situated on Bukit Nanas. The tower is open every day from 10 AM until 10 PM, and costs RM8 for adults and RM3 for children. In case you tire of the view, there are two levels of shops for you to browse through. If you can, try visiting on a Sunday or at the end of a long weekend when the accumulation of pollution is likely to have dropped. Then you may seen how close

the beautiful forested hills of the Titiwangsa Range really are.

CHINATOWN

Chinatown is a small area around Jalan Petaling just south of the Central Market. At night an open-air market springs up with stalls crowded with clothes, belts, cassettes and watches, and occasionally something novel makes an appearance — jewelry or fossils from Nepal for instance. During the day it is still a hive of activity, and there are

a number of places here to rest and have a drink or meal. A block away on Jalan Bandar rests the **Sri Maha Mariamman Temple**, one of the most spectacular Hindu temples in Malaysia because of its richly layered *gopuram* (gateway). Leave your footwear outside and feel free to wander in.

An alternative afternoon's sightseeing can be had at the Lake Gardens (Taman Tasik Perdana), particularly suited to those who need some peace and quiet or have children. Along Jalan Parliamen is the Lake itself, originally created in 1888, and for those who feel

ABOVE: Merdeka Square, Kuala Lumpur, by night, showing the Federal Secretariat building and clock tower. OPPOSITE: Masjid Jame stands on the spot where the first tin trading began in Kuala Lumpur.

energetic enough, paddle boats wait patiently at the bank. Also in the Gardens is the national monument, created by Felix de Weldon, creator of the famous Iwo Jima statue in Washington. The National Museum is close by, as are the orchid garden and deer park, where you can see the native Malaysian mouse deer, the smallest hoofed animal in the world. In the gardens is also a bird park, built into a natural valley. The entire area of over three hectares (eight acres) is covered in netting stretched from one side of the valley to the other and birds fly around freely. The

site has made maximum use of the natural surroundings, including the stream at the bottom which provides habitat for waterfowl. A few birds are caged, however. The hornbills glare balefully out from their prisons wondering what they did to deserve incarceration while the other birds enjoy the pleasure of relative freedom. The park is open from 9 AM to 6 PM; early morning or late afternoons are best, as both the birds and humans are livelier during the cooler hours.

OUT OF TOWN

A few kilometers out of Kuala Lumpur and easily accessed by public transport (bus N° 66, N° 78 or N° 77 from Pudu Raya Bus

Station) is **Templer Park**, 1,214 hectares (3,000 acres) of jungle and park land which offers many different types of activity. Pools fed by natural waterfalls, peaceful walks in the forest, birds of many species, caves and cliffs are just a few of the attractions here. The area is sufficiently large that a good amount of time can be spent here without seeing very many other visitors. Most people tend to collect at the swimming pools which have been created at various points along the fall of the river, but during weekdays even these areas are sparsely populated. There are some food stalls near the entrance to the park, ample parking, and easy access to the main road, where one can find a cab or a bus going into Kuala Lumpur.

Other out of town spots are best seen as part of a countryside tour. There are many such tours easily booked at your hotel (or at Malaysia Tourist Information Complex, where a tour operator offers good value with a wide range of places for $9). Most tours will include the **Selangor Pewter Showroom and Factory**.

This is one of the largest pewter (97 percent tin and three percent copper and antimony) factories in the world, and while there are shops everywhere in Malaysia selling pewter ware, you can be assured of finding legitimate prices here, as well as having the opportunity to view the factory and a large showroom.

BATU CAVES

The tour should also include the **Batu Caves**, 13 km (eight miles) north of Kuala Lumpur. These sacred Hindu caves contain various shrines, and the relatively easy 272-step ascent should not dissuade anyone from visiting the cathedral-like main cavern. During the Thaipusam festival the caves attract well over half-a-million devotees in the space of 48 hours. This is the time to visit if you want to view the penitents skewering their flesh and walking on fire (see TOP SPOTS). The caves are millions of years old, and tigers and bears

ABOVE: Most people go to the Genting Highlands for its casinos and cool air, but this pagoda provides a scenic diversion. OPPOSITE: Batu Caves, outside Kuala Lumpur, are a Hindu shrine as well as a tourist attraction.

once prowled the ground now trod by devotees. During the Japanese Occupation, a mass execution of communists took place here. Local buses leave from the Pudu Raya terminal in town.

THEME PARKS

Theme parks which are often part of an integrated development of hotels, condominiums and shopping complexes are increasingly popular in Peninsular Malaysia. One of the newest is located to the south of the city, adjacent to the relocated race course and a golf course. This is the **Mines Resort City**, Jalan Sungai Besi, Selangor, which imaginatively makes use of the world's largest opencast tin mine, filling it in to make a lake. A very pleasant hotel, the **Mines Beach Resort** ((03) 943-6633 FAX (03) 943-6622 (doubles from $119) is ideally located on one side of the lake, next to the "family playground" of **Mines Wonderland** ((03) 942-5010 where the attractions include of a snow house (complete with real snow) a musical fountain, water taxis and so forth (see FAMILY FUN, page 42). A package ticket giving admission to all the places of interest costs RM25 for adults, RM15 for children. To get there, take bus Nº 65 from Kota Raya, or a Toong Fong bus Nº 10. There is a coach service to major hotels in the city which sells packages including transportation for RM30 or RM22; call BTT Travel at ((03) 248-8820.

Another theme park, which has lost much of its glitter to the Mines Wonderland, is **Sunway Lagoon** (735-6000 in Petaling Jaya. Main attractions are the Water Park (with many wild and wonderful ways to get wet) and **Fort Lagoon Wild Wild West**. Admission to both parks is RM40 for adults, RM25 for children, or you can opt to visit one only for a lower price.

GENTING HIGHLANDS

Further afield is Genting Highlands, a rather brash and unpeaceful gambling resort with its own 18-hole golf course and bowling alley. It has, as well, the only casino in this predominantly Muslim country. If you want to play blackjack or baccarat, remember to pack a long-sleeved shirt and tie in order to gain entry to the casino. Genting operates its own daily coaches from the Pekeliling bus terminal and the journey takes over an hour. The best deal is to arrange a package with any travel agent in town.

FRASER'S HILL

Fraser's Hill is infinitely preferable as an out of town trip although, because it can take three hours to drive the 100-km (62-mile) journey, you might want to plan to spend at least one night there before returning to the capital. See INTO THE INTERIOR, page 170, for more details on Fraser's Hill.

OFF THE BEATEN TRACK

Contact the Malaysian Nature Society ((03) 616-5259, to see if any interesting trips are being organized. At Batu Caves, for instance, there is a network of caverns not open to the public, but the Nature Society has permission to organize visits. There is also a reputable tour company, **Asian Overland** ((03) 452-9100, FAX (03) 452-9800 that specializes in out of the ordinary trips like a one-day cave exploration that involves wading through waist-deep water, a day's basic rock climbing or a trip involving rafting along rapids. It also conducts jungle walks and various nature tours that all start from Kuala Lumpur. Another smaller adventure tour operator is **Tracks Outdoor** ((03) 777-8363 FAX (03) 777-8363 which has a good four-day, three-night trip which includes abseiling, trekking, camping and white-water rafting. The price per person (minimum of four per trip) is $300 per person. Alternatively, you could choose to go on a one-day rafting trip on the Selangor River for $60 per person.

Only half-an-hour's drive west of Kuala Lumpur, out toward the airport, is the satellite town of **Shah Alam**, and the **Sultan Abdul Aziz Shah Mosque**. This mosque is stupendous in size and design, with a prayer hall that accommodates over 12,000 worshippers. Although Muslims only can enter the actual chambers, the mosque is still worth viewing because of its commanding presence and the way that its sparkling blue color somehow avoids being garish.

A whole day could be planned in Shah Alam by combining a visit to the mosque with a longer stay at the 1,330-hectare (over 3,000 acres) Agricultural Park or **Taman Alam**. One of the most interesting features here is the paddy field with six plots in various stages of cultivation and the rice mill nearby. The whole process of rice growing can be observed in progress, and the rice mill is a little museum in itself with a guide who will be happy to talk about agricultural matters. The park has many other features, including a suspension bridge.

cost about $12, but getting one back could be tricky. Hiring a car would be best and it would also allow you to take in the nearby mosque. The mosque is right next to the **Holiday Inn Shah Alam** ((03) 550-3696 FAX (03) 550-3913, and the hotel would provide the ideal place for a decent meal in the vicinity as well as an alternative source of accommodation to the park chalets. A double in the Holiday Inn is $118.

Further afield is **Carey Island**, home to the Mah Meri aborigines, the only group of *Orang Asli* who do wood carving. Carey

There is no entrance fee, just RM2 for the regular buses that traverse the area. Hiring a bicycle would be more fun, though this wouldn't get you to the top of the 788-m (2,585-ft) Sapu Tangan Hill. This requires a stiff walk and is more fun early in the morning. There is accommodation in a resthouse at only $6, while chalets cost $16. You need to bring your own food to make use of the cooking facilities. To make reservations, call ((03) 550-6922 FAX (03) 291-3758. At weekends and public holidays the park and chalets are full but during the week the place is your own.

From Kuala Lumpur take the Sri Jaya N° 338 bus, or the Klang bus N° 222 or 206, from the Kelang Bus Terminal. A taxi would

Island, located in Kuala Langat some 60 km (37 miles) west of Kuala Lumpur, takes nearly two hours to reach. The island (slightly smaller than Singapore) is linked to the mainland by a 100-m (328-ft) bridge. It's a good idea to get a guide by contacting the *Orang Asli* Affairs Department (Jabatan Hal Ehwal *Orang Asli* Malaysia), 16th and 17th floors, Bangunan Tabung Haji, Kuala Lumpur ((03) 261-0577. If you are interested in learning more about the *Orang Asli*, you could visit the Muzium *Orang Asli* Gombak, (03) 689-2122 open Sunday to Thursday from 9 AM to 5 PM.

From sleepy capital to economic metropolis, Kuala Lumpur is developing at a accelerating rate.

NIGHTLIFE

The best clubs, pubs and discos are found in the area known as the Golden Triangle although there's also a lively scene out in areas such as Bangsar and Petaling Jaya. Closing times imposed in 1997 (to "prevent social ills") now means everything closes up at the ridiculously early hour of 1 AM, but it remains to be seen how long this will be enforced.

One of the oldest discos in Kuala Lumpur still holding its own is the **Tin Mine** in the

Kuala Lumpur Hilton, Jalan Sultan Ismail. **Musictheque** in the Hotel Istana, in the same road as the Hilton, has something for all tastes including a lounge with its own karaoke theme rooms, a lounge bar with live entertainment and the **197** discotheque. Still in the same area, the **Hard Rock Café** in the Concorde Hotel is a rocker's paradise with a bar and dance floor. The music alternates between a live band and a DJ spinning disks. This is one of the most popular places in Kuala Lumpur (and has one of the loudest decibel levels too).

For outrageous entertainment featuring a floor show, with a disco to while away the time both before and after, visit the popular **Boom Boom Room**, 11 Lebuh Ampang. The popular **Branigan's** pub, 1 Lorong Perak off Jalan P. Ramlee offers live entertainment to go with your drinks. **Uncle Chilli's Fun Pub** is a five-in-one spot with bar, restaurant, disco, karaoke and life music. It's an informal and friendly place where you're made to feel at home. Irish pubs, quite the rage in Singapore, have also opened up in Kuala

Lumpur. Try **Delaney's** in the GF Parkroyal Hotel, Jalan Sultan Ismail.

The **Barn Thai** offers hot Thai cuisine soothed with cool jazz. It's located in the Micasa Hotel Apartments, Jalan Tun Razak. Another place for both food and a mixture of live music plus jazz and blues via the DJ is the **Wall Street** on the ground floor of Menara TA One, 22 Jalan P. Ramlee. You can have pasta or pizza downstairs or fine dining upstairs, and the choice of cocktails here must be second to none.

WHERE TO STAY

EXPENSIVE

For unashamed luxury, sheer class and history, the **Carcosa Seri Negara** ((03) 282-1888 FAX (03) 282-7888, wins hands down (see YOUR CHOICE). Two romantic colonial bungalows set in 16 hectares (40 acres) of lush forest and gardens above Kuala Lumpur's Lake Gardens offer a total of 13 suites ranging from $380 to $1,040. The address is Taman Tasik Perdana, 50480 Kuala Lumpur. This is without doubt the ultimate place to stay in all of Malaysia.

A cluster of five-star hotels can be found along Jalan Sultan Ismail, among which the **Shangri-La** ((03) 232-2388 FAX (03) 230-1514, most consistently and deservedly wins awards for its standard of service. Ask for a room with a view of the hills, although you'll also get the Petronas Twin Towers standing on what used to be the race course. For $214, you get a double room, airport transfers, breakfast and laundry, although it is possible to negotiate for a lower rate without the extras. The **Hotel Equatorial** ((03) 261-7777 FAX (03) 261-9020, is close by and offers less expensive ($120, although you can negotiate less) but more homely rooms plus a coffee-house that is very popular with locals. The **Kuala Lumpur Hilton** ((03) 242-2222 FAX (03) 243-8069, is next door and the **Holiday Inn On The Park** ((03) 248-1066 FAX (03) 248-1930, in Jalan Pinang, P.O. Box 10983, is just behind the Hilton with good doubles for $144. Even closer to the big shopping centers is the relatively new and highly regarded **Regent Kuala Lumpur** ((03) 241-8000 FAX (03) 242-1441, 160 Jalan Bukit Bintang, where doubles start at $192. The advantage of staying in this area is your proximity to the largest shopping area in Kuala Lumpur, and there are numerous classy restaurants and nightclubs in the vicinity.

Well located for access to the airport and a large shopping complex (but with a small swimming pool) is the **Pan Pacific** ((03) 442-5555 FAX (03) 441-7236, adjacent to the Putra World Trade Centre and easily recognizable at night due to the lifts that climb the exterior wall like caterpillars. The postal address is P.O. Box 11468, 50746 Kuala Lumpur, and doubles start at $168.

Other well established hotels in this category are **Hotel Malaya** ((03) 232-7722, FAX (03) 230-0980 on Jalan Hang Lekir in Chinatown, the **Lodge Hotel** ((03) 242-0122, FAX (03) 241-6819 on Jalan Sultan Ismail and the **Champagne Hotel** ((03) 298-6333, well situated in the downtown area off Jalan Masjid India. But for sheer good value, a wide choice of rooms and excellent location, it is difficult to beat the **Hotel Pudu Raya**. This modern hotel is located on the fourth floor Bus Station in Jalan Pudu near Chinatown. Their basic standard double costs $41. The hotel has most of the

MODERATE

Melia Kuala Lumpur ((03) 242-8333 FAX (03) 242-6623, enjoys an excellent location in the heart of the shopping district at 16 Jalan Imbi. Rooms are small but adequate and you get all you need without the frills for $104 (negotiable) a double. The **Kowloon Hotel** ((03) 293-4246 FAX (03) 292-6548, is well situated at the town end of Jalan Tuanku Abdul Rahman (N° 142–146) and has modern, good rooms at $39. The **Asia Hotel** ((03) 292-6077 FAX (03) 292-7734, is similar but at the other end of the same main road— 69 Jalan Haji Hussein. **Kuala Lumpur Mandarin** ((03) 274-7433, 2–8 on Jalan Sultan, has singles and doubles at $42.

services you would normally associate with room rates double those of the Pudu Raya. The set meals are also a good value and if you are leaving by taxi or bus for other parts of Malaysia, then this hotel is perfect: the bus and taxi stations are literally below the hotel in the same building.

INEXPENSIVE

Always worth trying is the historic **Coliseum** ((03) 292-6270, but with only 10 rooms ($10 and shared bathrooms) it takes some luck to

OPPOSITE: Popular Eden Village restaurant seafood dining alfresco with a cultural show. ABOVE: Traditional religious buildings rub shoulders with Kuala Lumpur's colonial and modern architecture.

get a room. Just a little further up Abdul Rahman is the **Rex** ($8), but while the restaurant serves decent, inexpensive western food the rooms are depressingly bare. **Paradise Bed & Breakfast** ((03) 293-2322, offers very spartan but clean rooms ($10) with continental breakfast included. The Kuala Lumpur **International Youth Hostel** ((03) 230-6870 21 Jalan Kampung Attap, has rooms for the same price. The Tourist Information Centres have a useful booklet listing budget accommodation in Kuala Lumpur and other regions of Malaysia.

WHERE TO EAT

You can get almost anything you want in Kuala Lumpur when it comes to food. Malay cuisine is often better at the simple food stalls (where it still has that home-cooked flavor) although there are a few good restaurants. Chinese cuisine is everywhere, while there is no dearth of a variety of Indian cuisines. You can enjoy Thai, Japanese, Vietnamese and Korean food, or if you want to go Western, there's French, Italian, German, American and even Brazilian to choose from. The major shopping complexes such as Star Hill, Lot 10 or The Mall have air-conditioned food stalls (almost invariably in the basement) where its possible to get a good range of inexpensive and usually very good local as well as western food.

A favorite place for Malay cuisine and other food from around the region is the attractive **Spices** ((03) 244-2200 at the Concorde Hotel, Two Jalan Sultan Ismail. If you're not visiting Penang or Melaka and want to sample Nonya cuisine, visit the **Restoran Dondang Sayang** ((03) 261-8888 in the Ming Court Hotel, Jalan Ampang for delicious food that is a fusion of Malay and Chinese. Leave a space for one of the excellent and invariably sweet Nonya desserts.

Among the most highly regarded upmarket Chinese restaurants in Kuala Lumpur is the sophisticated **Hai Tien Lo** ((03) 442-5555 in the Pan Pacific Hotel, Jalan Putra, which serves superb Cantonese cuisine. For lesser known, generally light (and diet-conscious) Teochew cuisine, the **Restoran Teochew,** 272 Jalan Pudu is worth a visit, especially for their seafood and *dim sum* (steamed and deep-fried tidbits). Spicy Sichuan cuisine is featured in the **Ming Palace** ((03) 261-8888 at the Ming Court Hotel on Jalan Ampang.

Annalakshmi ((03) 282-3799, 44/46 Jalan Maroof, Bangsar is associated with the Temple of Fine Arts, a charity organization linked to a Hindu sect. The restaurant offers very good, refined Indian vegetarian cuisine and is staffed entirely by volunteers. Smoking and alcohol are unacceptable anytime.

Decidedly meat and poultry oriented, the cuisine of northern India is featured at the **Taj** in the Federal Hotel ((03) 248-9166 in Jalan Bukit Bintang; the same management runs another **Taj** with the same excellent tandoori foods, rich curries and Indian breads at the Crown Princess Inter-Continental ((03) 248-9166 at City Square Centre, Jalan Tun Razak. Similar food is served at the **Omar Khayyam**, Halan Dang Wangi at Medan Tuanku, off Jalan Tuanku Abdul Rahman. For good Indian Muslim food try the old stalwart **Bilal Restaurant,** 33 Jalan Ampang, which has really gutsy mutton and chicken curries. Lots of simple coffeeshop–restaurants serving inexpensive Indian food — particularly stuffed griddle-fried Indian bread known as *murtabak* — can be found in the Jalan Masjid area.

There is also a **Devi Annapoorna** ((03) 291-2705 in the city, very close to the Omar Khayyam restaurant in Lorong Medan Tuanku Satu, but it is closed on Sundays. Another excellent place is **Gandhi's Corner**, near the junction of Jalan Thambypillay and Jalan Berhala in Brickfields. Local gourmets travel from far and wide to savor vegan kebab, "Bruce Lee" rice and other unique dishes created by a chef born on the day Mahatma Gandhi was assassinated. Open from 6 PM.

LOCAL FAVORITES

For inexpensive local food try the top floor of the Central Market where excellent Indian curries are available at the **Kampung Pandan** restaurant. On the fourth floor of the Mall, next to the Pan Pacific hotel and the Putra World Trade Centre, is the **Medan Hang Tuah** food court. Lots of local favorites here: *bak kut teh* (pork ribs soup) and *tom yam* (hot sour) soup from Thailand, to name just two.

Below Parkson's in the basement of Bukit Bintang Plaza is a supermarket and air-conditioned food court which might be a good way to try local food. About 15 stalls each offer a different type of local food, from banana leaf curries to noodles or *yong tau fu*, a delicious local soup made from vegetables and tofu fishballs. There are also very good food stalls in the basement of Star Hill nearby, with not only local food but Middle Eastern doner kebab and Thai cuisine.

Thai restaurants are very popular, one of the "in" places at the moment being the **Barn Thai Jazzaurant**, whose name says it all: Thai food together with live jazz served up at the **Micasa Hotel Apartments** ((03) 244-6699, 370B Jalan Tun Razak. Alternatively, you might like to try less fiery but no less delicious Vietnamese cuisine at **Vietnamhouse** ((03) 294-1726, 6th floor, Sogo Pernas Department Store, Jalan Tuanku Abdul Rahman, where the chefs are (like many of the ingredients) from Vietnam.

GREAT DINING

Unlike in Singapore, many colonial-style buildings have survived in Kuala Lumpur. One such building houses one of Kuala Lumpur's best restaurants, the stylish yet utterly unpretentious **Bon Ton** ((03) 241-3614, 7 Jalan Kia Peng. Interesting East-West cuisine as well as carefully selected local and Western favorites are featured on the menu, which changes every couple of months. The cakes here are the result of the owner's passionate testing of literally hundreds of recipes to find the yummiest imaginable carrot cake, the most sinful chocolate cake and so on. Another colonial building not far away is the home of the **Kapitan's Club** ((03) 201-0242 in 35 Jalan Ampang, which serves the sort of food reminiscent of the colonial days. Good curries, especially the Kapitan Chicken Curry and the Nonya dishes.

For a unique dining experience, try the **Carcosa Seri Negara** ((03) 282-1888, a century-old mansion set above the Lake Gardens. Fine Continental cuisine with a creative modern touch features in the elegant Mahsuri dining room. Afternoon tea, which can be enjoyed in the air-conditioned comfort of the restaurant or in a comfy wicker chair on the wide verandahs, is almost a meal in itself. The Sunday curry tiffin, a spread of the Anglo-Indian favorites beloved during colonial days, has become an institution among a number of Kuala Lumpur residents and is a habit one could easily adopt.

Another classic restaurant and bar of a very different nature is **The Coliseum** ((03) 292-6270 situated at the town end of Jalan Tuanku Abdul Rahman, not far from the Masjid Jame and next door to the cinema of the same name. It was opened in 1921 and, despite a brief hiatus during the early days

of the Japanese occupation, it has remained open for business ever since. The framed drawing on the wall is an original by Malaysia's most famous cartoonist, Lat, and the artist can sometimes be seen at the bar. The ancient fans on the ceiling are purely decorative, for the place is pleasantly air-conditioned and makes for a lovely watering hole. The restaurant is a separate area and the menu offers sound western favorites, including great sizzling steaks.

There's no dearth of restaurants serving American food. The **Hard Rock Café** in the Concorde Hotel, Jalan Sultan Ismail ((03) 244-2200 is still acknowledged as the best place in town to get a hamburger (provided you don't mind the incredibly loud music). **Chilli Buddy's** ((03) 241-2426, 1D Jalan U Thant serves plenty of ribs and other American favorites. Unlimited amounts of barbecued meat which is sliced and constantly added to your plate plus an excellent salad bar for

You can try the fare at one of Kuala Lumpur's many hawker stalls.

RM45 ($18) a head bring hungry diners back to the **Rio Churascaria Brazil** ((03) 241-0080, One Jalan Pinang.

SHOPPING

Once upon a time, affluent Malaysians used to go down to Singapore to shop, taking advantage of the lower prices and wider range of quality goods. Now the roles have reversed, with far more competitive prices and dozens of quality boutiques and departments stores attracting Singaporeans to

and boutiques, including a Parkson Grand department store.

In Jalan Tuanku Abdul Rahman, the 10-level **Sogo Pernas** Department store has an amusement level with restaurants and even a waterfall to complement the usual range of boutiques. **Central Market** is the place to go for inexpensive local clothing, handmade goods and souvenirs. In Jalan Ampang, the linked complexes of Plaza Ampang and City Square are known for antiques, curios, jewelry and designer goods. An enormous range of batik fabric, made up and sold as clothing

Kuala Lumpur. The biggest cluster of stores with the widest range of shops is at the junction of Jalan Sultan Ismail and Jalan Bukit Bintang. Latest and glitziest is **Star Hill**, opposite The Regent, which has a branch of the Singapore department store **Tang's** and dozens of boutiques selling international labels. Nearby, **Lot 10** is a showplace of designer clothing with some nice shops and the Japanese Isetan department store. It also has a Delifrance for pastry addicts. **BB Plaza** and **Sungai Wang Plaza** are both in **Jalan Sultan Ismail**. The former has a Metrojaya department store and dozens of other stores, travel agents and tailors (where you can get a local *baju kurung* (Malay women's outfit) made to order. **Sungai Wang Plaza** has over 500 stores

or in individual lengths is available at **Batek Malaysia Berhad** ((03) 984-0205, 15 Jalan Cahaya, 15 Taman Cahaya, Ampang; this place even has a do-it-yourself corner where you can try doing your own batik.

The countryside tours that operate from all the big hotels may include a shopping trip as most usually stop at a batik/souvenir shop as well as the **Selangor Pewter** factory. If you are interested in buying paintings or sculpture by Malaysian and other Southeast Asian artists, head for **Valentine Willie Fine Art** on the 1st floor, 17 Jalan Telawi 3, Bangsar Baru. They are the experts on local art and deal with many corporate clients and top collectors, as well as encouraging the sale of lesser known artists at affordable prices.

GETTING THERE AND AWAY

BY TRAIN

From Singapore there's a night train that leaves at 10 PM and arrives at Kuala Lumpur at 7 AM, and a day train that departs at 8 AM and arrives at Kuala Lumpur at 2:30 PM. A similar service operates in the opposite direction.

From Thailand, the International Express departs Bangkok at 3 PM, arrives at Butter-

Lumpur you need the Kelang Bus Terminal on Jalan Sultan Mohammed. Buses to and from the East Coast use more than one location, the most common station being the Mara on Jalan Medan Tuanku.

BY LONG DISTANCE TAXI

There's also a taxi station in the Pudu Raya Station so you can compare prices and times of departure. Basically, a taxi will leave as soon as one to four people are prepared to pay or share the cost. Do consider taking one

worth around midday the next day, where a connection can be made with the afternoon train leaving at 2 PM and reaching Kuala Lumpur at 8:30 PM the same night. To leave Kuala Lumpur for Thailand, catch the 7:30 AM train for the first leg of the journey. Phone the railway station for details ((03) 274-6063.

BY BUS

Coach buses arrive and depart from Kuala Lumpur's Pudu Raya Bus Terminal near Chinatown. This is the station for buses to Singapore, the north and the west coasts and the fast ones leave early in the morning. For details ((03) 230-0145. For buses to and from the airport and places in the vicinity of Kuala

of these "outstation" taxis as they are very efficient, even if the drivers are often reckless. The taxis occupy a floor of the car park and there are clear signs indicating the various destinations. Just front up and engage the drivers in discussion; politely ignore the touts who may approach you outside the station.

BY AIR

See GETTING THERE under TRAVELERS' TIPS (page 249) for comprehensive information on airlines and flights.

OPPOSITE: The impressive Islamic-style Railway Station. ABOVE: Modern trains connect the capital with the provinces, and neighboring Singapore.

The East Coast

THE EAST COAST, with its magnificent beaches, tiny fishing villages and resort hotels can be a fine introduction to Malaysia. There are an increasing number of excellent resorts that do not suffer from the kind of overdevelopment found in comparable parts of Thailand. The local people are gentle and helpful, often to the point of tolerating visitors whose dress defies Muslim sensibilities. This section of the book will assume a journey northward from Johor Bahru, but the trip can be, and is often, done in the reverse order by tourists traveling south from Thailand. There are excellent tourist offices in Kuala Terengganu and Kota Bharu, but most of the journey is through very small towns. It is well worth stopping in some of the smaller places and possibly enduring a little discomfort in order to experience the culture and lifestyle of this part of Malaysia.

JOHOR BAHRU

Johor Bahru is not the most picturesque town in Malaysia, and its surrounding areas are a sprawl of factories and housing estates. Although little now remains of its rich past, when its sultan governed the southern half of the peninsula including the then unimportant island of Singapore, the main road running along the waterfront houses a number of impressive buildings that convey an air of majesty quite appropriate to its past history and present importance to the national economy.

Singaporeans come to Johor Bahru, or JB as it is commonly called, in droves, they say because the seafood and the shopping is cheap. Don't believe them. They come for a good healthy dose of chaos. Gone, for them, are the carefully regimented and well-drained pavements, the numbered and pruned trees and the well-ordered traffic flow. A Singaporean writer once wrote an amusing story about the government of Singapore buying a piece of JB to send its stressed-out executives to when things get too much for them in overregulated Singapore. At this rest home for overorganized government servants they would be able to spit on the ground, jaywalk, drop litter, pick the flowers and then return to squeaky clean Singapore refreshed and ready to start anew.

However, JB is beginning to clean up its act, both in terms of surroundings and its raunchy night life, so Singaporeans may have to switch to Jakarta in future.

GENERAL INFORMATION

There is a tourist information office ((07) 224-9485 on the Johor side of the Causeway, but the main information office ((07) 223-4590 is on the ground floor of KOMTAR on Jalan Wong Ah Fook. Car hire firms have offices in the Holiday Inn Crowne Plaza ((07)

332-3800, the Hyatt Regency ((07) 222-1234, and the Tropical Inn ((07) 224-7888. Taxis are readily available, and inexpensive. Travel agents in Johor Bahru offer sightseeing tours around town, as well as trips to the fishing village of Kukup (great for seafood) and a rubber plantation. Contact the tourist information office for details.

WHAT TO SEE

In January 1942, after withdrawing steadily in the wake of the Japanese advance down Malaya, the last Australian and British troops crossed the **Causeway** at 5 AM, with the remains of the 2nd Argyll and Sutherland Highlanders playing their pipes behind them. Once the pipers had crossed, explosives were laid and detonated and after the roar and smoke of the explosion settled, a 20-m (66-ft) chasm was awash with water.

OPPOSITE: Women pounding rice together on Malaysia's East Coast. ABOVE: Idyllic offshore isles, like Rawa, entice visitors to the East Coast.

Somehow no one remembered until it was too late that they were cutting off Singapore's major water supply at the same time. The **Istana Besar**, the main palace of the Johore royal family, was where General Yamashita installed his advance headquarters. He used the palace tower as an observation post where he sat with a large-scale map of Singapore to direct operations. The palace now houses the **Royal Abu Bakar Museum**, a collection of royal treasures from all around the world, open daily except Friday. The entrance fee for non-Malaysians is $7.

esting differences between the two countries and the noise that seems to be an essential accompaniment to the shopping is very typical of life in Malaysia. There are also various craft stalls plying wares, and some nice leather items are available. The most popular shopping complexes are **Plaza Pelangi**, off Jalan Tebrau; **Plaza Kota Raya** and the Holiday Plaza in Jalan Dato Sulaiman, Century Garden. With the exception of Plaza Kota Raya, which is in the heart of town, you'll need to take a taxi from the Causeway to reach these complexes.

Johor Bahru really comes alive at night. Restaurants and street stalls are crowded and a random walk often turns up something unexpected: a salesman with live snakes demonstrating the virtue of snake blood and selected organs, transvestites in their home ground near where the Putri Pan Pacific stands, food stalls tucked away in alleyways serving delicious *roti* at 1 AM or 2 AM.

SHOPPING

Holiday Plaza is immensely popular with Singaporeans who flock here to take advantage of the exchange rate between the Singapore dollar and the Malaysian ringgit. An hour spent here does throw up some inter-

NIGHTCLUBS

The nightclubs in the Wisma Abad Complex, just across the road from the Holiday Inn Crowne Plaza and Holiday Plaza, offer Chinese night entertainment at its very best, and outside of Hong Kong, places like the **Golden Palace** cannot be seen elsewhere. As you step into the place it's the sheer size of the interior that takes your breath away. It's cavernous and electric, with a rooftop that stretches into the distance with not a single pillar supporting it. This is what allows the uninterrupted space and the tremendous atmosphere of the place. The shows begin at 11:40 PM, 12:40 and 1:45 AM and you won't see them anywhere else in Malaysia or Singapore. A strip show usually accompanies the feature show, with the main one at 12:40 AM. In between there will be songs and dances. No matter that they sing in Mandarin or Cantonese. The style is what counts and the Golden Palace has that in plenty, and at reasonable prices. There is no cover charge (except when a big star from overseas is brought in). Weekends are the best time to visit (it will be full up by midnight) but the Golden Palace ((07) 33112077, is open throughout the week and you could have just as good a time on a quiet midweek night.

The Metropolis is in the same building and has a similar setup — no cover charge and similar prices to the Golden Palace, but you would be advised to get the prices settled clearly. Negotiation might be called for and the cost of brandy varies between weekdays and weekends. The shows begin around 11:30 PM, 1 AM and last show at 2:45 AM. The atmosphere at the Metropolis is just as frenzied as the Golden Palace but the feel of the place is more Chinese. Well worth a visit though non-oriental visitors might blend in more easily at the Golden Palace.

The Great Eastern ((07) 331-6094, is situated in the basement of the building and as you travel downstairs you could be forgiven for thinking the place is going to turn out to be some real sleaze pit. One couldn't be more mistaken. The place is friendly and cozy, not too crowded and with a quaint English/American feel to the music. This is the place to visit if you fancy dancing to some oldies and watching a modest show. The Great Eastern is a delightful place and closes at 12:45 AM most nights, around 2:30 AM at weekends.

WHERE TO STAY

Expensive

Johor has a number of relatively new five-star hotel, reflecting its increasing importance as a business city. **Hyatt Regency** ((07) 222-1234 FAX (07)222-9234 is the newest of these. Located out of the town center, double rooms here start at $94. The **Puteri Pan Pacific** ((07) 223-3333 FAX (07) 236622.

Moderate

With rates from $88 is within walking distance of the Causeway. The **Holiday Inn**

The East Coast

Crowne Plaza ((07) 332-3800 is on Jalan Dato Sulaiman, Taman Century, and is right next to the popular Holiday Plaza. A double is $80. **Hotel Sofitel** ((07) 599-600; FAX (07) 599-7028 located some distance from the city center, has doubles from $79. The **Rasa Sayang** ((07) 224-7888 FAX (07) 224-1544, in Jalan Dato Dalam enjoys a pleasant, quiet location but is far from the nearest shops and restaurants. Doubles from $46. The **Tropical Inn** ((07) 224-7888 FAX (07) 224-1544, 15 Jalan Gereja, is a popular place at $54, but like many of the hotels in Johor Bahru it lacks architec-

tural charm and the immediate environment is uncongenial.

Inexpensive

The best of the rest is the **Hotel Malaya** ((07) 222-1691 with rooms at $20, located on Jalan Bukit Meldrum and a few minutes walk from the causeway.

WHERE TO EAT

The best place for typical Johor Malay food is the **Tepian Tebrau** food center along Jalan Abu Bakar. Here you'll find seafood steamboat (you cook the seafood in a type of fondue), *nasi biryani* (spicy rice with chicken or mutton) and fish grilled in banana leaf (*ikan bakar*).

Straits Garden Restaurant ((07) 237-5788 is situated in Jalan Skudai, along the coast road from the town center and a taxi should

OPPOSITE: The sultan's palace in Johor Bahru, now houses the Royal Abu Bakar Museum which displays some of the sultan's many treasures. ABOVE: On Malaysia's East Coast, tourists are always greeted with smiles.

cost RM5. The restaurant is renowned for its seafood, especially the tiger prawns, and is open from 3 PM to just after midnight. From 8 PM to 11 PM there is live music in the form of a Filipino band on stage. Ask for a seat near the fishing ponds at the back if you want a quieter meal (an air-conditioned room is also available). The menu is extensive, and two people could eat well for $20.

Midland Garden, also in Jalan Skudai, has drunken prawns, delicious grilled fish and the ever-popular Chinese shark's fin soup. Another good seafood restaurant is **Jaws 5** situated on the main road that heads out west from town along the seafront. At weekends the place gets so crowded it's positively uncomfortable if you are looking for a quiet meal.

Just up the small road that runs alongside the Jaws 5 restaurant there is **Mechinta** ((07) 223-1400 an old-style colonial house once owned by royalty and now housing an entertainment center. The open air restaurant is called Ani Ani Seafood and its prices are quite reasonable. Dishes cost $5 on average and they are available in two sizes. A mouthwatering meal for two could begin with the buttermilk prawns, a house specialty, deep fried with curry leaves till crunchy and swimming in deliciously cholesterol-laden buttermilk sauce. Follow this by the special bean curd with fish, *sotong* (cuttlefish), and prawns, fried to perfect crispness on the outside while melting inside. On weekends a reservation is a good idea.

For good Indian food, try the **Rang Mahal** on the main road north (68 Jalan Padi Satu, Bandar Baru Udara), where you can find *tandoori* specialties including good *naan*.

Less expensive Indian food is to be found in the small cafés in the vicinity of the Pan Pacific. It would be unfair to recommend one rather than another, as the food is equally delicious. A meal for two should cost less than $5.

A good place to eat near Holiday Plaza is the **Holiday Inn Crowne Plaza**. There is a Sichuan restaurant ((07) 332-3800, as well as a reasonably priced coffeeshop serving light meals. If you hanker for western food, try the Manhattan **Grill**, Level 5, Plaza Kotaraya, for steaks, prime rib roast, salads and yummy desserts.

GETTING THERE

Singapore's proximity has helped to make Johor Bahru a major interchange for coaches to and from every part of Malaysia. Along Jalan Meldrum there is a whole chain of agents handling bus and coach tickets. Johor Bahru's airport is 20 minutes out of town and flights connect with Kuala Lumpur, the East Coast towns and Sarawak and Sabah. From Singapore bus N° 170 leaves Queen Street or Bukit Timah Road every 15 minutes. You can get board the bus at the stop in Jalan Tun Abdul Razak, just beside the railway station, although the brand new bus terminus is about 10 minutes away from here. There are daily shuttle trains departing for Singapore are at 7:00 and 10:00 AM, 12:30 and 5:00 PM. The return journey departs Singapore at 8:40 and 11:35 AM, 2:15 and 6:40 PM. As well as stopping at the main station in town the shuttle also serves Holiday Plaza. It is also possible to drive between Johor Bahru and Singapore. Luckily, the buses have a special lane and avoid the worst of the regular traffic jams on the Causeway. An hour's wait for private cars is not uncommon during the evening rush hour, and the weekend is always best avoided. It is often quicker to just walk across, as many people do. A new causeway linking the northwest of Singapore with Johor is due to open in late 1997, although this is mainly of interest to those heading for the west coast of Johore and not Johor Bahru or the East Coast.

DESARU

Desaru is the most popular beach resort in the state of Johore consequently, it attracts a large number of local visitors, especially during school holidays, weekends and public holidays. The beach is large enough to still give you the space to wander off and find your own patch but finding accommodation at these times can be tricky. The beach itself is glorious but not suitable for swimming because of the fierce currents. Children will have fun ducking the big waves but you do need to keep an eye on them all the time. The biggest hotel is the **Desaru View Hotel** ((07) 822-1221, P.O. Box 71, 81907 Kota Tinggi, with doubles starting at $82. **The Desaru Golf Hotel (** (07) 822-1107 FAX (07) 822-1480, P.O. Box 50, 81907 Kota Tinggi, named after the 18-hole golf course, has doubles that start at $80, **Desaru Holiday Resort (** (07) 822-1240 has chalets from $40. Book at **(** (07) 821-1101 FAX (07) 822-1480. Unlike most other places in Malaysia, there are only a few food stalls and these are open only during the day so you are pretty dependent on your hotel.

There is alternative accommodation just of five kilometers (three miles) from Desaru called the Tanjung Balau Fishing Village. This is a resettlement village planned by the Johore government and gives you a chance to experience the daily lives of the fishermen and their families by opting for the homestay at $64 for a two-days, one-night package including all meals for two persons. Alternatively, there are dormitories with rooms complete with dining-kitchen area and bathroom. If you come to Tanjung Balau, be sure to visit the unique Fishing Museum.

Desaru is just under 100 km (60 miles) from Johor Bahru and can be reached by taxi from Johor Bahru, via Kota Tinggi. From Singapore there are various companies offering packages that include transport by ferry from Changi across to Tanjung Belukor in southeastern Johore, and then by hired car up to Desaru. This is quicker and cheaper than traveling by yourself in a taxi. **Ferrylink** at **(** (02) 545-3600 or (02 733-6744 has four ferry trips a day.

MERSING

Mersing is best known as the place where ferries leave for the smaller islands off the coast of Johore and this is why the majority of visitors are here. But Mersing has a pleasant atmosphere, some good seafood restaurants, a charmingly dilapidated government resthouse at very reasonable prices and some decent beaches of its own.

WHAT TO SEE

Not much here in the way of sights but there are two good beaches, one south of the town and the other, more popular one, to the north at Air Papan. It is about 15 km (nine miles) north of Mersing, past the Merlin Inn, and

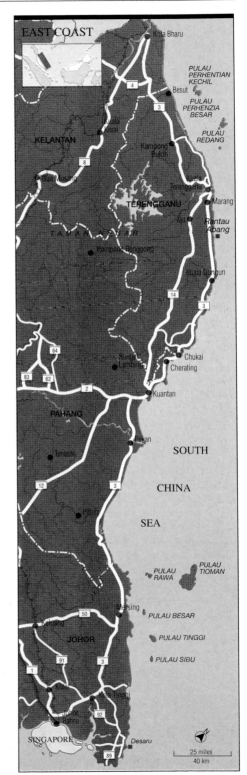

well signposted. A taxi will take you there for a few dollars and there is also a bus service. The beach to the south of town can be reached by driving up the hill past the mosque along the coastline until you see some old brick kilns where you can park your car. Locals tend to shun the place, but it has an enormous expanse of shallow gentle water, white beaches and interesting plant life, including some mangroves. On foot, the beach can be approached from the resthouse, but it is quite a long walk.

WHERE TO STAY

Just a little way north of Mersing is the **Merlin Inn** ((07) 799-1312 FAX (07) 799-3177 at Two Jalan Endau, 86807 Mersing, with comfortable rooms at reasonable prices ($40). It has a small pool and restaurant and is very quiet.

Alternatively, there is the wonderfully shabby **Government Resthouse** ((07) 799-2101 at 490 Jalan Ismail, 86800 Mersing, standing on its own on a long-abandoned and waterlogged golf course. The vast rooms are air-conditioned and many open onto the garden with fine views over the bay. There are only 18 rooms, a terrific value for $18, but reservations are often essential. In Mersing town itself, there are a number of inexpensive hotels, all equally unattractive, with the **Embassy** ((07) 799-1301, being the best of a bad bunch

WHERE TO EAT

Mersing's seafood restaurants are regularly patronized by Singaporeans on their way to and from the islands and there are a couple of Muslim places doing *murtabak* and curries. My favorite is the one directly opposite the supermarket in the main street of the town. It is clean and modern and always full of locals and visitors. The restaurant at the government resthouse serves inexpensive but disappointing Western, Malay and Chinese food. But you can have the food served on the open verandah and the view helps compensate. There's good and inexpensive seafood in the restaurant of the Hotel Embassy, and you could try the Taj Mahal on Jalan Abu Bakar for Northern Indian food.

GETTING THERE

It takes around two hours by taxi from Johor Bahru and usually it is not difficult to share the cost of a taxi. Buses and coaches also ply the route, but not on a very regular basis, so it's best to checkout the times and fares from various coach operators in Johor Bahru.

Ferries to the Islands

Several ferries and privately chartered passenger boats leave here for the many islands off the coast of this part of Malaysia and it is best to just turn up at the jetty and make inquiries. All the ferry companies and most of the island resorts have offices near the jetty so it is easy to compare prices and times of departure. Apart from weekends, and especially holiday weekends, there is usually no problem in just booking passage and accommodation there and then. There is a tourist center near the jetty ((07) 799-1204.

TIOMAN ISLAND

Despite its high profile, Tioman is still the best of the islands off Mersing, if only because it's larger and there is more to do there. There is also a greater range of accommodation and places to eat. The smaller islands are fine for very short visits, or if you want that Robinson Crusoe ambiance, but Tioman has a modest infrastructure for the visitor.

Tourist information is a little haphazard on the island. At the ferry terminal, by the airport at Tekek, the ticket booths will dispense information regarding the sea bus and accommodation, but life on the island is so simple that really there is little information to get.

WHAT TO SEE

With gorgeous beaches and limestone peaks thrusting up through virgin forest, Tioman is perhaps the loveliest of all the islands off Peninsular Malaysia's East Coast. It's dramatic beauty caught the attention of Hollywood film makers who used background shots of Tioman to portray the idyllic Bali Hai in the musical film, *South Pacific*. Although Tioman is reached via Mersing, or by boat directly from Singapore, it is not in Johore but actually in Pahang State. Marine life is the most interesting sight on the island and that abounds just about everywhere. If you want to see marine life that other people don't see, you can go to an inaccessible beach, but the same fish and coral are lurking about right in front of the Swiss Cottages or the Berjaya Tioman Beach Resort. Boats can be hired by the hour or for the day and there are a number of deserted beaches to spend the day on.

A sea bus travels around the island several times daily. Fares are minimal but you must be aware of the times if you want a ride back. It will take you to Juara village on the east side of the island where there are a few fairly simple places to stay and food is available. There is no snorkeling or scuba equipment to hire there though. Alternatively you can trek across the island's mountains to Juara and get the boat back. It is a pleasant walk through kampongs at first, and then through primary rainforest where you may catch sight of birds, squirrels and some spectacular lizards.

The sea bus will also take you from Tekek to Ayer Batang, where there is a good selection of places to stay, or further along to Salang where there is accommodation and a scuba center. In the other direction the sea bus stops at the resort's jetty and Genting Village which has a pleasant beach.

Starting from the north side of the island, **Monkey Bay** is a regular stopping point for chartered boats. It has a agreable beach and snorkeling is possible. Traveling clockwise from Monkey Bay another pleasant stopping point is **Teluk Dalam** where there is an abundance of marine life to see. Good snorkeling is also possible at the beach at Juara. Traveling south a good stopping point is the refreshingly cool waterfall at **Mukut**. Close by Tioman are several smaller islands including **Tulai** and **Renggis**. Hiring a boat for the day can be an expensive business, but the resort that you stay at can arrange it for you. A half day trip to Tulai will cost around $80 per boat. Many resorts also offer SCUBA instruction packages and equipment rental.

For dyed-in-the-wool landlubbers, the Tioman Beach Resort has a glass-bottomed boat which goes out daily for hour-long trips.

WHERE TO STAY

Moderate

At the top end of the market is the large **Berjaya Tioman Beach Resort** ((09) 419-1000 FAX (09) 419-1718, P.O. Box 4, 86807 Mersing, Johore, Malaysia, which has looked like an enormous building site for several years but now appears to be reaching its expansion limit. Getting around the resort requires a small golf cart, and room service is delivered by bicycle. The resort offers luxury accommodation and is frequently full, so book ahead. It has a golf course, sea activities, horse riding and more activities. A double room here costs $136. Chalets are nicer but more expensive.

The rest of the accommodation, and there is an almost uncountable amount of it, is spread along the bays to the north and south of Kampung Tekek, where the **Tioman Beach Resort** is located.

The **Tioman Horizon Condotel** ((09) 419-1909 FAX contact the same as Tioman Beach Resort, FAX (09) 419-1718, near Bunut beach, is managed by the same company as Tioman Beach Resort and offers pleasant one- and two-bedroom apartments, the one-bedroom costing $172.

Inexpensive

Next to the Tioman Beach Resort is the **Samudra Swiss Cottage** ((07) 224-8728 FAX (07) 223-2293. It is pleasantly small, has a very well organized scuba shop and training center, and has chalets at $30.

A little further north is **Sri Tioman Chalets**, with similar rooms for $16. It has a good restaurant, a little shop selling many of the things that you forgot to bring and some locally painted T-shirts, but it lacks Swiss Cottage's community atmosphere.

Pesona Island Resorts ((09) 414-6213 FAX (09) 414-6213 does not have chalets but offers double rooms at $44.

Beyond the jetty, about 15 minutes walk, is **Ramli's** ((09) 414-5347, with pleasant A-frames for $6 and chalets at $12. Next door is a diving shop, **Dive Asia**, which offers a five-day diving course. The beach here is a little scruffy and you are right under the flight path of incoming planes.

Further north again is **Mango Grove**, set on a rise in the ground above the beach, with lots of shade and cool breezes. It started as a restaurant and has now expanded into chalets with fans and little shower rooms for about $4. It sells batik T-shirts which are made while you watch.

Still hiking northward is **Nazri's**, Kampung Air Batang, Pulau Tioman, Pahang ((011) 349-534, which is highly organized and very popular. It offers a whole range of chalets and longhouse rooms with varying prices depending on proximity to the sea. Sea view bungalows go for around $20 and offer four beds, fans and bathroom, all nicely decorated. The beach here is good, particularly if you walk a little way south through the trees. Right outside Nazri's it looks a little like Kuta Beach on Bali.

Along the beach all the way to the last of the tourist ghettos are any number of small settlements. The **ABC**, near the very end of the strip, has chalets for $20, **Salang Indah Chalet** (07) 799-1407 FAX (07) 799-1407 is at the very end of this are and has non-air-conditioned chalets at $16 and air-conditioned doubles at $68.

WHERE TO EAT

Only the **Tioman Beach Resort** can offer international standard cuisine, and at a price. But if you come to Tioman prepared to live fairly simply, the quality of the local food available is remarkably good. Each of the sets of chalets has its own restaurant, serving western breakfasts and Malay dishes. Sri Tioman has a particularly nice restaurant with remarkably quick service. Swiss Cottage serves food until about 8:30 in the evening. Its menu is limited but it has a good-value special each night and often does barbecues. Best of all is **Liza Restaurant**, beside the police station, some five minutes north of Swiss Cottage. It serves a vast array of dishes to suit all tastes and does it quickly and at very reasonable rates. Two people could eat here for $18.

Smaller Isles

Further southeast of Pulau Tioman they are other glorious islands where you can stay. On **Pulau Aur**, you have the choice of accommodation at Aur Holiday Resort or Samudra

Holidays. Separated from Aur by a channel is the exquisite little isle of Dayang, where boat transfers to and from Mersing, three days and two nights in a chalet plus all meals costs $270 per person. For more information call ((07) 799-4407.

GETTING THERE

Tioman is accessible by air from Kuala Lumpur, Kuantan and Singapore. SilkAir has a daily 30-minute flight from Singapore. Watching it land, one worries about the coco-

nut trees it neatly skims but they are all still intact. Pelangi Air also flies in and whichever airline you fly with, it's an amazing experience, particularly landing at Tioman. **SilkAir** ((02) 221-2221, has flights daily from Seletar Airport in Singapore, while Pelangi Air flies daily from Kuala Lumpur and Kuantan. Book Pelangi flights through **Malaysia Airlines** ((03) 955-3937 in Kuala Lumpur or ((02) 336-6777 in Singapore.

The sea journey can be made from Mersing either by regular boat, which takes about four hours, or on the Tioman Beach Resort's hydrofoil, which is more expensive but halves the traveling time. This can be a rough journey if you encounter a Sumatra, one of the storms which may suddenly hit this part of the coast at any time of year. Tioman Island Resort Ferries runs fast air-conditioned ferries daily from Singapore except during the northeast monsoon months (mid-October to the first week of March) ((02) 271-4866 FAX (02) 273-3573, and offers a package trip including transport and accommodation from $150.

Tioman is pretty short on shops so bring anything unusual that you need with you. On the island you can buy regular things like mosquito coils, suntan cream, etc., but they are more expensive than on the mainland.

for around $30 but the beach is not great at low tide. The information center at the Mersing jetty will be able to provide details of other possibilities.

Do not confuse Pulau Besar (which is more properly known as Pulau Babi Besar) with **Pulau Sibu Besar**, usually referred to as Pulau Sibu, another delightful tropical isle with white beaches and coral reefs that make snorkeling irresistible. **Sea Gypsy Village Resort** ((07) 799-3125, the first resort on Pulau Sibu, has wooden chalets for $18; contact via the tourist office at Mersing jetty. Another more

OTHER ISLANDS

Pulau Besar is about an hour's journey from Mersing and, in recent years, the accommodation scene has grown here as well as in other Johore islands further south such as Pulau Tinggi, Pulau Sibu and Pulau Sibu Tengah. Pulau Besar's **White Sand Beach Resort**, which has fan-cooled doubles at $76, and the Sun Dancer Island Resort, with fan-cooled doubles at $67 and air-conditioned doubles at $91, can both be booked at **Sun and Sand Holiday**, Jalan Ismail, Mersing ((07) 799-4995 FAX (07) 799-5279. **Radin Island Resort** ((011) 325-935 has simple A-frame chalets for $15. **Hillside Chalets** ((07) 223-6603 has chalets with a great view

upmarket resort is **Rimba Resort** ((07) 223-1753, with chalets at $120. **Sibu Island Cabanas**, accessible via Tanjung Leman, have fan-cooled chalets at $53.

There is a nearby island called **Pulau Sibu Tengah**, where **Sibu Island Resort** ((07) 223-1188, has comfortable chalets with prices of $232 for a three-day, two-night package including boat transfers and two meals a day. Departure is from Tanjung Leman, south of Mersing.

About 16 km (10 miles) from Mersing lies the tiny but pretty **Pulau Rawa** with bungalows and chalets for hire. Reservations are

Horses and ponies for hire on the beach at Terengganu.

made through Rawa Safaris at the tourist center in Mersing ((07) 799-1204. No other accommodation is available on the island. Some 32 km (20 miles) southeast of Mersing is **Pulau Tinggi**, inhabited by a few Malay fishing families. Accommodation is available at the luxurious **Smailing Island Resort** and there is a range of packages from Singapore ((02) 733-3555, Johor Bahru ((07) 224-6490 and Kuala Lumpur ((03) 298-0772. Nadia's Inn, also on Pulau Tinggi, has air-conditioned chalets at $56; book at ((07) 799-5582 FAX (07) 799-5797.

KUANTAN

Kuantan is at the end of the long beach strip that stretches unbroken from Kelantan down along the East Coast of the Malay peninsula. Although it is the capital of the state of Pahang, the town of Kuantan itself is pretty nondescript. Kuantan's popularity with tourists is in its beaches at Teluk Chempedak, about four kilometers (two-and-a-half miles) from the main town. The town itself is hardly worth a visit but you will arrive there if you come by bus. The actual beach area is a short taxi ride away. The tourist office ((09) 513-3026, is on the 15th floor, Kompleks Teruntum, Jalan Mahkota, 25000 Kuantan, Pahang.

WHAT TO SEE

The beach at Teluk Chempedak is pleasant and the strong waves make for happy frolics, but are not very safe for swimming. There are several jungle walks to be done here, notably the 45-minute walk which goes behind the Merlin Inn Resort to a mini zoo on the hillside. If you are staying at one of the hotels, there are several day trips which you can take which the hotels regularly organize.

Beserah is a small fishing village 10 km (six miles) north of Kuantan where you will be able to watch the activities of the local fishermen, arrange a fishing trip for yourself, watch batik being made and possibly watch top spinning and kite flying competitions. Accommodation here is rudimentary so it is best done as a trip out of Kuantan. Local buses (N° 27, 28 and 30) pass through and can be boarded at the bus station in Kuantan.

A day's trip out from Kuantan are two interesting sights, the Gua Cheras cave near Panching and, 13 km (eight miles) further on, the Sungei Pandan Waterfalls;. The road passes through rubber and oil palm plantations. To get to the caves one has to climb an external stairway of 170 stone steps. The caves were lived in by a visiting Thai monk and have attracted Buddhists ever since. Inside among other statuary is a nine meter-long (30 ft) reclining Buddha. Torches are necessary. To get there on public transport, you should take a bus to Sungei Lembing, a ghost town which is the home of Malaysia's only large underground tin mine, and hitch a ride for the last three-and-a-half kilometers (two miles). From Panching, the Pandan Waterfalls are reached by taking a turn-off

back on the road to Kuantan and then a 13-km (eight-mile) journey along a laterite road. A picnic area is laid out by the falls, which are 150 m (500 ft) high. Many of the local hotels will organize trips lasting usually about five hours to these two spots.

Fifty-six kilometers (34 miles) west of Kuantan on the Temerloh road, a small side road south brings you to Kampung Chini from where you can cross the Pahang River to trek the rest of the way to Lake Chini, a lotus-covered lake said to contain a monster guarding a sunken Khmer city. There are *Orang Asli* settlements around the lake and some chalets and camping spots. Unfortunately, the erection of a small dam at one end of the lake has done untold environmental damage, with many of the trees and fish dying. It would be wise to check on whether the situation has been reversed before taking the trouble to visit.

WHERE TO STAY

Expensive

The **Hyatt Regency Kuantan** ((09) 566-1234 FAX (09) 567-7577, at P.O. Box 250, 25730 Kuantan, Pahang, provides all the luxury you could ask for in a beach resort, including beautifully designed surroundings which somehow suggest primitive jungle conditions while simultaneously providing every amenity. There are three restaurants including a rooftop steamboat, a converted

A glorious sunset on the East Coast of Malaysia.

Vietnamese refugee boat offering drinks on the beach, a nice pool and a great beachfront view which becomes magnificent in rough weather when the waves are high. Prices are from $85.

Moderate

Somewhat down-market is the **Merlin Inn Kuantan** ((09) 514-1388 FAX (09) 513-3001, designed primarily as a motel and with pleasant family rooms with verandahs leading straight on to the gardens and the pool on the beach. Standard doubles, at $50, are smaller and further away from the beach with less pleasant views. The hotel has a restaurant serving western and local dishes and organizes coconut collections by monkeys and a weekly cultural show. Opposite the Hyatt is the **Hotel Kuantan** ((09) 567-4980, with doubles from $35–$40. This is an excellent hotel with a good restaurant and clean if unspectacular rooms.

Inexpensive

Asrama Bendehara, tucked in between the two resort hotels, has dormitory beds from $3, and fan-cooled rooms at $7 a double. It has a small inexpensive restaurant.

WHERE TO EAT

Excellent seafood can be found at the food stalls and restaurants at Teluk Chempedak, not far from the Hyatt. The most popular are the open-air Pattaya and the **Katong Seafood Restaurant**, which specializes in fish-head curry. Nearby is **Nisha's**, serving good North Indian cuisine. The Hyatt Regency Kuantan has an excellent (if expensive) buffet. In the town of Kuantan, you can find good Malay and Western cuisine at **Restaurant Tiki**.

GETTING THERE

Kuantan can be reached by air on SilkAir from Singapore ((02) 221-2221, or by Malaysia Airlines from Kuala Lumpur. There is a MAS office in town ((09) 515-0055. Roads link Kuantan with Mersing, Kuala Lumpur and Segamat. If you choose to drive, take a taxi or get a bus you will find the roads are pleasant enough, even if a little short on places to stop for a rest. Kuantan's long-distance bus

station is in Jalan Besar, from where buses leave for towns to the north. Nearby is the long-distance taxi station.

CHERATING

GENERAL INFORMATION

The name Cherating applies to an extremely large area covering several kilometers of beach and three or four big resorts. The village after which the area is named is in fact a tiny place which seems to make its living largely from the many budget homestays and chalets scattered around it. Cherating experiences the monsoon season during November to February so prices are seasonal at the small locally owned places.

WHAT TO SEE

From the hotels and resorts in Cherating the same visits can be made that were described in the Kuantan section, page 108. In addition you can visit a nearby island called **Pulau Ular** (Snake Island), which is about 20 minutes away by boat, for some unspoiled scenery and clear blue seas. In the village itself you can watch hand-drawn batik being made and even try your hand at this in craft some of the homestay places. Some of the guest houses also arrange trips up the river to visit a tiny *kampung* followed by a nature walk. If you are not planning to stop again before Khota Bharu then you should consider making the trip to **Kapas Island** from here (see MARANG, page 113). Most of the hotels arrange trips, although from here it will involve a long bus ride north and then back again. If you don't stay in one of the budget places in Cherating village, then you could spend a day in the village itself just soaking up the laid-back atmosphere, watching the craft work going on, visiting the craft shops that spring up and eating very fresh seafood at very reasonable prices.

WHERE TO STAY

From Kuantan northward, there are a few beach resorts which offer sports and facilities typical of beach resorts with typical prices, or there is the much more primitive accommodation at Cherating Village which offers a lack of luxury but local flavor.

Moderate

Starting from the south, at Balok beach there is the **Coral Beach Resort** ((09) 544-7544, which offers sea-facing rooms from $43 to $104. It has a pretty beach, safe for children although the waves can be quite strong. Further north about four kilometers (two-and-a-half miles) south of Cherating is the **Cherating Holiday Villa** ((09) 581-9500 Lot 1303, Mukim Sungei Karang, Cherating,

2608, an even more luxuriously appointed resort where a double room with a sea view is $82. Book in Kuala Lumpur ((03) 261-4599. North of the village is the **Club Méditerranée Holiday Village** ((09) 589-1131 FAX (09) 581-9172, at Cherating Lama, 26080 Kuantan, which offers packages at $94 a day on week days, increasing to $114 on weekends per person including meals and sports facilities.

Inexpensive

In Cherating Village itself, what you are likely to find is a chalet with a fan, mosquito net

Kuantan, which offers rooms overlooking the pool at $72 or chalets with a sea view at $78. Each chalet is fashioned after a style indigenous to a Malaysian state. The beach is excellent, there is a supply of gadgets and equipment for sea sports, and a good tour agency within the hotel. The disadvantages of both these places is, of course, that unless you have transport of your own, getting to other places can be difficult, and so holiday-makers tend to stay where they are. From the Holiday Villa it is possible to walk along the beach toward Cherating Village, but do so only when the tide is out as the Cherating River can only be waded across at low tide. Right next door to Cherating Holiday Villa is another resort, **Palm Grove**, Kampung Baru, Cherating,

and primitive bathroom. The **Coconut Inn** ((09) 581-9299, is right on the beach and has pleasant rooms with fans and bathrooms at around $8 to $11. There are many more places, very small and without telephones, and more are opening up all the time, each one offering slightly more than its predecessors in comfort and facilities. If you intend to stay there, the best thing to do is walk around and choose a place which suits your mood.

On the main road are two places which are highly recommended by those who stay there, **Mak Long Teh** and **Mak De**, board-

Malaysia's smooth East Coast waters are perfect for windsurfing.

ing houses with a family atmosphere. Full board with three meals a day is around $8.

WHERE TO EAT

Eating at the resorts is a comparatively expensive business. Breakfast at the Cherating Holiday Villa is about $6 while a meal for two would work out at about $20–25. The restaurant serves a variety of local dishes and western items. The Coral Beach Resort has two restaurants, both with good reputations,

serving Chinese and Japanese cuisine. In Cherating Lama itself there are many restaurants which spring up and disappear. The **Sayang Inn** serves Indian food, and a meal for two would cost about $10. **Mimi** restaurant serves *roti canai* when it feels like it, as well as many tourist staples like boiled eggs and fish and chips.

GETTING THERE

Buses to Cherating depart from the bus station at Kuantan, (look for Kemaman bus Nº 27). If you are staying at any of the resorts south of the *kampung* itself, the local bus, run by a company called Sihat, reputedly travels in that direction at half-hourly intervals. Other means of transport are car hire and taxi hire. Cabs have no meters, and fares seem to depend on how rich you look. Your hotel will be able to tell you how much you should pay.

On the East Coast, turtles' eggs are lovingly collected and protected in hatcheries until the newborn are ready to return to the sea.

KUALA DUNGUN AND RANTAU ABANG

The town of Dungun itself is a depressing place, but nearby are some lovely beaches and pleasant resorts. SCUBA divers praise the island of **Tenggol**, reached via Kuala Dungun, as the best dive spot in all of Peninsular Malaysia. The **Tenggol Aqua Resort (** (09) 844-4862 FAX (09) 844-4862, offers packages which include boat transfers to the island, accommodation and all meals. Naturally, the price for divers, which includes tank, weights and dive boat, is higher. A three-day, two-night package for non-divers, for example, costs $168 per person on a twin-sharing basis, and $258 for divers. The address is Tenggol Aqua Resort, Jati Embun Sdn. Bhd., 8 Bangunan UDA, Jalan Sungai Penaga, 23000 Kuala Dungun, Terengganu.

TURTLE WATCHING

The most famous activity along this stretch of coastline is watching giant Leatherback turtles heave themselves up on to the beach to lay their eggs (see TOP SPOTS). The peak egg laying season is August but turtles come ashore from May to September. Leatherbacks are a highly endangered species which have only a few locations worldwide where they choose to lay their eggs, so don't miss this opportunity to witness this event. If you are visiting Sabah you will have the opportunity of seeing Green turtles, which are more common there than the Leatherbacks.

WHERE TO STAY

Thirteen kilometers (eight miles) north of Dungun is the magnificent **Tanjung Jara Beach Hotel (** (09) 844-1801 FAX (09) 844-2653, 8th mile of Dungun, Terengganu, 23009, built in the style of an eighteenth-century Malay sultanate, and recipient of awards for architectural design. Accommodation is in two-story buildings built entirely of wood with beautiful moldings, every convenience and a great view of the sea from the large balconies. There are the usual beach facilities, lovely gardens, a lagoon and a pleasant pool, although not as big as their publicity material suggests! The restaurant is adequate though expensive for what it offers. The hotel was closed in 1997 for renovation and is due to reopen some time in 1998. Rates have not been finalized, but are likely to be at least $100 for a double.

A few kilometers further north is the **Merantau Inn ℂ** (09) 844-1131, Kuala Abang, Dungun, 23050, Terengganu, which has an interesting fish farm on its premises, a small restaurant and clean air-conditioned bungalows right on the idyllic, if shadeless, beach. The beach is deserted for most of the day though you are likely to have gigantic turtles lumbering about it in the early hours. Double rooms are $26.

Further to the north again is **Rantau Abang**, where most of the turtle watching organizations are located. The **Rantau Abang Visitor's Centre**, 13th mile of Dungun, 23009, Terengganu ℂ (09) 844-1533 is built in a similar style to Tanjung Jara, with a museum, restaurant and chalet accommodation. It is open throughout the year, and rates vary according to whether it's peak season for turtle viewing. Rates range from $30 per room (sleeping six) in the off season (October to March) and $52 during the rest of the year. Cheap accommodation is available at Awang's, close to the information centre ℂ (09) 844-2236, with chalets for around $5. All around this part of the beach are many small budget bungalows built on to the beach, which is however quite untidy and crowded, particularly in the turtle watching season.

WHERE TO EAT

Not much joy here. Tanjung Jara has an adequate but unexciting restaurant, there are some Malay food stalls in Dungun and near the information centre in Rantau Abang which do tasty dishes catering to the budget traveler.

GETTING THERE

Getting there from Cherating involves changing buses at Chukai, a one-horse-town about half-an-hour north of Cherating, just inside the Terengganu border. The only tourists that see this place are those getting buses to

Terengganu and the rest haven't missed much. If you want to go to Tanjung Jara, the bus to Terengganu will drop you off a sweaty 500 m (550 yards) up the road. For the other places to stay, the bus will stop on the main road close by your destination. Getting away means flagging down another Terengganu-bound bus. Or flag down a relatively empty cab and ask for an estimate. To reach Rantau Abang from Kuala Terengganu, take a local bus or taxi ($10 if you wish to charter it, or $2.50 on a share basis) for the 58-km (23-mile) journey south.

MARANG

Heading further north from Dungun and Rantau Abang you can hail any of the buses marked Terengganu, negotiate a cab from your hotel or just flag one down. From hotels, cabs are expensive; if you stop one on the road which already has someone in it you can travel a long way for very little. Avoid mentioning the name of the hotel you are traveling to if it is an expensive one until after you have negotiated the price.

Marang is the next interesting stop on the journey north. If you didn't stop at Cherating or if you found there that you love the small-town Malaysian life, Marang is a must. Marang has that scruffy but relaxing quality that only a small town in Malaysia seems to possess. Those who knew it in the old days say Marang has lost a lot of its charm due to development by the national oil company in the region, but first-time visitors will still find it worth a visit.

WHAT TO SEE

What to see in Marang is chiefly the town itself. It is built along a river which runs through the village, separating the one road from the beach. At one end is the hub of life of the village, where the boats hang out waiting for the good weather, longhaired young men lounge about pretending they can play the guitar and listening to heavy metal music or oldies from the 1970s like 'Hotel California', and the newly built market and hawker centers confront the crumbling and crazily leaning wooden buildings of an earlier era. Unlike many of the small towns further

der white sand. The islands range from **Pulau Tenggol** in the south up through Kapas, **Bidong**, **Redang** and the two **Perhentian Islands**. A rash of resorts and other more simple accommodation has been built on all the islands recently. The **Primula Kapas Island Beach Resort (** (09) 623-3360, has luxurious Malay-style chalets from $60 and offers a swimming pool plus snorkeling, fishing and scuba facilities. **Kapas Garden Resort (** (010) 984-1686 FAX (09) 6245162, is a small but pleasant place where doubles cost from $24 to $30. **Tutypuri Island Resort** has

south, this is almost like Malaysia proper, the Chinese running the small stores catering mainly to the many backpackers hanging out in the Marang Inn or **Kamal's**, the Malays manning the fishing and tourist boats. But there are some other sights to be seen from Marang and all the hotels organize trips.

One good half-day's adventure is to take a boat up the river and go wildlife spotting. The boat travels up the river to a tiny kampong where a brief walk will show you local women making *atap*, the rows of thatch which cover many of the roofs in the village, and men making *gula melaka*, a gorgeously sweet sugar made from boiling down the sap tapped from coconut flowers. Along the way the keen-eyed boatmen will spot monitor lizards, monkeys and other wildlife and there will be a trek to a batik factory. The trip costs around $8 per head from the smaller hotels in Marang but much more from the upmarket hotels.

Another reason for a stay in Marang is the trip out to the clear waters and white sandy beaches of **Pulau Kapas**, about half-an-hour out from the village. Terengganu is blessed by a scattering of fabulous islands with turquoise or emerald waters and pow-

doubles from $34; book at **(** (010) 223-4917. Considerably less expensive at $10–$12 a night are the fan-cooled chalets at Zaki Beach Chalet **(** (09) 654-5121, and the amusingly named Mak Cik Gemuk (literally "fat aunty") Resort, where the rooms cost the same as at Zaki. Several boats go over to the island daily except in bad weather. The trip costs $6 in a regular wooden boat, and $10 by speedboat.

Another trip which might be nicer made from the calm of Marang is a trip into Kuala Terengganu which is a noisy place to stay in but has some pleasant sights. A bus plies between Marang and Kuala Terengganu, and costs 40 cents. Alternatively you can walk to the far end of the village where it meets the main road and flag down one of the express

Beautiful faces of young Malays from the country's East Coast.

buses which don't seem to need an official bus stop to pull into. Or again flag down an already occupied cab or just look pathetic and somebody will offer you a lift.

WHERE TO STAY

The new **Marang Resort & Safaris ℂ** (09) 618-2588 FAX (09) 618-2334, won a prestigious international award for its efforts in preserving authentic Malay culture and the natural beauty of its environment. A hundred *kampung*-style chalets sprawl along the sea or river over a huge 32-hectare site. Fishing, trekking, diving, snorkeling and sailing all available. Most of the accommodation in the village of Marang itself is very simple and inexpensive. South of the village, but away from the atmosphere that makes this place so interesting, are one or two resorts which approach a comfortable style. As in Cherating, here one has to decide between luxury and atmosphere.

At Kampung Rhu Muda, two kilometers (1.2 miles) south of the village, are the **Mare Nostrum Beach Resort ℂ** (09) 618-1433, Nº 313 Jalan Pantai, Seberang Marang, 21600, Terengganu, which has small chalets with no view for $6 or big rooms with views and a verandah for $25. **Beach House ℂ** (09) 618-

2403, 12th mile, Kampung Rhu Muda, Marang has air-conditioned chalets for $32, and cheaper fan-cooled chalets for $10.

Back in the village, the best accommodation you'll find is a fan-cooled chalet with a fairly primitive bathroom and mosquito nets. The nicest of these is at the **Marang Guest House ℂ** (09) 618-2277, Lot 1367–8, Kampung Paya, Bukit Batu Merah, Marang, 21600, Terengganu which, as its address suggests, is on a small hill which gives great views over the beach. It has a tidy and very flexible restaurant, fascinating travelers' comments books and extremely helpful staff. Loved by shoestring travelers but without many fans, which can be disastrous on a hot night, is **Kamal's ℂ** (09) 618-2181, B23 Kampung Paya, Marang, 21600, Terengganu, which is friendly but primitive. In the village itself is the **Marang Inn ℂ** (09) 618-2132 FAX (09) 618-1878, 132–3 Bandar Marang, 21600 Marang, offering rooms with a fan but shared bathroom for $4. The Inn is the most popular place to stay since it is centrally located, making boat trips easier and also because it serves alcohol, a rare event in a largely Muslim community. It also has lots of information, a good notice board, some pretty batik items for sale and organizes trips to suit its customers.

KUALA TERENGGANU

GENERAL INFORMATION

Kuala Terengganu is a bustling little town, about 15 minutes north of Marang, made rich by the discovery of offshore oil but still retaining some of its original fishing village charm. Travel within the town is largely by trishaw; all the taxis you see are long distance ones. Terengganu has its own beaches and many interesting places to visit but many travelers prefer to stay out of town and make visits to the town itself. The Terengganu state government is now actively promoting tourism and even declared 1997 "Visit Terengganu Year", so you should find plenty of leaflets and other information at the Tourist Information Centre opposite the central market.

WHAT TO SEE

The waterfront presents an interesting walk around Kuala Terengganu, starting at the central market, which sells both fresh produce and craftware, including locally made brassware, cane items and woven and printed cloth. Right outside the market is the jetty from where fish make the journey on to the market stalls, still flapping in some cases. After exploring the market, a pleasant walk is along Jalan Bandar, which follows the curve of the river and has many old fashioned shops along it selling fishermen's gear, spices, Chinese medicines and other unusual items. Between the buildings quaint little alleyways lead down to the river. You might like to break for a while at N° 224, Kedai Kopi Cheng, which serves excellent Chinese food or just coffee or soft drinks if you need a rest. At the end of this road is the long distance taxi rank where you can negotiate a cab to Kota Bharu or south to your next destination. Since the new bus station was built, though, cabs tend to lurk around there collecting enough passengers to make the long journeys profitable. At the junction of Jalan Bandar and Jalan Sultan Ismail, the old town merges into the new so if you hate traffic and noise, turn back here past the central market to the jetties and the tourist office which has now moved closer to the center.

Close by here is **Bukit Puteri**, a small hill on which stands the remains of a nineteenth-century fort, some cannons and a bell whose function was to warn the town of approaching danger such as an *amok*, and a lighthouse marking the entrance to the Sungei Terengganu. Entry to the fort is 50 cents and it is open until 6 PM.

The cultural center or **Pengkalan Budaya** displays Terengganu's recreational and cultural activities. It is on Pantai Batu Buruk, the esplanade in front of the beach south of town and close by a hawker center. Shows of *seni silat* (self defense), dances, top spinning, and other pastimes can be seen on Thursdays, Fridays and Saturdays from 5 PM to 6:30 PM and from 9 PM to 11 PM between April and October. Check at the tourist office, particularly during Ramadan, since these performances are often canceled on public holidays or other festivals.

The **Terengganu State Museum**, Jalan Cherong Lanjut, 20300, Kuala Terengganu, is a trishaw ride away from the tourist office and other attractions. It has many interesting exhibits, perhaps the most quirky being one of the bicycles that the invading Japanese used to travel down towards Singapore. There are also four traditional palaces which have been moved to the museum site, and a maritime museum.

In the river estuary are several islands, one of which, **Pulau Duyung**, the largest, is the home of the local boat-building industry. Ferries regularly go over to the island and you can watch boats being built using techniques which have changed very little in generations. At Chendering, five kilometers (three miles) south of town you will find Sutera Semai, where you can watch the process of *songket* weaving, where patterns are woven into silk with gold and silver thread. Also in the area are manufacturers of wooden carvings and brassware, These are carried out in people's homes and so there are very few, if any, signs pointing out their presence.

Rhusila is a small village about 12 km (seven-and-a-half miles) south of Kuala Terengganu where there is a handicraft center. Here you can watch basket-weaving

Making kites and flying them is serious business in Malaysia's East Coast.

demonstrations. Close by are two batik factories The tourist office in Kuala Terengganu can provide you addresses. *Songket* weaving is also practiced in this region. Desacraft ((09) 636627 close to the outstation taxi rank is one good outlet to buy this.

WHERE TO STAY

Expensive
The new **Awana Kijal Beach and Golf Resort** ((09) 864-1188 FAX (09) 864-1688, boasts of having the longest private beach on the East Coast. At 3.5 km (two miles), it seems like a reasonable claim. It also has the largest landscaped swimming pool on the East Coast, an 18-hole golf course and a host of other impressive facilities. It puts the previous leading hotel, **Primula Beach Resort** ((09) 622-2100 FAX (09) 623-3360, Jalan Persinggahan, Kuala Terengganu 20904, P.O. Box 43 in the shade. Overlooking the Batu Buruk beach, Primula Beach Resort has a swimming pool, tennis courts and grillroom beside a waterfall. A double room with all mod cons here is $90. **Motel Desa** ((09) 6222100 at Bukit Pak Apil overlooks the town and has a pool. Large rooms cost $52.

Moderate
Back in the bustle of town there are some good-value hotels which offer good room facilities. The centrally located **Sri Hoover Hotel** ((09) 623-3823 FAX (09) 622-5975, 49 Jalan Sultan Ismail, offers basic double rooms for $20. The **Seaview Hotel** ((09) 622-1911, 18A Jalan Masjid Abidin, 20100 Kuala Terengganu offers air-conditioned doubles for $30. It is very pleasant, has nice views of the Istana, and is close to the tourist center, central market, etc. Top spot for budget travelers is **Ping Anchorage** ((09) 622-0851, 77A Jalan Dato Isaac. Fan-cooled rooms and dormitories from $2 to $6. Again, nice as Terengganu is though, if you are going to spend any time in the area, Marang would be a better choice.

WHERE TO EAT

Kuala Terengganu has the usual quota of small, very reasonably priced restaurants and coffeeshops. If by now you are a *uroti canai*

addict, the **Taufik Restaurant** in Jalan Masjid is good. The **Rhu Sila** coffeehouse at the Pantai Primula has good buffets of Malay food in pleasant surroundings. Great spicy Nasi Padang can be had for lunch at **Sofinaz Restoran**, 38 Jalan Masjid Abidin. A good deal on Malay seafood dishes can be found at the open-air restaurants along Batu Buruk beach. If you are desperate for fast food, there are a couple of copy places, one called the **Whimpy Fried Chicken Restaurant** in Jalan Air Jernih, and another called **MacDota Fried Chicken Restaurant** in Jalan Kota Llama, but somehow fast food doesn't to take to Malaysia too well and ends up neither fast nor finger lickin' good.

OUT OF TOWN

Redang Island
EXPENSIVE
Located about 50 km (31 miles) from Kuala Terengganu, Pulau Redang is actually a whole group of tiny, largely uninhabited islands, Redang itself being the home of a fishing village built on stilts over the sea. The pristine beauty of the island, which is set in one of Malaysia's few marine parks, has been threatened by the construction of a golf course on the island (as if the country needed yet another golf course!). There are more than half a dozen luxurious resorts scattered about the Redang islands, offering packages which include meals and, in most cases, transfer by speedboat. The **Redang Beach Resort** ((09) 623-8188 FAX (09) 623-0224, has 60 rooms and has a wide range of water sports including SCUBA diving; a three-day, two-night package costs $156 per person on a twin-sharing basis. The **Berjaya Redang** ((09) 697-1111 FAX (09) 697-1100, largest of all the resorts, is considerably more expensive at $140 a night for a double for accommodation only; all meals are extra.

MODERATE
Coral Redang ((09) 623-6200 FAX (09) 623-6300, is smaller and more intimate, and offers a three-day, two-night package at $148 per person on a twin-sharing basis. A two-day, one-night stay in a chalet at **Redang Lagoon** ((09) 827-2116 FAX (09) 827-2116 will set you back $88 per person.

Perhentian Island

On the very border of Terengganu and Kelantan is the small village of Kuala Besut, from where ferries travel regularly to the two islands, **Perhentian Besar** and **Perhential Kercil**. These islands are truly idyllic, except during the northeast monsoon season from November through March, when the crossing is rough and the surrounding seas murky. The Perhentian islands are much closer to the coast than Redang and offer a range of accommodation.

On **Perhentian Kecil** (Little Perhentian) there are a number of small, inexpensive places, one or two having as few as six rooms and the largest offering 35 rooms. Prices range from $12 up to a maximum of $20 per night, the latter for Rajawali Chalet ((09) 691-0818. Other options include D'Lagoon ((09) 691-0105, Long Beach Cottage Hut ((011) 987-7252, Rock Garden ((09) 691-0290, Matahari Chalet ((011) 987-7968, Rosly's Chalet ((09) 691-0155, Coral Bay ((09) 691-0189 and Moonlight Chalet ((010) 984-2065.

Perhentian Besar, the larger of the two islands, offers one upmarket resort as well as a range of less expensive chalets and beach huts. The **Perhentian Island Resort** ((03) 244-8530 FAX (03) 243-4984, which has scuba diving facilities, has doubles from $100. Cozy Chalet ((09) 691-0090 has rooms from $20 to $28; similarly priced is the Coral View Island Resort ((09) 695-6943. You could, of course, just take your chances, turn up at the beach and wander around until you find the place that suits you and lie about for a few days. Most are have only basic facilities: no electricity, water drawn from a well, kerosene lamps at night and basic home cooking. If you're staying several days, you'd be well advised to bring a few tins, biscuits and fruits to ensure a little variety. Some of the cheaper places include Coco Hut, IBI Chalet, Mama's Place, Rosli Chalet and Hamid's.

GETTING THERE

Getting to Perhentian is fairly simple and getting easier all the time as the place develops more and more tourist-oriented services. The bus to Kota Bharu will stop at Jerteh where you can either get another bus to Kuala Besut or negotiate a cab. From Kuala Besut, fishing boats or ferries leave regularly throughout the day for the two-hour trip to Perhentian, which costs $15 return. Getting back, just wait for an incoming ferry or organize for the boatman to pick you up if it's not peak season. If, during your visit to Malaysia, you plan to stay at only one of the offshore islands, then you should choose this one. It is more primitive than Tioman and a longer journey than Kapas, but as yet is unspoiled. If you are staying at any of the budget places in Kota Bharu, Terengganu or Marang, you will find that each of them will recommend a place to stay and even arrange the details of the trip

for you. If you need an even easier trip, many of the big travel agencies will organize the whole trip for you including, SCUBA equipment and instructor — for the right price, of course. There can't be many nicer places to learn SCUBA diving.

Kenyir Lake

Fifty-five kilometers west of Terengganu, this is a man-made lake and hydro-electric dam. It is about 369 sq km (142 sq miles) and has many islands created when the area was dammed in and flooded. It is rapidly turning into a leisure center for boating, fishing and trekking and has some pretty waterfalls and caves. The lake is increasingly popular with Malaysians, but many foreign visitors will not enjoy the sight of dead trees lining the foreshores, nor enjoy the sound of jet skis zooming across the waters. There is a Tasik Kenyir Express bus which departs daily from Kuala Lumpur and picks up passengers at

One of the myriad of traditional dress styles, this one from the East Coast.

Kuala Berang, south of Kuala Terengganu. For further information on this service, contact ((09) 822-1276 or (03) 444-4276. The newly opened **Tasik Kenyir Golf Resort** ((03) 202-8822 FAX (03) 202-8833 for reservations, has 150 chalets and other accommodation on the lakeside. It also offers, predictably, an 18-hole golf course plus a two-tiered pool, Children's Village and rope and obstacle courses. There are a several places offering accommodation in the region of $20–$30, while at the other end of the scale is the Kenyir Lake Resort, where you can

two-night package, which includes all meals, boat transfer and free use of non-motorized watersport facilities, costs $110 per person. Contact Uncle John's Resort ((09) 622-9564 FAX (09) 622-9569, PO Box 117, Kuala Terengganu, 20710 Malaysia.

Sekayu Waterfall

At the southern end of the system which feeds Kenyir Lake is the **Sekayu Waterfall**, another point from where you can approach the interior of Malaysia. Both the waterfall and the lake are on the borders of Terengganu's seg-

stay in a houseboat or floating chalet. **Kenyir Lake Resort** ((09) 514-6002 Kenyir Dam, Kuala Terengganu. Package stays here consist of a three-day trip for $92 including full board and organized trips to the waterfall, jungle treks and fishing. The resort has its own floating restaurant, a television room and just what you'd want in an idyllic country retreat — a karaoke set.

For something more simple, try **Uncle John's Resort**, copied from a floating restaurant on the River Kwai in Thailand. Accommodation is either in the main split bamboo and thatch roof building, or in houseboats. One of the best things about this place is the way they organize hikes, waterfall trips and other adventure activities. Their three-day,

ment of **Taman Negara**, so if you aren't making the trip to the National Park this might give you a good, if slightly commercialized, picture of what a stay there would be like. The waterfall is situated inside a recreational forest, has a government resthouse, some fairly well equipped chalets, including electricity and regular bathrooms, a mini-zoo and bird park. Some walks are marked out, and rumor has it that tigers have been seen in this area.

To get there, take the same road toward Berang but take the left fork, following signs for the waterfall. A regular bus service goes to Berang from Terengganu. The Terengganu-based South China Sea Travel offers a five-hour tour to Kenyir Lake and Sekayu Waterfalls for $28. The chalets at Sekayu can be booked by phone at ((09) 622-1433. They are about $15 a night.

GETTING THERE

Most express buses terminate in Kuala Terengganu, and bus users should note there are two bus stations, one for express buses and the other for local services. If you are traveling north to Kota Bharu from Marang on a local bus, you must go to the other station in order to continue your trip. Both Malaysia Airlines and Pelangi Air fly from Kuala Lumpur to Terengganu; there are also two MAS flights a week from Singapore, and daily Asia Pacific Airlines flights from Langkawi and Johor Bahru.

KOTA BHARU

BACKGROUND

The coastline from Kuala Besut northward is in the state of Kelantan, Since 1990, Kelantan has been ruled by the ultraconservative PAS, a fundamentalist Islamic party which has banned alcohol and countless seemingly harmless pursuits such as karaoke, and has even introduced separate check-outs for women in supermarkets. Be warned than liberal Western attitudes won't be well received here. The state has had a checkered past, finding itself under the influence of assorted foreign states from Majapahit, a Javanese kingdom in the fourteenth century, Thailand during the nineteenth century and Britain until 1948, when it became part of the Federated Malay States. These varying influences can be seen in many aspects of present day Kelantanese life, from the shadow-puppet shows to the batik printing and silk weaving whose influence is that of Thailand. The countryside, as you will notice on your journey through Kelantan, is decidedly different from the oil palm and rubber plantations further south and west. Bounded by the sea and mountains, Kelantan has retained its culture in a way that cannot be seen anywhere else in Malaysia. Top spinning, kite flying and traditional dances are not just things that get trooped out for the tourists, but are a genuine part of daily life.

GENERAL INFORMATION

The Tourist Information Centre is a good one and has lists of accommodation as well as some very useful leaflets about the area. It is at Jalan Sultan Ibrahim ((09) 748-5534 or 748-3543, beside the museum. It is closed on Fridays and public holidays; on other days, it is open from 8 AM to 12:45 PM, and from 2 PM to 4:30 PM. Finding your way about town is fairly easy, partly because the tourist office has decent maps and partly because a good effort has been made to erect large maps in public places.

If you are going from here to Thailand, the Thai Consulate ((09) 748-2545, is on Jalan Pengkalan Chepa.

WHAT TO SEE

Merdeka Square

Kota Bharu has grown a little too large to be a real pleasure to walk around in but bicycles can be hired cheaply from most travelers' budget hotels. Alternatively, rent a taxi for around $6 per hour. Merdeka Square, the busiest quarter of the town, has a long history predating its new name which it was given in 1957. In 1915 the body of the Malay freedom fighter, Tok Janggut, was displayed here after being executed by the British. Around the square are some other buildings with tales to tell. The old Hong Kong and Shanghai Bank, now a craft shop, was built in 1912 and served as the headquarters for the Japanese army during the Occupation. The Istana Balai Besar is nearby, built in 1844 as a palace for Sultan Muhamad II. Also nearby is the Istana Jahar, recently the home of the state museum but now the Royal Museum. It was built in 1887 and only part of it still stands. There is also a Museum of Royal Traditions and Customs, housed in a former palace built in 1887 and showing the intricate wood carvings typical of Kelantan. This and other museums as well as the Handicraft Village are open from 10:30 AM until 5:45 PM daily except Fridays.

The tightly bound feet of Chinese gentlewomen created the need for pretty little shoes.

The Handicraft Village and Craft Museum

This complex built in traditional Kelantanese style displays the state's various crafts such as weaving of *songket* fabric, batik painting and woodcarvings. Items on display are also for sale.

Cultural Centre

The Cultural Centre or Gelanggang Seni is the best place to get an overview of Kelantan's cultural heritage, most likely the richest you will find in Peninsular Malaysia.

Central Market

Kota Bharu's huge Central Market (Pasar Besar) is probably the most colorful market in all of Malaysia. Don't miss it. The sellers are all women, dressed in batik, their heads modestly veiled, their gold jewelry immodestly flashing. They preside over mounds of brilliantly colored fruits and vegetables on the ground floor of the market, while upstairs, there are great food stalls where you can try local specialties such as *nasi dangang* (rice with tuna) and *nasi kerabu* (rice with herbs).

A program listing the date and time of events happening here from March through to October (except during the fasting month of Ramadan) is available from the Kelantan Tourist Information Centre. Events include kite flying, the art of self defense or *silat*, shadow puppet plays, traditional music and dance.

The Cultural Centre or the Tourist Information Centre can put you in touch with a number of craftsmen who conduct one-day workshops in such skills as batik making, kite making, silver working and creation of traditional puppets. They also have a homestay program where you can actually stay in the home of various artisans and even a rice farmer.

If you're looking for souvenirs, textiles, brassware, gold and jewelry, try Jalan Temenggong in town, or if you're interested in something a little less upmarket, try the Buluh Kubu Bazaar, a three-story shopping complex crammed with clothing, knick-knacks and souvenirs.

Wat Phothivihan

Reputedly the longest Buddha in Malaysia, Wat Phothivihan was built in 1973 and is 40 m (131 ft) long. Possibly more interesting than the statue itself is the journey out to it. The road passes through many small villages, strongly influenced by their proximity to Thailand and the importance of rice to the local economy. Water buffalo lounge about, beautifully tended rice paddies add color, and the houses are up on stilts to protect them against flooding during the rainy season. If you are in the area in April or during the national holiday for Vesak day, inquire about festivals that are held at the religious center. There are also other smaller Buddha statues in the area. The statue is situated about 12 km (seven miles) north of Kota Bharu near to Kampung Berok. Buses N° 19 or N° 27 from the central bus station go to Chabang Empat, from where you can walk or take a taxi for the final two kilometers. From town a return cab will cost about $11 including waiting time.

WHERE TO STAY

If you want to make the town your base of operations, there are many good hotels to choose from at rates ranging from luxury to shoestring. But if you prefer beach life, you should be aware that there is accommodation out at Pantai Cinta Berahi from where you can make the trip into town on the local bus, which is very reliable, or on the organized buses from the hotels. As mentioned above, you might like to take advantage of the homestay program where you can actually spend time living with various craftsmen or a rice farmer; check with the Tourist Information Centre ((09) 748-5534.

Expensive
At the top of the range is the **Hotel Perdana** ((09) 748-5000 FAX (09) 744-7621, on Jalan Mahmud, 15720 Kota Bharu which offers accommodation, a good range of recreational facilities as well as a pool and a coffeeshop. It is nicely situated close to the cultural center and some hawker stalls and within easy walking distance of the center of town. Doubles from $76–$84. No alcohol is available here.

Moderate
In the middle range there is the **Temenggong Hotel** ((09) 748-3844 FAX (09) 744-1481, Jalan Tok Hakim, 15000, Kota Bharu, where a deluxe twin is $30, well worth the extra cost over a standard double. Opposite Merdeka Square is the **Hotel Indah** ((09) 748-5081 FAX (09) 748-2788, 236B Jalan Tengku Besar,

15000 Kota Bharu, where a double room is $27. Rooms are air-conditioned, have hot water, television on request. There is also a coffeeshop in the hotel.

Of the middle range hotels the nicest has to be the **Tokyo Baru** ((09) 744-9488 3945, 6 Jalan Tok Hakim, where rooms are large and comfortable. The **Hotel Murni** ((09) 748-2399, centrally located in Jalan Dato Pati, has comfortable air-conditioned doubles at $28.

Inexpensive
At the budget range there are many small places to choose from. Opposite the Thai consulate is **Mummy Brown's** which has a good reputation and has rooms for $7, breakfast included. Nearby is **Rainbow Inn Guest House**, 4423A Jalan Pengkalan Chepa, 15400 Kota Bharu, with rooms at the same price.

WHERE TO EAT

Kelantan, and Kota Bharu in particular, have some culinary delights not available anywhere else in Malaysia. Some of the best Malay food is to be found in Kota Bharu and the best place to try some is the **night market**, opposite the Central Market. There is a terrific range of seafood, *murtabaks*, satay and lots more (see below). A good meal for two couldn't cost more than $12 and it would be silly to visit Kelantan without having at least one dinner here in the open.

For a small outlay here, or on the upper level of the **Central Market** during the daytime, you can eat some of the most unusual and delicious food and try different dishes each night for a month. Instead of trying the old favorites of *roti* or satay go for some of the less familiar items like *nasi kerabau*, rice cooked with ground coconut, fish, and local herbs and spices, *ayam percik* the local specialty which is chicken marinated in coconut milk and spices and then roasted over charcoal and served with thick gravy. Especially local are the many sweets such as *akok* cooked from duck and chicken eggs, brown sugar and flour.

If you want air conditioning with your meal, try the **Perdana**'s Chinese restaurant which serves Cantonese food.

The market at Khota Bharu is probably the country's most colorful.

There are also some reasonable banana leaf restaurants in Jalan Gaja Mati, a Kentucky Fried Chicken if you've got several hours to kill, and an A&W by the bus station.

OUT OF TOWN

If you're interested in seeing the famous *songket* weaving (see TOP SPOTS), you could visit Kampung Penambang, three kilometers (two miles) from Kota Bharu. Many other crafts for which Kelantan is renowned are produced along the road to the well known beach, Pantai Cinta Berahi.

Pantai Cinta Berahi translates as the Beach of Passionate Love, although this should definitely not be taken as any kind of suggestion in this staunchly Muslim area. In fact, the current puritanical government is trying to change the name of this beach, referred to locally by its initials, PCB, to Pantai Cahaya Bulan (Moolight Beach)! This is very much a local holiday resort, and during weekdays when the schools are operating, it is almost uncannily deserted. This is quite a pretty beach, although compared to beaches further south it's pretty average really. All the way out from town there are many batik factories and shops selling *songket*, silverware, and other handicrafts. The beach itself is the site of a historic occasion in the annals of the British Empire. It was on this stretch of beach that on December 7, 1941, the Japanese landed and began their blistering movement south that was to end in the dramatic surrender of Singapore. There is little evidence of the historic battle that was fought here, since all the earthworks and gun emplacements have long been swept away by the encroaching sea, but the Perdana Beach Resort, built on the actual site of the landing, has a display of memorabilia and some interesting photographs.

There's not much to do here besides battle it out with the ultra violet rays on the beach and wander along back toward town looking in the craft shops, but if you like beach life this is as good as any. Foreigners tend to get ignored here so if you really want to experience life in a beach village you should try one of those further south.

Where to Stay

The Perdana Resort ((09) 774-4000 FAX (09) 774-4980, Jalan Kuala Pa'amat, Pantai Cinta Berahi, P.O. Box 121, 15710 Kota Bharu, is the most recent and poshest of the resorts here. It has a pool, a lagoon with boat rides for children, tennis courts, wind surfing and other water activities, beautiful chalets built in a traditional Malay style and a decent but pricey restaurant which is frequented by townspeople who come for the buffets which are quite a good value. Double rooms cost $60, while a semi-detached double chalet with all mod cons costs $72.

Just along the beach further south toward town is the **Pantai Cinta Berahi Resort (** (09) 773-2307 FAX (09) 773-2605, P.O. Box 131 Kota Bharu, Kelantan which has semi-detached chalets at $45 and detached chalets from $54 to $68 but no swimming pool. The restaurant there is much cheaper than the Perdana and offers a good breakfast and snacks.

On the other side of the Perdana heading further away from town is **H.B. Village (** (09) 773-4993, offering lots of fun things like a mini-zoo, bicycles for hire and a boating lagoon. An air-conditioned chalet which sleeps four will cost you $20.

FURTHER AFIELD

From Kota Bharu it is possible to explore the interior of **Kelantan** by taking a boat along the Sungei Kelantan to visit various points along the river. Most of these journeys are rarely done by tourists and involve some planning on the visitor's part. The tourist information office organizes a number of tours, one of which is a trip by train to **Gua Musang** inside the boundary of Taman Negara. If you feel like a trip on your own steam, you could try getting the 7:45 AM bus N° 5 to Kuala Krai, then the 10 AM boat from near the police station to Dabong. The boat passes through lovely rainforest on the way to Dabong. Three kilometers east of Dabong is **Gua Ikan**, some caves and a waterfall. There is a government resthouse at Dabong. If you want to return to Kota Bharu the same day, catch the 5:45 PM train back. Alternatively, you could travel on to Jelawang and stay overnight in a chalet ($10 including meals), and take a one-and-a-half-hour trek to the spectacular **Jelawang Waterfall**. There are some lovely waterfalls not far from Kota Bharu, most of them in the Pasir Putih district about 35 km (21 miles) from town. Take the bus N°3 from the main terminal to Padang Pakamat, and then a taxi for the eight-kilometer (five-mile) journey to the falls. Or you could take the same bus and get off at Pasir Putih, then take a taxi to Jeram Lenang where there is a popular waterfall. The Tourist Information Centre at Kota Bharu will give you assistance in organizing any of these trips.

and Singapore with Wakaf Bharu, just south of Kota Bharu. Take a bus N° 19 or N° 27 to reach the station from Kota Bharu. Best book your rail ticket in advance if possible. There are also daily MAS flights from Kuala Lumpur, Penang and Alor Setar.

Kota Bharu is another town with a confusing network of bus stations. South of town are two bus stations, one in Jalan Hamzah for Ipoh, Seremban and Melaka buses, another in Jalan Pasir Puteh, where SKMK buses depart both south and west, and two in town, one at Jalan Pendek for

GETTING THERE

If you are coming from the south it will take about three hours in a taxi from Kuala Terranganu, longer on a bus of course. From Penang a bus will take about five hours. The bus travels through interesting countryside which was once home to communist insurgents left over from the troubles of the 1950s. Now it is living testimony to the disappearance of the rainforest, the only signs of wildlife being signs warning motorists against passing herds of elephants. The East-West highway, which starts at Grik, has speeded up traveling time considerably.

It is possible to take one of the two daily express trains which connect Kuala Lumpur

travel inside Kelantan and the other for more local buses. How definite that description is remains debatable. If you get confused, inquire at the Tourist Information Centre or ask one of the locals.

Perhentian Island is becoming popular as a get-away-from-it-all destination off the East Coast.

The West Coast

LANGKAWI

Just off the northwest coast of Malaysia is a group of 99 islands, 104 if you include the five that disappear when the tide comes in, that are just beginning to make their presence felt. The whole group of islands is named after the largest and most populated one, Langkawi.

Until relatively recently, Langkawi was a tranquil spot with a few Malay fishing villages and not much else. All that has changed as one luxury hotel chain after another opens up its doors, and as various theme parks, malls and other attractions open, primarily for Asian visitors who aren't keen on just lying around on a beach and relaxing. If you love just luxuriating at a resort as you gaze upon dozens of forest-clad islands, you'll probably enjoy Langkawi, but don't expect a rich indigenous culture as in the northeastern states of Peninsular Malaysia, the historic buildings and great food of Penang's Georgetown, or the vibrant night life of Phuket over the border in Thailand.

BACKGROUND

Many legends are associated with the island, but the one that has a hold on people's imagination concerns Mahsuri, a young woman falsely accused of adultery and ordered to be punished with *sula* — burying the guilty up to the waist in sand and plunging a *kris* between the shoulder blades into the stomach. Protesting her innocence, Mahsuri was put to death, but the blood that flowed from her body was white and in her dying breath she cursed the island of Langkawi for seven generations. The legend was recalled when one of Malaysia's largest construction companies decided to invest millions in a giant tourist complex in the 1980s. The whole plan failed badly and was never completed.

Dr. Mahathir, Malaysia's current prime minister, is from the state of Kedah under whose jurisdiction Langkawi falls, and the decision to turn the island into a duty-free haven in 1987 in order to stimulate trade and tourism has been seen as one of his pet projects. When the money was poured into Langkawi to build roads, an international airport and hotels, the economic boom that was expected never materialized. The curse of Mahsuri was blamed for the failure. The seven generations are now said to have run their course and there is now optimism and confidence for the island's future. The decision to hold the Commonwealth Government Heads of State conference, and the staging of the big annual Aerospace and Maritime Exhibition at Langkawi ensure that its luxurious hotels are not always under utilized.

GENERAL INFORMATION

There is a tourism information counter at Langkawi's airport; if no one is on duty (which often seems to be the case), just help yourself to the brochures displayed at the counter. The main tourism information office is located in a small building along the waterfront in the main town of Kuah, just past the mosque and almost opposite the Sime Darby duty-free shopping complex ((04) 966-7789. The office is open from 9 AM until 5 PM daily. Note, however, that banks and government offices are closed Thursday and Friday, and are open Saturday and Sunday.

The island is best appreciated by traveling around it and by taking a boat out to some of the smaller islands. The roads are in excellent condition, there are special bicycle trails with occasional signboard maps in some areas. There is very little traffic, but watch out for buffaloes, especially at night, as they often wander across the road and have caused a number of accidents. Cars, motorbikes and bicycles are easily hired, the rates are reasonable, and petrol is tax-free. Cars go for as little as $28 a day, small motorbikes are $12 and bicycles, $6. Most of the big hotels will insist on seeing your license but the smaller places are not so fussy and will rent out motorbikes regardless.

If you are not staying at one of the big hotels it may be worth remembering that local establishments run by Muslim Malays do not have a license to sell alcohol, and many eating stalls and restaurants, even at the main resort strip of Pantai Cenang, do not sell beer. Remember to bring your own from Kuah or

Sardine fishing and drying is a cottage industry in Tanjong Rhu on the island of Langkawi.

the airport shops. The airport shop also sells
a useful tourist map of the island, although
the brochure on Langkawi published by the
Malaysian Tourism Promotion Board has a
perfectly adequate map showing major
places of interest and some of the major
resorts.

As the Muslim day of worship is on Friday and Langkawi's population is resolutely
Muslim, banks and government offices are
closed on Thursday afternoon and Friday,
but open throughout the weekend.

WHAT TO SEE

The main town of Langkawi is **Kuah**, on the
southeast corner of the island. This is where
ferries from Penang, from the mainland
(Kuala Kedah and Kuala Perlis) and from
Thailand arrive and depart. A large **duty-free
shopping centre** occupies most of the ferry
terminal, called Jetty Point, though it has little
of interest to foreign visitors apart from the
duty-free alcohol. Nearby, a massive stone
sea eagle — the real thing is often seen flying
overhead — dominates Dataran Lang (Eagle
Square), which has a number of ponds,
bridges, terraces and a couple of restaurants.
Just next to this is a park known as **Taman
Legenda**, with a range of souvenir shops and
numerous stone depictions of Langkawi's
legends. If this sort of thing interests you, go
in the cooler hours of the afternoon as this
place is incredibly hot during the middle of
the day. Open daily from 9 AM until 9 PM, it
costs $2 for adults.

Looking from here across the bay one sees
a sort of bizarre Sleeping Beauty castle, the
Tiara hotel, at the far end of Kuah. The waterfront area right in front of Kuah is home to
several groups of food stalls offering inexpensive Malay food. Kuah itself has nothing
of interest for the tourist, apart from a good
Chinese restaurant inside the City Bayview
Hotel. Like all other restaurants on Langkawi,
this is not permitted to serve pork.

It is a short trip from Kuah to Mahsuri's
Mausoleum The white marble tomb itself is
not that memorable, but there is an attractive traditional Malay house in the complex.
The west coast beaches of **Pantai Tengah**,
Pantai Cenang and **Pantai Kok**, as well as at
those of **Datai Bay** and **Tanjung Rhu** on the

north coast of Langkawi, are the best on the
island, and this is where most of Langkawi's
resort hotels are located. Although the sand
is fine, soft and white, don't expect the crystal clear waters and coral reefs typical of the
islands off the eastern coast of the Malaysia
Peninsula.

The best coral in the Langkawi region is
located south at **Pulau Payar Marine Park**,
although if you have a chance to see the reefs
off Peninsular Malaysia's East Coast, don't
bother going there. **Langkawi Coral** organizes cruises in a high-speed catamaran to
the marine park almost an hour away, where
a huge floating platform with a roof has been
moored over the reef. The platform has an
underwater observatory, dining area and sun
deck, and there are also glass-bottom boats

and snorkeling and diving equipment available. A day here is not cheap, costing $152 for adults and $76 for children, which covers transport, lunch and coral viewing (but not hire of scuba equipment). Many visitors complain that it's very hot out on the floating platform, and that apart from viewing the coral and taking a dip, there's not much else to do.

Telaga Tujuh or the Seven Wells is a series of seven waterfalls set in lovely forest in the northwest corner of Langkawi. The falls are accessible after a fairly stiff hike. Be warned, the area is dangerous and more than one visitor has fallen to his death or been severely injured here.

A number of manufactured attractions of varying degrees of interest to the visitor are scattered about the island. The Galleri Perdana, at Kilim in the north east of the island, houses a collection of over 10,000 state gifts and awards presented to the Malaysian prime minister. The gallery is open from 10 AM to 5 PM daily (except Mondays), and is closed from 12:15 PM until 3 PM Fridays.

On the north coast, at Teluk Yu, not far east of the industrial area and port of Telok Ewa, you'll find the **Handicraft Centre** or Kompleks Budaya Kraf Langkawi. A wide range of handicrafts from all over Malaysia is displayed in a series of lavish white stone halls which remind one of a mosque or minor palace rather than a craft center. Many

On the west coast of Malaysia, boat building and fishing are traditional skills handed down from father to son for many generations.

The West Coast

may feel the buildings themselves are more interesting than the contents on sale within, but the same is not true for the Langkawi Crystal glass blowing centre tucked away at the back of the craft center. Here you can see glass items being created and purchase the result.

Just south of the airport, at Pantai Cenang, is the popular **Underwater World**, billed as one of the largest marine and freshwater aquariums in Asia. Open from 10 AM until 6 PM daily, entry costs RM12 for adults and RM8 for children.

A **Crocodile Farm** with more than 1,000 reptiles can be found at Kubang Badak, 32 km (20 miles) from Kuah. Probably more interesting to most visitors is the **Sangkar Ikan Langkawi**, a floating platform in the sea where fish are bred for restaurant tables; this is located on the east side of Kuah. An indoor water theme park, **Aquabeat**, has a number of water rides and is a popular place for kids; there are also outdoor jacuzzis for the less energetic. Pricey at RM20 per head, Aquabeat is open daily from 9 AM until 9 PM.

Visiting the Islands

Most visitors would find it far more interesting to take a local boat out on an island cruise. Round trips of about four hours usually cover three main islands, including **Pulau Dayang Bunting** where the waters of a lake are believed to help infertile women conceive; on the same island is the **Cave of the Banshee**, inhabited by thousands of bats. The trip also includes **Pulau Singa Besar**, which is a wildlife sanctuary. A boat holding eight to ten passengers costs between RM200 to RM300. Arrange with your hotel or resort, or go to where the boats are tied up between the ferry terminal and the Langkawi Yacht Club. You can also arrange to charter a boat and choose your own island; try the motor yacht *Melreni*, through ((04) 955-3837 or (04) 955-3643.

If you have your own transport and would like a glimpse of what real life is like in Langkawi, drive up to the night market held every Friday from about 5 PM to 8 PM at **Padang Lalang**, which is near the big roundabout on the road to Tanjung Rhu. This is where the locals do their shopping and enjoy a wide variety of food at the stalls.

WHERE TO STAY

Expensive

Top of the range and arguably the best resort in all Malaysia is **The Datai**, an exquisite place tucked in the rainforest on a hill sloping down to a beautiful white sandy beach (see LIVING IT UP in YOUR CHOICE). Exclusivity is the keynote here, with 68 deluxe rooms and suites located in the main body of the resort, and 40 villas scattered in the surrounding rainforest. The Datai has a couple of pools and two dining areas, and guests can also stroll down the beach or take a lift to the nearby Andaman (run by the same group) which has a good Japanese restaurant. (Non-guests, however, are not permitted to use The Datai's restaurants.) **The Datai Bay Golf Club** ((04) 959-2500 FAX (04) 959-2600, is literally just down the road from the resort. Rates begin at $276 for a double.

The **Andaman** ((04) 959-1088 FAX (04) 959-1168, is at the other end of Datai Bay on Langkawi's northwest coast, and offers a different style to the exclusive Datai. The vast entrance lobby looks down over the forest to the sea, with the 187 rooms and suites located in two wings. All the facilities expected of a five-star resort can be found here, with tennis courts, non-motorized water sports, a large swimming pool and access to the Datai Bay Golf Club. Rates begin at $192.

Also located on the north coast but towards the eastern corner is the **Radisson Tanjung Rhu Resort** ((04) 959-1033 FAX (04) 959-1899, which occupies one of the loveliest beaches in Langkawi with powder white sand fringed by casuarina trees, facing blue-green islands seemingly within touching distance (see LIVING IT UP in YOUR CHOICE). The luxurious yet understated resort has doubles starting at $240.

There are several resorts nestled between the sea and the forest-covered hills that dominate the northwest corner of Langkawi. These include the **Berjaya Langkawi Beach and Spa Resort** ((04) 959-1888 FAX (04) 959-1886, on Burau Bay, where doubles start at $193. The Japanese-style spa here is excellent, and even if you're not staying at the hotel, you are welcome to use this state-of-the-art spa where aromatherapy, shiatsu, facials, hydro-therapy and a relaxing flotation tank are all available.

Nearby the Berjaya is the **Burau Bay Resort** ((04) 959-1061 FAX (04) 959-1172 where the Malay-style chalets of the resort are scattered in the rainforest at the edge of the beach. Doubles from $140. The large **Sheraton Langkawi Beach Resort** ((04) 955-1901 FAX (04) 955-1968, in the same area, has doubles from $242.

Along the west coast, from Pantai Tengah in the south up through Pantai Cenang to Pantai Kok, you will find a large variety of accommodation and, at Pantai Cenang, a few independent restaurants and food stalls. Upmarket resorts in this area include the well-established **Pelangi Beach Resort** ((04) 955-1011 FAX (04) 955-1122, at Pantai Cenang, built in wood in traditional Malay style. Plenty of recreational options here, as well as a pool. Doubles from $193.

The less expensive **Beach Garden Resort** at Pantai Cenang ((04) 955-1363 FAX (04) 955-1221, is small but popular. Run by a German couple, this spotlessly clean place on the beachfront has doubles for $121, including a large breakfast for two.

Moderate

The **Semarak Langkawi Beach Resort** ((04) 955-1377 FAX (04) 955-1159, Pantai Cenang, has only 26 rooms, with the option of fan-cooled ($60) or air-conditioned ($82). **Cenang Beach Resort** ((04) 955-1395, is a budget place with doubles at around $40.

Inexpensive

Two or three small beachside resorts nestle along the water's edge at Pantai Kok; these offer a pleasant place to relax for a very modest price, but as the area is threatened with demolition so that more expensive resorts can be constructed, telephone first to check they're still open. Perhaps the nicest and popular with travelers is **The Last Resort** ((04) 955-1046 FAX (04) 955-1046, with a variety of options from terraced rooms to detached air-conditioned rooms and beach-view chalets with fan. Prices range from $24 to $55. The neighboring **Kok Bay Beach Motel** ((04) 955-1407, has simple beachside chalets with fans for around $28.

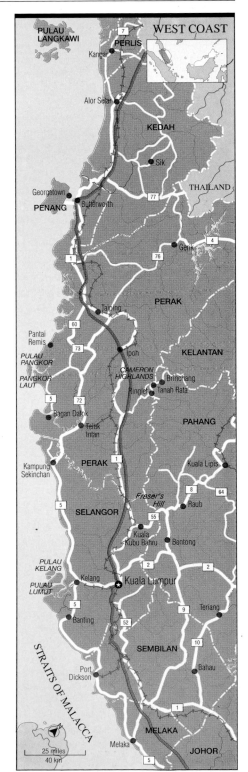

WHERE TO EAT

What follows is organized around the various locations on the island.

Kuah

Located behind the multistory City Bayview Hotel, you will find the modestly fronted **Domino** Restaurant, 10 Pandak Mayah Enam. The food is Western, with New Zealand steaks the house specialty.

On the main road in Kuah, behind the government souvenir and craft shop, is the **Sari Seafood Restaurant**, built on stilts. There is a great view of the sea from the tables, and the menu is large enough to support snacks or dinners. Wine is available and a good seafood dinner for two (without alcohol) averages about $25. Across the road from the Sari there are a couple of Indian cafés serving inexpensive but tasty food. The Langkawi **Yacht Club**, just beyond Jetty Point, has a very agreeable open-sided restaurant on the water's edge which is open to the public for lunch and dinner. Further east of Jetty Point, you can find pizzas plus the nightclub cum bar, **Someplace Else**, at the Sheraton Perdana. For inexpensive local cusine, try any of the food stalls that set up late afternoon along the waterfront. Most of these vendors offer Malay food, but some have Thai dishes, too.

Pantai Cenang

The Spice Market Restaurant at the Pelangi Beach Resort has good local and continental dishes, but the resort's Thai restaurant is disappointing. For better Thai food, go to the simple open restaurant of **Haji Ramli**, at Jalan Pantai Tengah (basically the southern end of Pantai Cenang). The *haji's* wife is Thai and the food here is both delicious and cheap; only drawback is that beer is not served. There's a palm-thatched open stall known as the **Breakfast Bar** at Pantai Cenang, where you can get good local breakfasts such as *roti, nasif* and chicken rice from 8 AM until midday. The **Beach Garden Resort** has a German restaurant on the beach with good food at reasonable prices, with alcohol available.

Kek Lok Si Buddhist Temple, Penang.

Oasis Beach Bar and Restaurant offers simple food and is a popular hangout spot at night.

One of the best places for both food and ambiance in all of Langkawi is **Bon Ton At The Beach**, a branch of the popular Kuala Lumpur restaurant. Set in a Balinese-style pavilion, where there is also a gift shop with a wide range of items, Bon Ton is an oasis of good taste and good food. Open for both lunch and dinner, with local and Western specialties plus a range of the sinfully delicious cakes that have made Bon Ton famous. Bon Ton At The Beach is at the northern end of Pantai Cenang, heading in the direction of the airport.

Pantai Kok and North Coast

At Pantai Kok, all the eating places are attached to the few remaining inexpensive hotels and they all serve modestly priced local food as well as some basic Western dishes. **The Last Resort** comes well recommended. On the northern end of the island, at **The Andaman**, you will find a good Japanese restaurant as well as a restaurant featuring Mediterranean cuisine and a poolside bar with pizzas, sandwiches and salads. (Note that The Datai's restaurants are, as mentioned above, for the exclusive use of guests staying at the resort). The delightful Radisson Tanjung Rhu features east-west seafood at the elegant Rhu Restaurant, but you can also eat at the Sands Beach Restaurant which offers a range of Western and Malaysian cuisine throughout the day.

GETTING THERE

By Air

MAS and AirAsia fly directly from Kuala Lumpur, while SilkAir flies in from Singapore. MAS also has a flight between Penang and Langkawi. The airport number is ((04) 955-1311. A taxi from the airport into Kuah will cost $8.

By Rail

Malayan Railway runs the Ekspres Langkawi rail service from Kuala Lumpur to Alor Setar in Kedah, where you take a taxi to Kuala Kedah for the ferry across to Langkawi.

By Ferry

There are plenty of boats crossing to and from Kuala Kedah (8 AM until 7:30 PM) and Kuala Perlis (8 AM until 8 PM) on the mainland. The one-hour journey costs $9. Boats to and from Penang cost $24 and take a little under three hours. The ferry departs from Penang at 8 AM daily, and leaves Langkawi on the return trip at 6:15 PM. The **Star Cruise Company** was planning to introduce a fast ferry service between Langkawi and Phuket some time in late 1997 or early 1998; check if this is already in operation.

PENANG

BACKGROUND

Like Melaka and Singapore, Penang was recognized at an early stage in its history as a strategic point for trade. Occupied in the sixteenth century by the Portuguese, in the seventeenth by local pirates, and then in the eighteenth century by the British, it has witnessed many battles and played many roles. In 1786 Francis Light, working for a trading company, took control of the island with the permission of the local sultan. Later he had to defend the island from the same sultan who began to feel that he wasn't getting his money's worth out of the British. The British settled and prospered, finding rich deposits of tin in nearby states and making Penang the trading post for those wishing to buy and sell. Millionaire's Row, a little shabby now, stands as testimony to the wealth created here.

By 1835 Penang was part of the Straits Settlements, with a large Chinese population as well as Malays and foreigners. Trouble between two different dialect groups of Chinese broke out in 1865 and lasted for a decade before it was finally settled. The motor car brought more wealth to Penang, boost-

moved aggressively to become an area for light industry and dozens of gleaming factories (many making computer parts) cluster around the airport in the southeast of the island. Since the rise of Langkawi, Penang has been losing out to the tourist industry, which is a pity since it still has much to offer. The dozens of luxurious resorts and hotels in the Batu Ferringhi region tend to give the place an air of an oriental Costa Brava, but Georgetown remains one of the most fascinating place to explore in all of Peninsular Malaysia.

ing its port facilities with the massive demand for rubber and the First World War brought even more riches to the traders. The depression also hit Penang, followed a decade later by Penang's abandonment by the British to the Japanese who took the whole Malay peninsula in just three months.

Apart from the fact that Penang's occupiers were Japanese rather than English, business went on as usual here, the only difference being the destination of the rubber and tin. The Japanese left, and the British sheepishly returned, but it was never the same. By the fifties Malaya was independent and rubber plus the tin that Penang's port shipped out became less and less profitable. During the past decade or so, Penang has

GENERAL INFORMATION

Penang's climate seems to be a fraction cooler than that of the mainland, although perhaps this is because one is never far from the sea breezes. The island itself is about 24 km (15 miles) by 14.5 km (nine miles), smaller than Singapore and less built up, although this is changing fast on the eastern side. Penang is predominantly Chinese, and some of the local Malays and Indians even speak Chinese dialect. It is renowned throughout Malaysia for its fantastic food, and much of its magnificent colonial architecture still

Wat Chayamangkalaram Temple, Penang. Its gilded Buddha figure is claimed to be the biggest in the country.

remains. Transport around Georgetown is by local bus, which is quite efficient, taxi, which gets more expensive depending on the label on your luggage, or trishaw. Traffic in Georgetown itself is comparatively light, so a trishaw ride to places of interest is not the death-defeating activity carried out by the caravans of trishaws which duck and dive their way around Singapore each night (see YOUR CHOICE). Bicycles can be hired at Batu Ferringhi and a possible day trip is a motor cycle ride around the island. The ferry to Butterworth operates around the clock. The

Malaysian Tourism Promotion Board information office ((04) 262-0066, Jalan Tun Syed Sheh Barakbah, opposite the clock tower, is quite helpful and well situated next door to the booking office for boats to Langkawi and opposite Fort Cornwallis. There is an information center run by the Penang Tourism Association almost next door to the government run office, but their information is limited. Another government tourism information center is located on the third level of KOMTAR, the giant tower building by the bus station; be warned that this office does not open until 10 AM, whereas the one near the clock tower is open by 8:15 AM.

Before arriving at Penang, some decision-making has to be done about what kind of a holiday you want to have here. Penang's beaches are not fantastic, and if you have the time to enjoy the beaches of Langkawi or, better still, those of the East Coast, you'd be better off staying in Georgetown and concentrating on the cultural aspects of Penang, with a couple of day trips to see attractions in other parts of the island. The medium-

priced and budget accommodation is in town, and if you choose to stay at the beach, where most of the hotels are very definitely in the luxury class, your holiday will be considerably more expensive.

WHAT TO SEE

A Trip Around Georgetown

A pleasant two-hour sightseeing trip will show you the sights of the town and help you get your bearings. Starting from the tourist office, the first point of interest is right outside, the **Clocktower**. Erected at the personal expense of one of Penang's many millionaires, it marks the Diamond Jubilee of Britain's Queen Victoria. Beside it is **Fort Cornwallis**, built in the early nineteenth century by convict labor. One of the cannons, Seri Rambai, is said to grant fertility to barren women. Around the rest of the Padang can be seen what were once the major municipal buildings. In Lebuh Farquhar is the **Museum and Art Gallery**, once an English school which started undergoing renovation in 1995 and was still not reopened in 1998. However, the original exhibits were fascinating (especially those devoted to Peranakan culture) and the refurbished museum should be worth a visit. Next door is **St. George's Church**, built in 1811 by the same obliging set of convicts who built the fort. This exquisite building is one of Southeast Asia's oldest churches and has a lovely pavilion in front devoted to the memory of Francis Light.

Carrying on up Lebuh Farquhar to Lebuh Leith you will come across a magnificent old private house, **Cheong Fat Tze Mansion**, built in 1860 and surrounded by high walls. The gates are firmly closed against visitors, and the future of the building (owned by the same man who owns the blue-painted houses containing a bar and restaurant opposite, 20 Leith Street) is uncertain. This remarkably ornate building is one of the two remaining examples in Southeast Asia of Ching Dynasty architecture. Back up Lebuh Leith to Farquhar Street is the old **Christian cemetery** where Francis Light is buried alongside many of his countrymen.

A slightly longer trishaw ride will bring you to **Khoo Kongsi**, a highly ornate clan house in Cannon Square built by the Khoo clan in 1906. There are many clan houses in Penang, but this is the most impressive. The purpose of the clan house is to act as a meeting house for the extended family of that name and to extend charity and help to all other Khoos. Inside in the central room is an altar dedicated to Tua Sai Yeah, the family's particular deity, while other rooms bear the names of past members of the clan. The clan house is open to the public from 9 AM to 5 PM on weekdays and 9 AM to 1 PM on Saturdays. Before you finish your ride or walk around the town, you should go down some of the older roads such as **Lebuh Chulia, Lebuh Muntri** and **Lorong Stewart** where the old tile work, architecture and peculiar items for sale offer hours of interest.

Out of Town

Further out of town are places which would take at least a half day to visit. The **Botanic Gardens**, on Waterfall Road, are a good wheeze. Much wilder than Singapore's tidy and well labeled park, the gardens are ruled by several troupes of extremely sneaky macaque monkeys, each of which guards its own territory. They have a cute habit of coming close, pretending to take the peanut out of your hand, and while you are engaged in giggling at it, snatching the whole packet and biting you if you try to get it back. Going through the park empty-handed, especially if you are small, is asking for trouble. One tribe has been thrown out of the gardens by the others and hangs around outside getting more food than those deep in the park who only get the few leftovers. The gardens also have a small zoo and a waterfall. For $6, a cab will take you to the park and wait, or you can take bus N° 7 from the Weld Quay bus terminal.

From the Botanic Gardens you can find your way up **Penang Hill**. To reach the top of the hill, you ride up the funicular railway, begun in 1899, with its carriages having the same angle as that of the hill slope. The railway works by the weight of the descending carriage pulling the ascending one up. After the funicular failed to move on its maiden voyage, it took 20 years, until 1923, to get it actually started. The hill itself is very pretty and cool, with an aviary, lots of stalls selling fake designer goods, and a hotel. The views

from the hill are spectacular. To get to the funicular railway, take a green bus N° 91 from the jetty terminal on Pengkalan Weld or bus N° 1 from the KOMTAR bus station to Air Hitam, where you transfer to a N° 8 bus. Alternatively, stop off at the **Kek Lok Si Temple**, worth a visit in its own right, and from there bus N° 8 to the funicular station. This Buddhist temple's architecture is a mix of Thai, Chinese and Burmese.

In the past, no visit to Penang was considered complete without a trip to its famous **Snake Temple**, on the way to the

airport. However, for reasons no one can explain, the snakes (many of them highly poisonous) have been dying out. The temple itself was built in 1850 and is dedicated to the memory of Chor Soo Kong, a priest who was said to have healing powers.

On the north coast, on the way from Batu Feringghi towards Teluk Bahang, the **Pinang Cultural Centre** offers three cultural tours daily (except Friday) between 9:30 AM and 5 PM. The two-and-a-half hour show gives demonstrations of various Malaysian arts, games and handicrafts, as well as a 45-minute cultural show with dances from all over

---

OPPOSITE: Batu Ferringhi beach, Malaysia's answer to the Costa Brava. ABOVE: A rooftop scene.

Malaysia. Just past Teluk Bahang is the **Butterfly Farm** and an interesting batik factory. The Butterfly Farm is 22 km (14 miles) from Georgetown, about $8 by cab, and has butterflies and other insects from all over Malaysia. Everything in its shop has a butterfly motif. Just before it is a batik factory, where one can witness this amazing and beautiful art created first-hand. South of the Butterfly Farm is the 100-hectare (240-acre) **Recreational Forest** or Taman Rimba, with a interesting Forestry Museum and some lovely walks along clear streams.

Batu Ferringhi is worth a visit. In the 1960s and 1970s this was an important stop on the route to Thailand and Burma for the many young people who sought alternative lifestyles. Now they've all grown up, and perhaps some return to stay in the expensive hotels built on the beach where they once stayed for next to nothing. More and more package-holidays from Europe are organized every year. The beach is quite pleasant, although sunbathers tend to get hassled by beach boys selling rides on speedboats, massages, hair-braiding and even the odd bit of illegal substances. Keep in mind that there is a mandatory death penalty for anyone caught handling even small amounts of drugs.

WHERE TO STAY

Beach Hotels
EXPENSIVE

Luxury hotels abound in Penang. Your biggest decision is whether to stay at the beach or in Georgetown. At the far end of the strip of beach hotels, in a little *kampung* called Teluk Bahang, is the **Penang Mutiara Beach Resort** ((04) 885-2828 FAX (04) 885-2829, One Jalan Teluk Bahang, 1150 Penang. This is the only five-star resort at Teluk Bahang The basic double room will set you back $135, but if you arrive there after an eight-hour bus journey from the East Coast, as I did, the magnificent bathroom makes it seem perfectly reasonable. The trouble is getting out of your room long enough to enjoy the other aspects of the resort which are also pretty impressive. They have a great service for taking young children off your hands, including camps, video games, a water slide and enter-tainment park. All the rooms look over the sea which is littered with the paraphernalia of the marina. The restaurants are good.

One of the best hotels, architecturally at least, is Shangri-La's **Rasa Sayang Resort** ((04) 881-1811 FAX (04) 881-1984, P.O. Box 735, Penang, where double rooms are $116. Rooms on the ground floor have tiny gardens opening out to the swimming pool and are excellent if you have children. The grounds are well laid out with a very large pool and all the regular beach facilities, and guests have access to the facilities of the other two places owned by the same hotel chain. Shangri-La's **Golden Sands Resort** ((04) 881-1911 FAX (04) 881-1880, is more of a family hotel, with room rates similar to the Rasa Sayang. All these hotels have pleasant gardens but face onto a public beach. The **Park Royal Penang** ((04) 890-8808 FAX (04) 881-2233, at Batu Ferringhi, has an excellent range of cuisine with Malaysian, Indian and Japanese plus a Continental deli. There are the usual water sports and other facilities. Doubles from $130.

INEXPENSIVE

Budget hotels are few now that the big hotels have moved in. The **Lone Pine** ((04) 881-1511 FAX (04) 881-1282, has basic rooms with television and 'fridge, and the cheapest double is $31. The hotel is on the beachfront, has a tiny pool and a pleasant atmosphere. Below this is very primitive accommodation consisting of rooms with fans and shared bathrooms, e.g., **Ali's** ((04) 881-1316, 53–4 Batu Ferringhi, For $12 you get lots of atmosphere, Seventies music and the usual travelers' tales. **Shalini's Guest House** ((04) 881-1859, 56 Batu Ferringhi Road not far from Ali's, has a Malay family atmosphere and great Penang Malay food for breakfast and dinner. A double with fan costs $12; if you want air conditioning it'll be $24. Nearby **Beng Keat Guest House** offers similar but less pleasant accommodation for the same price or rooms with a bathroom, television and 'fridge for $15. A cooker and washing machine are available for guests' use. Out at Teluk Bahang there is less to choose from. **Rama's** ((04) 881-1179, is a tiny guest house run by an Indian family and has a couple of double rooms at $6 which have shared bathrooms, fans and are pretty cramped. Guests are treated as one of the family and can use the 'fridge and cooker. They have room for 12 people in all and are usually full.

Town Hotels

The City Bay View ((04) 263-3161 FAX (04) 2634124, 25A Farquhar Street, 10200 Penang, is a good value at $48 including breakfast, has a pool, great views from the revolving restaurant, and is perfectly placed for trips around the city. The old **E & O**, a classic hotel in the genre of Raffles in Singapore and the Strand in Rangoon, is undergoing reconstruction and when it opens in late 1998 or early 1999, promises to be the grandest hotel in Penang, with an unrivaled waterfront location as well.

The hotels which offer more simple air-conditioned comfort are all in the area of Penang Road, and typical of these is the **Oriental** ((04) 263-4211 FAX (04) 263-5395, where a standard double is $30. At the **Hotel Malaysia** ((04) 236-3311 FAX (04) 237-1621, standard doubles are $38, including breakfast.

INEXPENSIVE

At the budget level there are some excellent Chinese hotels redolent with the atmosphere of an age long-gone, and a number of popular traveler's hangouts in Lebuh Chulia. Best place of all for atmosphere, and right opposite the spectacular Cheong Fat Sze Mansion in Lebuh Leith is the **Cathay** ((04) 262-6271. It offers huge high-ceilinged rooms at $27 for an air-conditioned double, spacious and airy lobby areas, and an atmosphere somewhere between a nineteenth century railway station (without the noise) and a stately old mansion.

WHERE TO EAT

Penang is justifiably renowned throughout Malaysia as one of the best places to eat. You get excellent seafood, great Chinese and Indian cuisine, plus some of the cross-cultural cuisine produced by the Peranakans. Penang's Chinese food often shows a Thai influence, and many dishes (such as their famous *laksa* noodle soup) tend to be sour rather than rich in coconut milk. All over the island, and especially in Georgetown, food stalls spring up either early morning or in

the evening, depending on the location and what they are offering. In addition to this, dozens of simple open-fronted restaurants as well as more elegant air-conditioned places make choosing where to have your next meal a matter of exquisite agony.

For breakfast in Georgetown, you could try some of the **Chinese noodle stalls** along Lebuh Carnavon, towards the northern (Lebuh Chulia) end, or some of the Chinese coffeeshops along Jalan Penang or near the waterfront on **Pengkalan Weld**. One of Penang's specialties in *nasi kandar*, a range of spicy southern Indian Muslim dishes served with rice. Many *nasi kandar* stalls are clustered in the lane next to the Kapitan Kling mosque and open early in the morning. Most famous of all is the stall known as **Line Clear Nasi Kandar Stall**, off Jalan Penang not far from the Odeon cinema and Hotel Oriental. You can get great chicken or mutton *biryani* rice, and a range of 20 different dishes of chicken, beef, seafood, eggs and vegetables. They also have *murtabak* and *roti canai*.

Later in the day, you can get *nasi kandar* at the popular **Dawood Restaurant**, 63 Lebuh Queen, next to the Sri Mariamman temple, and at Hameediyah, 164A Lebuh Campbell.

Great Penang Chinese food with a strong Malay influence is sold at **Sin Kheang Aun Restaurant,** Two Lorong Chulia, off Lebuh Chulia towards Lebuh Pantai. Don't miss their *gulai ikan*, hot sour fish curry.

An interesting place for lunch, which is about a $3 taxi ride from the heart of Georgetown, is the **Sa Chew Restaurant,** 37B Jalan Cantoment, at Pulau Tikus (turn right into Jalan Cantonment off Burma Road). This small, fan-cooled restaurant specializes in Nonya cuisine and has a range of ready-cooked dishes including *otak otak* (a spicy fish mousse), laksa and a very good *purut ikan* fish soup. Their homemade soy bean drink is very good, and so is the *cendol* for dessert. Unfortunately, Sa Chew is closed at night. Another place offering Nonya food is the **Hot Wok**, 12D Desa Tanjung, next to the Island Plaza in Jalan Tanjung, about $5 by taxi from Georgetown. At any time during the day, the **Beach Blanket Babylon**, an upmarket café/restaurant in 16 Bishop Street, offers a very Western ambiance, good food, coffee and magazines. It's open 11 AM until midnight.

You can get very reasonably priced Japanese food at the **Japanese Bistro** inside the attractive blue bar / restaurant complex known by its postal address, **20 Leith Street**; *teppanyaki* lunches cost from only $5 to $7.

Still in Georgetown, the **Supertanker Restaurant** in the KOMTAR building has good Teowchew Chinese food. The **Mayflower Restaurant** in Jalan Penang is also highly regarded for its Chinese cuisine.

A collection of food stalls can be found within KOMTAR, offering a wide range of local cuisines. These stalls are better for lunch than for dinner.

One of Penang's most famous collections of stalls, which set up in the late afternoon, is known by the name of its location, **Gurney Drive**. A taxi from Georgetown should cost around $3 to 4. There is an excellent range of Malay and Chinese specialties, the Malay stalls grouped together closer to the roundabout. Best things to sample here are the Penang *rojak*, a salad of sour local fruits and some crisp vegetables slathered with a black prawn paste, and the wonderful sour *laksa* soup. Everything is good, and surprisingly cheap. A lavish meal (provided you don't eat all seafood) will cost as little as $2.

Up at Batu Ferringhi, all the resort hotels have their own restaurants. However, it's worth getting out and try some of the local cuisine. The **House of Malay Kampung Food** in Batu Ferringhi, opposite the Rasa Sayang, has very good Malay food, including rich coconut beef *rendang* and *ulam*, a herbal salad. The **Ferringhi Village Restaurant,** 157B Batu Ferringhi has good seafood dishes at a much more reasonable price than the nearby **Eden Seafood Village**, part of a restaurant group found in many parts of the country. Ferringhi Village also has very good steaks at prices well below what you'll pay in the luxurious resorts nearby.

Locals flock in their hundreds all the way up to Teluk Bahang for the seafood served at the simple **Fishing Village Seafood Restaurant,** one of three by the jetty. This restaurant, open only from 3 PM until 11 PM, sells the most fantastic black pepper crab with curry leaves, and many other excellent seafood dishes.

If you're staying in Georgetown and don't want to go all the way to Batu Ferringhi for seafood, head for Tanjung Tokong where

Hai Chu Hooi, located along the seafront, has good fresh prawns and crabs which can be cooked to your taste; their chilli crab is recommended.

GETTING THERE AND AWAY

Penang's international airport has flights from Singapore, Kuala Lumpur, Johor Bahru, Kota Bharu, Langkawi and Hat Yai in Thailand. From the airport, a cab to Georgetown is about $8. Malaysia Airlines can be contacted on ((04) 621403.

Penang has a reputation as a source for cheap air tickets although you should take care when buying.

There is a daily ferry service to Langkawi which can be booked at the office next door to the tourist information center.

By train, a service goes from Butterworth to Kuala Lumpur and Singapore daily.

Buses go daily to all destinations in Malaysia, Thailand and Singapore. Along Lebuh Chulia are many travel agents offering good prices for all means of transport to leave the island. Hotels will also arrange travel for you.

There is a road link back to the mainland along the ever-long **Penang Bridge**, but it doesn't seem to be used very much because of the toll fee and because it is quicker and much cheaper to use the ferry to Butterworth, which costs only RM.60. You could take a taxi to the ferry, followed by 30 minutes on the boat and a five-minute walk to the station. The ferry runs 24 hours a day. There are also ferries for cars.

IPOH

BACKGROUND

Like many other towns in the area, Ipoh owes its existence to tin mining, and crumbling

GENERAL INFORMATION

There are two tourist information offices in Ipoh. One is in the Royal Casuarina Hotel's shopping complex, 18 Jalan Gopeng ((05) 253-2008, extension 8123. The other is the Perak Tourism Information Centre at Jalan Tun Sambanthan ((05) 241-2958. The *padang* is still intact as are the law courts and government offices.

Outside the town are the well known **Buddhist temples** built into limestone mas-

mansions of tin millionaires dot the townscape, suggesting a little of the life of the past. Ipoh still has some of the best Cantonese cuisine in the country; add some startling cave temples, a pretty *padang* and some beautiful colonial architecture, and you have many good reasons to make your stop a little longer than overnight.

The best and most spectacular way to see Ipoh and its surroundings is from the air. What stands out is the scale of the tin mining and its effects on the landscape. Almost like a moonscape at times, the bare earth is littered with water-filled pits. The extraction process unfortunately involves the loss of much of the fertile quality of the soil, accounting for the wasteland visible from the sky.

sifs. The pillars are honeycombed with caves, and into these caves have been built temples and monasteries. Six kilometers south of the town in Gunung Rapat is the **Sam Poh Kong Temple**. The inside of the limestone tower is hollow, so one enters the caves and comes out into a garden completely enclosed by a towering wall of rock. Back inside the temple, alongside statues of Buddhist mythology and a Buddha, are staircases carved into the limestone going up to lookout points in the rock. Outside there is a pretty Chinese garden and a vegetarian restaurant.

OPPOSITE: Lunar landscapes, the result of Ipoh's extensive tin mining. ABOVE: Perak Tong Temple, one of several in caves above the naturally occurring limestone pillars around Ipoh.

North of the town is the **Perak Tong Temple**, built into the caves inside Gunung Tasek. Altogether more impressive, this set of caves holds two massive Buddhas and many smaller statues. The walls of the caves have been painted by the many artists who still come to fill the caves with Buddhist images. A climb of 385 steps brings you to the top of the rock with some magnificent views of the countryside. Should you choose to make a contribution to the temple, the huge bell will be sounded.

WHERE TO STAY

Expensive

The most luxurious and conveniently located for the airport and roads to Kuala Lumpur and Penang is the **Royal Casuarina** ((05) 250-5555 FAX (05) 250-8177, 18 Jalan Gopeng. It offers all the amenities of a top-class hotel, including two restaurants and a pool. A double room costs $104.

In town is the pool-less **Excelsior Hotel** ((05) 253-6666 FAX (05) 253-6912 at Jalan Clarke. Rooms here from $55 to $70 for a double. Around the hotel are some popular local restaurants and hawker centers. Offering very similar facilities, but again no pool, is the **Ritz Garden Hotel** ((05) 254-7777 FAX (05) 254-5222, 79 Jalan C M Yussuff. This place is right in the nightlife part of town and has its own disco which is very popular so it could be a little noisy, but at about $30 for a double room, it offers the best value in this range.

Moderate and Inexpensive

There are any number of hotels in the same neighborhood as the Ritz Garden, such as the **Hotel Mikado** ((05) 255-5855, 86–88 Jalan Yang Kalsom. There's no restaurant at the Mikado, but at $23 and up, it offers clean, rather over-furnished rooms with television and attached bathroom.

In the older part of town are several hotels, notably the faded and no longer splendid **Station Hotel** ((05) 251-2588 at the railway station, which offers huge rooms full of crumbling 1960s furniture at $28 a double, with suites at $69. The restaurant does a good breakfast for about $5. The lift is a museum piece and so are some of the employees, but

you get lots of atmosphere and a lot of space on the huge verandahs overlooking the other old colonial buildings. Closer to the new part of town are more hotels which are bland but reasonable. They all have restaurants and offer packages including breakfast or all three meals. One such is the **Hotel Eastern** ((05) 254-3936, 118 Jalan Sultan Idris Shah, with rooms at $32.

With all of the above, consider practising the gentle art of negotiation; if business is poor, they'll be willing to bargain.

WHERE TO EAT

This is the nightlife area and there is no shortage of good places to eat at reasonable prices. For the reputed best *kway teow* (flat rice noodles fried in black bean sauce with seafood, eggs and bean sprouts) try **Kedai Kopi Hong Keng** on Jalan Leech, near to the Padang. If you are an Indian food lover there are several good places, the best being **Restoran Pakeeza** ((05) 250-1057, 15–17 Persarian Green. It is slightly out of the bustle of town but within easy walking distance of the main hotels and serves Moghul food with a wide range of breads. Two people can eat here for about $15.

Another excellent and very inexpensive Indian Muslim restaurant is **Rahman Restaurant** on Jalan Chamberlain which does the typical *murtabak* and *biryani* range, as well as some *kurma* and *rendang* dishes. This establishment is very clean and is completely devoid of the cigarette advertisements that most of these places adorn their walls with.

A very popular Chinese restaurant is the **Oversea Restaurant** ((05) 253-8005, 57–65 Jalan Seenivasagam. Decorated in traditional deep reds with the supper selection swimming about in tanks, this restaurant requires reservations and can be best enjoyed with a large group.

Many of the hotels have good restaurants, the Royal Casuarina having a reasonably priced Italian restaurant, **Il Ritrovo**. At the Excelsior is **The Palace**, serving Cantonese and seafood dishes. The **Ritz Garden** has an inexpensive 24-hour coffeeshop serving western and local dishes.

A young boy dressed in traditional Malay dress.

For vegetarians there are some pleasant places, not all as far out as the cave temples. In Jalan Yang Kalsom is the **Bodhi-Lin** restaurant ((05) 251-3790, which is very reasonably priced.

GETTING THERE

Ipoh is on the main routes to and from Kuala Lumpur, Penang, Kuantan and the islands of Pangkor and Pangkor Laut. From Ipoh you can get the train to Thailand or Kuala Lumpur. Express buses go from the main coach station in Jalan Kidd to all destinations at regular intervals and are very inexpensive. Buses to Lumut, for Pangkor island, have a separate bus station across the road from the main one, also in Jalan Kidd.

From Ipoh, MAS has direct flights to Kuala Lumpur and Johor Bahru.

PANGKOR AND PANGKOR LAUT

Pangkor and its smaller sister island are places to enjoy a beach holiday. Both are tiny islands, situated close to the mainland, offering clear water, excellent and relatively empty beaches (as well as a crowded and rather dirty one), good food and quality accommodation.

BACKGROUND

Pangkor Island has been a holiday resort since the late 1960s because of its proximity to the mainland and pretty beaches. But Pangkor's history goes back much further. In the sixteenth century a battle was fought here between Sumatran invaders and local people. The Sumatran leader was killed on the beach and the story goes that his fiancée came to Pangkor to find his remains. Not finding them, she stayed on the beach to pine away and die for love of him. The beach Puteri Dewi is named after her.

In 1663 when the Dutch arrived they found a wilderness of mangrove swamps. By 1670 they had taken Pangkor as a storage depot and outpost against pirates. It was abandoned in 1748, and after that, the pirates ruled Pangkor, which was the scene of battles between the Indonesian Bugis pirates and the Malays. The little island visible out at sea between Pangkor and Pangkor Laut is called

Pulau Simpan, which means "storage island" and legend has it that pirates kept their stolen treasure there. After the Dutch came the British, and in 1874 the island hosted the Treaty of Pangkor, giving the British the sole rights to mine tin in Perak.

Pangkor's main industries were boat building and fishing, but tourism is now even more important than to the local economy as young people turn to hotels looking for employment.

GENERAL INFORMATION

Cabs on Pangkor are expensive by Malaysian standards: about $12 from the Pan Pacific hotel to town and back. There is a bus service running from Pasir Bogak, the main

tourist beach, to the ferry and on to the north-ernmost village at hourly intervals. Bicycles are for hire in town and from The Pan Pacific if you are a guest. Motor bikes can also be hired in town. The Pan Pacific organizes boats from its jetty to Pangkor village once a day. Having a good time on Pangkor is largely a question of timing. School holidays in December, June and September are not a good time unless you plan to stay at the luxury resorts, and even then they will make book-ings difficult. If your stay is going to be a short one you should try to avoid weekends.

WHAT TO SEE

If you want to spend some of your time exploring the island, there is the **Dutch fort**

to visit at the south end of the island near to Kampung Teluk Gedung. The fort has been rebuilt using what bricks could be found. Ten soldiers, a corporal and a slave were stationed on the island. In 1690 the fort was attacked by locals and destroyed, to be rebuilt in 1743 with a garrison of 60 soldiers. It was aban-doned in 1748 and gradually fell into ruin.

The two villages on the island are domi-nated by the Chinese community and pro-vide an interesting picture of small-town Malaysia. Between the two villages is the **Fu Lin Kung Temple** with a miniature Great Wall of China in a garden. Further along toward Sungai Pinang Kechil is an Indian

Conceived as a holiday playground, Langkawi capitalizes on its natural beauty.

Temple, an ancient Dutch tomb and one of the island's two mosques. All the sights of the island can be easily done in a two hour cab trip which will cost around $15. Cab drivers don't speak much English though.

WHERE TO STAY

Expensive

There are two luxury resorts, the **Pan Pacific Resort Pangkor** at Teluk Belanga on Pangkor and the **Pangkor Laut Resort** on the nearby island of Pangkor Laut.

Pangkor Laut Resort ((05) 699-1100 FAX (05) 699-1200, located on the smaller island of Pangkor Laut is, if anything, even more exclusive than the Pan Pacific. At one time it was common for holiday makers on Pangkor to hire a boat and go over to the beautiful Emerald bay on Pangkor Laut for the day, but now security guards patrol the beach, keeping out the riffraff. Pangkor Laut Resort offers traditional-style thatch-roofed chalets and rooms, most of them clustered around the reception area, with another beautifully designed group of bungalows

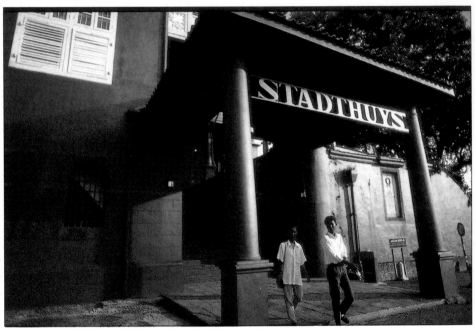

The **Pan Pacific Resort Pangkor** ((05) 685-1399, FAX (05) 685-2390 is isolated from the rest of the island. The resort is beautifully designed to blend in with its surroundings and offers a range of accommodation, from double rooms at about $140, to chalets and honeymoon bungalows at the end of the beach. The beach, the famous Pantai Puteri Dewi, is an idyll of white sand and palm trees backed by a golf course, and all the sea sports expected of these types of resorts are available. Many other activities are organized by the resort including jungle walks, trips by boat into the village and a boat tour around the island. Or you can lay about by the pool and swim over to the bar for a drink while the hornbills squawk overhead.

along the next bay. Some are built into the hillside on a stilts while others are out in the water with walkways connecting them with the land. Guests are transported by mini-bus from one site to the other or the 10-minute walk is pleasant enough. There are no televisions here, so it truly is a getaway holiday. Prices vary depending on where your room is and go upwards from $206 for a double.

Moderate and Inexpensive

After the two resorts, prices and exclusivity move rapidly down-market. A good place to stay is **Nippah Bay Villas** ((05) 685-2198 Lot 4442, Teluk Nippah, 32300 Pangkor, which lies out of the main hotel area in

Nippah Bay, two bays round from the highly populated and, at peak times, less than pristine Pasir Bogak Beach. This is a tiny settlement of 10 bungalows and a restaurant; no pool or water sports but lots of quiet and a completely deserted and idyllic beach. Rates include all meals, and the rooms are air-conditioned and comfortable, although there is no hot water. A room plus breakfast here is $36, going up to $60 during public holidays. You should try to book if you want to stay here because it is often fully occupied. Cabs charge $10 to bring you there and back.

of them are near the sea. Further along the main strip are two older and very popular places, **Khoo Holiday Resort** ((05) 685-1164 FAX (05) 685-1605, and **D'Village** ((05) 685-1951 at Pantai Pasir Bogak, Pangkor Island, Perak. Both offer a wide range of accommodation ranging from tents at $3 a night per person to air-conditioned rooms at Khoo's at $37 or beach chalets with a fan and shared bathroom at D'Village at $35, including all meals for two people. They both stand at the noisiest part of the island with the most crowded and least pleasant beach areas.

Back on Pasir Bogak, which these days looks a little like the Costa Brava there are two good hotels close together at the start of the Pasir Bogak Beach strip. **Beach Huts** ((05) 685-2198 is the smaller and quieter of the two establishments and has air-conditioned chalets fronting the beach with a verandah, large single beds, a television and 'fridge for about $43. **Sea View** ((05) 685-1605 at Pasir Bogak, 32300 Pangkor, Perak, is much bigger and has a range of room types, but the nicest are the chalets on the beach front at about $34 including breakfast for two. This place has a large Chinese/Western restaurant and a pretty garden along the beach front but gets noisy at peak times and the chalets are unimaginatively arranged, closely packed and not all

WHERE TO EAT

If you're staying at either of the two resort hotels this problem is solved for you by the inconvenience of getting into town. Both hotels have a choice of restaurants of international standard. Pangkor Laut Resort's continental restaurant, **Sri Legenda**, is one of the most beautifully located restaurants you are likely to see. Built on to a promontory of rock, it uses the natural lay of the land in its construction. Its huge verandahs offer magnificent views of the beautiful Coral Bay, and a meal for two with wine costs about $80.

Melaka still boasts the vivid colors associated with Portuguese colonial architecture. OPPOSITE Stadthuys and ABOVE a trishaw in a quiet street.

Back in town, many of the hotels offer meals and accommodation packages but there are plenty of reasonably priced local restaurants along the beach area.

The Fisherman's Place along Pasir Bogak is very popular for its seafood, and also its range of breakfast options. In town there are more restaurants, including some good Indian Muslim places.

GETTING THERE

Pangkor is approached from the small town of Lumut from where ferries leave to Pangkor regularly. Journey time is about half-an-hour. There is a separate service to the Pan Pacific Resort which goes less often. Pangkor Laut Resort also has its own ferry service which takes an hour, so if you miss one it is faster to take the ferry over to Pangkor and get a cab round to the Sea View Hotel from where a smaller ferry makes the five-minute journey over to Pangkor Laut and the resort.

Getting to Lumut is chiefly by express bus or taxi from Ipoh. Planes from Singapore, Melaka and Kuala Lumpur arrive at Sitiawan airport and from there it is a 15-minute drive in to Lumut. You can also fly from Kuala Lumpur and Singapore to Ipoh and catch the two-hour express bus from there.

The bus station at Lumut is within sight of the jetty, and close by are some good hawker stalls and low priced restaurants to hang around in if you have missed your ferry or are waiting for a bus. The ticket offices for the buses are situated around the bus station, so all you have to do is wander round looking for the name of your destination above a booth and find out the times. There are also small offices of the Malaysian Tourism Promotion Board and Pangkor Laut Resort close to the jetty.

MELAKA (MALACCA)

Melaka (previously spelled as Malacca) is Malaysia's most historic town. The place once known as Sleepy Hollow is sleepy no more, thanks to industrial development, the construction of a huge oil refinery, constant reclamation of the seafront and a surge in tourism. Despite all this, pockets in the heart of Melaka remain untouched, and each of the different quarters (Chinatown, the Indian area, the Malay Kampung and the Eurasian district — known as the Portuguese Settlement) retains a distinctive idiom of its own.

BACKGROUND

According to legend, a late fourteenth-century fugitive prince from Sumatra was resting under a tree at the mouth of the river when one of his dogs attacked a mousedeer. The deer drove the dog into the sea and the prince was led to exclaim, "This is a fortunate land where even the deer are full of courage!" He decided to found a new city and named it after the tree under which he sat, the *melaka*. True or not, the story is immortalized on the crest of the municipality of the town, while a couple of unappealing stone mousedeer graze under several giant red plastic hibiscus in a tasteless modern monument in front of the old Dutch Stadthuys.

Melaka gained the attention of the emperor of China, who sent Admiral Cheng Ho as an emissary there in 1403. The location of the town made it a natural entrepôt, for Indian merchants could sail across the Bay of Bengal while their Chinese counterparts could come down from China and Indonesian traders sailed across from the Spice Islands. All these traders converged at the meeting point of the monsoons: Melaka. The trade with India facilitated the conversion to Islam of Melaka's rulers, and the city grew to be the most important and cosmopolitan port in the whole of Asia.

By the beginning of the sixteenth century, the Portuguese had heard enough to know that capturing this port would wrest control of the lucrative European spice trade away from the Arabs. Under Alfonso de Albuquerque, Portuguese forces took control of the city in 1511.

Dutch imperialists captured the Portuguese fort in 1640 after a five month siege, but because their trade capital was Batavia (Jakarta) the economic importance of Melaka declined rapidly. From 1824 until Malaysia was granted independence in 1957, apart

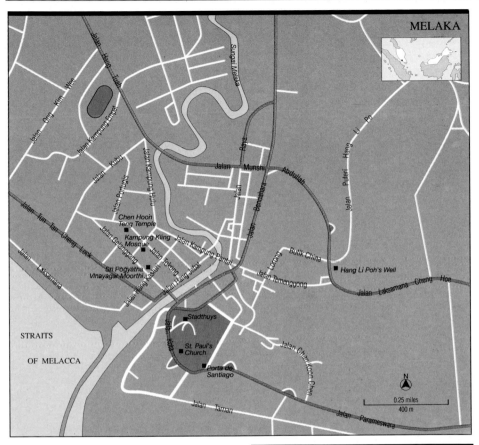

MELAKA

STRAITS

OF MELACCA

from a brief period of Japanese occupation during the Second World War, the English controlled the city.

Such basic historical facts are woven into the appeal of modern Melaka and it is impossible to ignore the past when visiting the city.

GENERAL INFORMATION

The Tourist Information Centre ((06) 283-6538, is just across the road from the Stadthuys, and booklets on Melaka and other parts of Malaysia are freely available here. Cars can be rented from Avis ((06) 263-2727. Sightseeing tours are also available through a number of agencies like Atlas Travel Services ((06) 282-0777, or through any of the bigger hotels. There is a quite a choice: historic Melaka tours, countryside tours, night trips by trishaw and a mediocre river cruise which departs from the back of the Tourist Information office. For further information, check with the Tourist Information Centre.

WHAT TO SEE

There is plenty to see in Melaka. Its unique blend of Dutch, English, Chinese, Indian and Malay cultural influences makes it an interesting city for sightseeing and I suggest you begin by heading straight for the salmon-pink-colored **Stadthuys** and **Christ Church**, two buildings that have survived remarkably well from the period of Dutch rule. Built around 1650, the Stadthuys has all the solidity of a Victorian bank but with a grace and elegance that the nineteenth century rarely expresses in its architecture. Inside there is one room left with the authentic wooden ceiling of the Dutch, and the whole interior that once housed the Dutch governors is now a museum. The exhibits are representative of Melaka's cultural mix, with some fine furniture and porcelain from Portugal, Holland and China. Christ Church, next door to the Stadthuys, was built a hundred years later and it is worth going inside just to see the original wooden pews and the 15-m (48-ft) rafters over the nave that must have been carved from single trees.

Porta de Santiago, only a short walk from the Stadthuys, is all that remains of the Portuguese fort that was laid siege to by the Dutch. But it wasn't the Dutch who destroyed the fortress, for even though it was damaged in the siege, they actually repaired the gateway, hence the date "Anno 1670" inscribed over the entranceway to the fort built which was actually built in 1512. It was the English who set about systematically demolishing

the fort when they took control in 1807 and it was only through the intervention of Stamford Raffles (who had not yet stepped foot on Singapore) that the gateway was preserved.

Another Portuguese building, at the top of St. Paul's hill and just a short walk away, is **St. Paul's Church**. Or at least what remains of it, for the Dutch took the roof away when they converted it into a military post. They used the hill as a burial ground, probably because of its proximity to Christ Church.

ABOVE: Two of Melaka's older buildings. OPPOSITE LEFT: The Stadthuys, dating back to the Dutch era. OPPOSITE RIGHT: This roofscape shows the Kampung Kling Mosque and some of the many well-preserved shophouses surrounding it.

The walk up the hill is worth your time because the top affords picturesque views and inside the ruins are some remarkable tombstones. Nearby the Fort, housed in what used to be the private Malacca Club, you will find the **Proclamation of Independence Memorial**, with memorabilia relating to Malaysia's fight for independence.

Along Jalan Kota is the reconstruction of the wooden fifteenth-century palace of **Sultan Mansur Shah**. The various dioramas inside the Melaka Sultanate Palace show the golden age of this Malay kingdom.

Retrace your steps back to the tourist information center and take time out to visit the reproduction of a Portuguese sailing boat permanently at rest beside the river and operating as a **Maritime Museum**. You may be surprised, in view of the type of boat, that most of the exhibits inside related to local rather than colonial maritime exploits. Opposite this is the museum of the Royal Malaysian Navy; the most interesting part of this is the separate area housing some of the porcelain recovered from the *Diana*, a British ship which foundered off Melaka during the nineteenth century.

Cross the bridge over the small river. It is very difficult today to imagine the flurry of commercial activity that must have once arisen from the coming and going of Chinese junks, Arab dhows and dealers from India, Java and Sumatra.

Chinatown

Chinatown, across the river, has a real historical identity of its own and retains a feel for the past that is stronger than Chinatowns in neighboring countries, primarily due to the relatively languid intrusion of modernity. **Jalan Tun Tan Cheng Lock,** running parallel on the coast side to Jalan Hang Jebat, is a good example, for here you will find

property laws that calculated the house tax according to the width of the front.

Also in Chinatown is **Jalan Hang Jebat**, sometimes still called by its Dutch name, Jonkers Street, and famous for its antique shops crammed with antiques and reproductions from Indonesia as well as the remains of what once made up the homes of the wealthy Dutch, Chinese and British. Prices are high these days so don't expect a bargain. Be aware that many of the items on sale come from other parts of Asia, and quite a lot of reproductions are displayed.

eighteenth- and nineteenth-century homes built for prosperous merchants. And at 48-50, the site of the **Baba Nyonya Heritage Museum** ((06) 283-1273, you can view the interior of one such home which is actually two houses linked by doorways. The term Baba refers to the descendants of interracial marriages between early Chinese settlers and Malays, and the resulting fusion of lifestyles was a unique blend of two quite different cultures. Guided tours of the museums are given from 10 AM to 12:30 PM, and from 2 PM until 4:30 PM daily. Incidentally, if you visit the museum you may wonder about the proportions—each house has a frontage of 7.3 m (24 ft) but a length of 36.5 m (120 ft) — a result of the Dutch

If you're a lover of classical antique Chinese furniture, be sure to look in at the **Old China Gallery,** 15 Jalan Hang Lekir, linking Jalan Tun Tan Cheng Lock and Jalan Hang Jebat (Jonkers Street). There are some exquisite pieces for sale, and if you go to the first floor traditional tea house, you'll see some fine paneling.

In the same part of town is the oldest Chinese temple in Malaysia, **Cheng Hoon Teng Temple**, founded during the Dutch period of control by a fugitive from China following the fall of the Ming Dynasty. The solid bronze statue of the Goddess of Mercy was brought from India, though the bulk of materials came in junks from China. Worshippers may be engrossed in prayer or quietly busy lighting joss-sticks, but you are free to discreetly wander around. On the same road rests the unusually shaped **Kampung Kling Mosque**, another typical piece of poly-stylistic Melakan architecture: a Hindu-like roof, Corinthian columns, colored tiles from Portugal and Britain and a Victorian chandelier. The **Sri Poyyatha Vinayagar Moorthi Temple** is just a few steps down Jalan Tukang Emas. The Indian god Vinayagar takes the form of a human body but with an elephant's head, hence the carving over the main altar.

Melaka's southern Indian population shops and eats in a corner of town bounded by Jalan Temenggong (which is less than five minutes up Jalan Laksamana from the Stadthuys), Jalan Bendahara and Jalan Buna Raya. You'll see shops selling spices and jasmine garlands, newspapers in Tamil, clay cooking pots and great vegetarian food.

There is still a Malay village known as **Kampung Mortem** not far up the river. This can be seen from Jalan Bunga Raya where it bends at the river bank or, better still, from the river cruise boat.

Out of the Town Center

A few places worth seeing are not exactly out of town, but walking there and back in the tropical heat can be exhausting (take a tip from the locals and use an umbrella to protect you from the sun; it makes an enormous difference). Driving or hiring a trishaw or bicycle would be more pleasant options.

Bukit China has a notable history, being a gift from Melaka's Sultan Mansur Shah back in 1459 to his new bride, Princess Hang Li

Poh, the daughter of the Chinese emperor Yung Lo. It was supposed to be her royal residence but *fung shui*, the Chinese art of geomancy, encouraged its use as a graveyard and the disintegrating graves date back to the seventeenth century. At the top of the hill which commands a fine view of Melaka, you can still find on the eastern side large flat stones, remnants of an old monastery and chapel built by the Portuguese in the 1590s.

At the foot of the hill is the **Sam Poh Kong Temple**, built in 1795 and later dedicated to Cheng Ho, the famous Chinese admiral who first came to Melaka in 1409 and firmly established commercial and cultural links. Just next to this temple is **Hang Li Poh's Well**, also known as the Sultan's Well. Admiral Cheng Ho is said to have bestowed it with powers of purity, but that didn't prevent it from being poisoned by neighboring Malays when they attacked the town in 1551. When the Dutch took over they fortified it. The remains can be seen today in the crumbling masonry around the well.

Further afield is **St. John's Fort**, once an important Dutch fortification of which now only the walls remain. It is still worth a visit, not least because of the splendid views afforded from the top of the hill.

Portuguese Settlement

St. John's Fort might best be seen as a short stopover on route to the **Portuguese Settlement**. It is situated three kilometers, or nearly two miles, south of the town, accessible by the N° 17 bus from the bus terminal or from in front of Stadthuys, at a cost of 60 *sen*, and since the 1930s has been home to Malaysians with names like Albuquerque, Santa Maria, De Costa, Dias — descendants of the Portuguese of the sixteenth century. When the Dutch community left Melaka in 1824, those remaining joined the Portuguese and gradually intermarried, and later some of the British Eurasians also joined in with this community. Despite all the pressures to change, these people retain their Catholic religion, although only a few are still able to speak Cristão, a patois based on the simple Portuguese spoken in the African colonies. Many Portuguese words (such as those for butter, cheese, shutters and cupboard) have become a part of the Malay language.

The community has its own school whose playground contains a statue of the Blessed Virgin. The land for this settlement was purchased by two Jesuit missionaries in the 1920s, and the movement of the disparate Eurasians in Melaka to this one area probably accounts for the successful survival of the culture of these people until today. In the 1930s this area consisted of *atap* houses, but it has gradually become positively suburban. In the early 1980s the Portuguese community was given the square, which is built on reclaimed land. The square, or Medan Portugis, is enclosed by buildings which house mostly restaurants and a community center. Inside the square is an open courtyard with a pier built out into the sea.

However, the area is due to change with a massive reclamation project right in front of the zone where the fishermen now beach their boats, sit for a chat under the shady trees while repairing their nets or have a drink at one of the food stalls nearby. Within the square is a floating population of restaurants, although the Lisbon remains a constant feature. There used to be regular performances of Portuguese folk dancing for the guests of the restaurants. These were discontinued but may at some point start up again, so check with the tourist information office when you arrive in Melaka. During the Festival of St. Peter (late June) the local fishermen decorate their boats before they are blessed by the priest. Call in at the **Restoran Lisbon** which has a collection of memorabilia and handicrafts of the Portuguese community, and whose owner, George Alcantra, is a local community leader and will be pleased to tell you about the Portuguese community in Melaka.

NIGHTLIFE AND SHOPPING

The major hotels in Melaka all have discos, but don't come here for a jet-set nightlife. A more pleasant evening could be spent eating at **Glutton's Corner**, which used to be on the waterfront but is now blocked off by the new development next to Mahkota Square. There is a whole bunch of handicraft and souvenir stalls next to Glutton's Corner, running up towards the hill, which are open during the day. This is a good

opportunity to purchase locally produced items made from rattan and pandanus. There is also a good selection of pottery and as long as you don't pay the first price asked, you should pay less than regular shop prices.

In the same area, but only at night, there is a **Light & Sound Spectacular** presenting the city's historical and cultural background. It takes place on the green opposite St. Paul's Hill and is well worth seeing. Unfortunately, the show rarely takes place these days and seems to depend on the presence of large tour

groups (and the state of the sound equipment). Check with the tourism information center first.

Melaka has an increasing number of modern shopping centres, but the most convenient for visitors is **Mahkota Parade**, about $1 by trishaw from the Stadthuys. Anchor tenant here is the department store Parksons, with a good supermarket in the basement. There are plenty of fast food outlets, including a Delifrance for those seeking something Western, and a fashion shop with incredible bargains called the **Reject Shop**.

OPPOSITE: Festival of the Hungry Ghosts, Penang. Food is left out for the wandering spirits and incense is lit. ABOVE: A traditional shophouse selling craftwork from all over Malaysia.

There's a surprisingly good book shop where you can pick up paperbacks, magazines and so forth just around the corner from the Stadthuys in Jalan Laksamana. Lim Brothers have been in the same spot since 1938 and are worth visiting.

OUT OF TOWN

If you have a car, the place to head for is **Tanjung Bidara**, a coastal location 35 km (21 miles) north of Melaka. Tanjung Bidara has a long beach with good shade and a resort hotel nearby with all the expected amenities.

Some 50 km (31 miles) from Melaka is **Mount Ophir**. The mountain requires no special skills to climb but you do need to be fit and climbing alone is not recommended. In 1988 a group from Singapore managed to get totaly lost for days before stumbling into a loggers' camp. If you are seriously thinking of climbing, do consult the book on mountain climbing in Malaysia, in RECOMMENDED READING towards the end of TRAVELERS' TIPS.

Without a car of your own, an alternative way to see the everyday rural life of Malaysia is through a countryside tour. The agriculture around Melaka is rich and varied and this can be a good opportunity to visit cocoa, rubber and oil palm plantations, as guided visits to the plantations are usually a feature of the countryside tours. Because of the relative prosperity of the area, there are some fine examples of authentic, traditional Malay homes and a late afternoon cycle tour would be a good way to take these in.

Air Keroh

Air Keroh, some 12 km (seven-and-a-half miles) east of the town, has been developed as a recreational area and has a number of attractions on either side of the main road, as well as a range of accommodation. The area is particularly popular with Malaysian families at weekends and school holidays, although is relatively quiet on week days. The **Recreational Forest (** (06) 232-8401 offers quiet walks through the trees and there are fan-cooled cabins for rent at $20. The **Mini Malaysia Cultural Village (** (06) 32849, is a collection of 13 houses representing the various regions of the country and sometimes

shows are staged here. A look at the cultures of the countries making up ASEAN (Malaysia, Singapore, Thailand, the Philippines and Indonesia — Vietnam, the latest country to join the association, is not yet represented), go to the **Mini Asean Cultural Village**.

Other attractions at Air Keroh include the **Melaka Zoo** which is situated near a lake with canoes and aqua-boats for hire. A visit to the zoo, which is open every day from 10 AM to 6 PM, will allow you to see the increasingly rare Sumatran rhinoceros. There's also a butterfly farm, a display of fresh and

saltwater fish in an aquarium called Malacca Fish World and the inevitable crocodile farm.

Air Keroh can be visited by bus (N° 19) or reached by bike along the main road running east out of town. The various attractions are spread out in green open spaces off the main road, but a few kilometers separate the first from the last, so a bit of walking is involved if you don't have your own transport.

Off the Beaten Track

Pulau Besar is a small island just four kilometers (just over two miles) off the coast of Melaka. Never occupied by the Portuguese, Pulau Besar is mentioned in old Chinese texts where Ming records refer to its use as a navigational aid for mariners. Nowadays, boats depart from the Umbai jetty, just out of town on the coast road to Singapore. There a couple of resorts here, and another on Upeh Island, which offer golf, sunset cruises, water sports and so-called jungle trekking. Although the sea is a lot clearer than right on the coastline of Melaka itself, unless this is you only chance to visit an island in Malaysia, you'd be better to look elsewhere. Should you decide you want to go, try the **Pandanusa Island Resort** ((06) 281-8057 FAX (06) 281-5941, which has standard chalets from as little as $40 when it's not the holiday season.

of high-class apartment blocks rather than a hotel, the **Century Makhota Hotel** ((06) 281-2828 FAX (06) 281-2323, has only 28 rooms and almost 600 apartment suites, with an extensive range of facilities including a lavish swimming pool. Promotional prices (which all Melaka hotels seem to offer) begin at $79 for a double. Toll free reservations can be made by calling (800-8161. The **Pan Pacific** is due to open at the end of 1997 and promises to be the most outstanding hotel in Melaka. The older **Renaissance Melaka Hotel** ((06) 248-8888 FAX (06) 284-9269, has undergone a total

WHERE TO STAY

There are three accommodation areas: the town of Melaka itself, the coastal area and an eastern strip at Air Keroh. It's worth remembering that most places in both the town and nearby areas increase their rates at weekends and public holidays; it would be a good idea to try to time your stay during the working week.

Expensive

If you want one of the newest hotels in town, head for the Century Makhota Hotel, located (until the next flurry of reclamation) on the new seafront behind the Mahkota Parade shopping centre. Looking more like a series

renovation. Conveniently situated off the main road that runs through Melaka, Jalan Munshi Abdullah, the postal address is Jalan Bendahara, P.O. Box 105, 75720 Melaka, although there is a sales office in Kuala Lumpur as well ((03) 2444-6822 FAX (03) 242-1493. Promotional room rates are $78 for a double. Ask for a room high up and overlooking the town and sea for you will be able to trace the course of the river as it snakes through the houses. The **City Bayview** ((06) 283-9888 FAX (06) 283-6699 on Jalan Bendahara, 75100, Melaka, offers doubles from $126. Similarly priced is the **Emperor Hotel** ((06) 284-0777

OPPOSITE: One of Melaka's many artists painting at Regency Hill. ABOVE: The oldest hotel in Melaka, full of character and faded splendor.

FAX (06) 283-8989 (formerly the Merlin), just behind the Renaissance on Bangunan Woo Hoe Kan, Jalan Munshi Abdullah, 75100. If you want a beach on your doorstep, there is the five-star **Tanjung Bidara Beach Resort** ((06) 384-2990 FAX (06) 384-2995 at Tanjung Bidara, 78300 Masjid Tanah. Doubles from $60.

Moderate
In town there is the usefully situated and well kept **Plaza Inn** ((06) 284-0881 FAX (06) 284-9357 (from around $40), located in a shopping complex, Two Jalan Munshi Abdullah,

There's another house converted into a hotel further up the same road, The Baba House, but rooms are claustrophobic and windowless, so this is not recommended. A fine house almost opposite this is currently undergoing transformation into a hotel and would be well worth checking out.

For space and greenery leave town and head for the **Air Keroh Country Resort** ((06) 232-5212 FAX (06) 232-0422, at Air Keroh, 75450 Melaka. There are good rooms ($44) and chalets with attached kitchens. Although 16 km (10 miles) out of town, the Nº 19 bus

75100, Some of the rooms have views of the river, and amenities close by include bicycle hire, money exchange, a bowling alley, a disco and several food spots. **The Palace Hotel** ((06)282-5115 FAX (06) 284-8833 is on the same road at 201 and has doubles at $46.

One of the nicest places to stay right within the old Chinatown area of Melaka is the converted Peranakan house on the corner of Jalan Tun Cheng Lock, **Heeren House** ((06) 281-4241 FAX (06) 281-4239. There are only six rooms, so be sure to book in advance and request one of the upstairs rooms overlooking the river. There's a pleasant restaurant downstairs, which is open to the public. Doubles are $47 on weekdays, including continental breakfast.

runs every 15 minutes and the place has its own 12-seater tripping into town. If your reason for coming to Melaka is solely to explore the town and historical sights, then staying at Air Keroh is not a good idea, but there is the attraction of peace and quiet as well as non-historical places of interest. If you want to relax and make occasional trips into town, Air Keroh is perfect, especially if you have a car. The **Air Keroh d'Village Melaka** ((06) 232-8000 FAX (06) 232-7541 has almost 300 chalets starting at $92.

The **Tanjung Bidara Beach Resort** ((06) 384-2990 FAX (06) 384-2995 on the beach some 35 km (21 miles) north of Melaka, has 50 motel rooms and 15 chalets, with a double room from $60 on weekdays.

Inexpensive

If you like an air of faded elegance and individuality, the **Majestic (** (06) 762-2506, has good-value doubles for $20–$25 — but skip the outside rooms at the front. This 20-room hotel, located at 188 Jalan Bunga Raya is tucked behind the Renaissance. The bar downstairs is open until midnight and it's a good place to meet fellow travelers.

Budget accommodation (around $14) is available at the **New Cathay (** (06) 282-3744, and the **May Chiang,** both on Jalan Munshi Abdullah or the **Chong Hoe Hotel (** (06) 282-6102, which is just opposite the Kampung Kling Mosque in Chinatown.

WHERE TO EAT

I warmly recommend the **Banana Leaf** for an Indian breakfast. *Roti canai* or *dosai* with coconut sauce and curry sauce are served hot and fresh from early in the morning to the accompaniment of Indian music. Evening curries are also available and at any time the food is cheap and good. The place is conveniently situated on the main street of Munshi Abdullah, just past the Bunga Raya junction and the Renaissance.

Another Indian favorite is **Restoran Selvam** at the top of Jalan Laksaman, between Jalan Bunga Raya and Jalan Bendahara. A good breakfast of *dosai* with a foaming *kopi tarik* (literally "pulled coffee") will cost you less than $1.

Another inexpensive and pleasant little place that serves Western and Asian food is **Kim Swee Huat,** 38 Jalan Laksamana. The average dish is $2 and the notice board bears testimonials from happy customers. All the bigger hotels have air-conditioned restaurants offering standard European fare, but if you want to go local, the most popular nightspot is **Glutton's Corner**. This cluster of stalls not far from the Porta de Santiago used to be along the waterfront, but reclamation has put paid to the sea breezes. Nonetheless, there are a number of open air food stalls, including the famous Madam Fatso's, more properly known as **Restoran Bunga Raya**, great for crabs and steamboat, and several stalls offering tasty home-style Malay food. Some stalls open for lunch or dinner only, others open at 11:30 AM and stay open until late.

More and more restaurants offering cross-cultural Peranakan cuisine are opening in Melaka. One of the oldest and most authentic is **Peranakan Town House Restaurant** in Jalan Tun Tan Cheng Lock, set inside a genuine old home and still bearing a somewhat faded air and the mixture of styles typical of the Peranakans. Very good *ayam buah keluak*, a chicken curry cooked with a black nut with an indescribably good flavor, and also excellent spicy prawns cooked with the strangely pungent *sambal udang petai*, made with Parkia beans.

Nonya or Peranakan food is just one of the options in the delightfully restored **Jonkers**, 17 Jalan Hang Jebat. Surely the prettiest restaurant in Melaka, this serves light meals and set lunches encompassing both East and West, and offers the best homemade cakes you'll find in town. Jonkers closes at 5 PM.

The **Old China Café** just around the corner, in Jalan Hang Lekir, has excellent Peranakan food as well as a wide range of teas (local, Chinese, Japanese, Ceylon) and fresh fruit juices. Breakfast is served from 9 AM, as well as soup and sandwiches for those who don't want to go local.

OPPOSITE: Children in traditional Malay dress, Terengganu. ABOVE: For this visitor from Borneo, earrings are part of her daily dress.

If you want a really local Chinatown experience, go to **Teo Soon Loong Chan**, a small air-conditioned Chinese restaurant tucked away at 55 Jalan Hang Kesturi (also known as Second Cross Street) just near the corner of the road leading to the Kampung Kling mosque. Careful you don't miss this place, which has the unusual feature of having an open kitchen right next to the pavement at the front of the restaurant, with the dining area (plus an array of alcohol, because this doubles as a liquor shop) inside. Be sure you don't miss their speciality, deep-fried soft-shelled crabs from Vietnam. Inexpensive and open for both lunch and dinner.

If you hanker for familiar Western cuisine such as steaks, fish and chips or an omelet, try **Bob's Tavern and Restaurant,** located between the bottom of Jalan Hang Jebat and Jalan Tun Tan Chan Loke.

Out at the Portuguese Settlement there are several restaurants claiming to offer "authentic Portuguese cuisine" but it's certainly nothing that a Portuguese would recognize. Behind the walls of the Medan Portugis, the restaurants seem to come and go, except for the stalwart **Restoran de Lisbon** where $10–15 will cover a basic but tasty meal for two. The **San Pedro** restaurant, set back on a small road opposite the Medan has all its tables inside. This place offers a more private atmosphere and has been serving up good food and a friendly welcome for the past 20 years. Tony, the owner, is a good person to chat with about the Eurasian community. There's a cluster of two or three simple stalls facing the muddy beach (although planned reclamation may by now have pushed the shoreline even closer to Sumatra). These stalls offer much the same food as you'll find elsewhere in the settlement, and at slightly cheaper prices. Look for devil curry and fried squid.

If you take the bus to the Portuguese Settlement (N° 17), get off at the first stop once you pass the first traffic light after the town center (about five to seven minutes beyond Stadthuys). Opposite you'll see a cluster of food stalls known as **Moon Luck**, with very good noodles, *popiah* (fresh spring roll) and the speciality *satay celop* where skewers of food are dipped into boiling stock. Inexpensive and good; go during the evening.

Out at Air Keroh the **Country Resort** has a pleasant restaurant and the Mini Asean Village includes food stalls featuring the various national cuisines.

Thai food is served at **My Place (** (06) 284-3848, 537 Taman Melaka Raya.

HOW TO GET THERE

By Bus or Taxi
Express buses run from Kuala Lumpur, Singapore and other major towns. The departure point for coaches, in Melaka, is the Express Bus Terminal at Jalan Tun Ali. Contact the taxi station in Melaka ((06) 282-3630, for details of long-distance taxis out of Melaka. See TRAVELERS' TIPS for more in-

formation on travel between Malaysia and Singapore.

By Air

The airport is located nine kilometers (five miles) from Melaka. Pelangi Air has daily flights from Singapore and Ipoh to Melaka, and three flights a week from Langkawi. Contact the airport at (06) 351-1175.

By Car

It takes 90 minutes from Kuala Lumpur along the Air Keroh expressway, passing thousands of rubber and oil-palm trees along the way. The car journey from Singapore takes around three hours, provided you don't get stuck in a jam on the Causeway.

By Train

You may take a train to Tampin and complete the 38-km (23-mile) journey by bus or taxi, but it's much more convenient and faster to travel by bus or air the entire distance.

By Ferry

A fast passenger service between Melaka and Dumai in Sumatra now runs from Melaka harbor. The journey lasts about five hours; the ferry leaves Melaka on Thursdays and returns from Dumai every Saturday. Contact Madai Shipping at ((06) 240671.

The Light & Sound Spectacular at Melaka is worth trying to see. It throws much light on the history of this old trading settlement.

Into the
Interior

SMALL TOWNS, kampongs and beaches make up the familiar terrain. But if you ever travel across Malaysia in a plane, the most astounding and characteristic sight is the vista of rainforests and dense jungle that make up the interior. You should try to find time in your itinerary for a trip that takes you away from the coastline and into the true heart of Malaysia.

CAMERON HIGHLANDS

Four hours by car from Kuala Lumpur, Cameron Highlands is distant enough to deter day-trippers but big enough to absorb all the tourists and holiday makers who choose to spend some time there. The Highlands offers a whole range of activities, all of them enhanced by the cool temperatures and burgeoning gardens of the area. There are many well-marked jungle walks here, a golf course, some tea plantations, a Buddhist temple and a good butterfly park with many interesting local plants and animals.

BACKGROUND

The place originally came into being when it was discovered by a surveyor called — you guessed it — Cameron, who first thought of the area now called Ringlet becoming a hill station. Further areas were cleared and now there are three distinct settlements in the Cameron Highlands all with a purpose and atmosphere of their own. Ringlet is now a center for flower nurseries, the next village, Tanah Rata, 13 km (eight miles) further up the road, is the tourist center and Brinchang, the highest of the villages, is a center for vegetable growing.

GENERAL INFORMATION

Readily available from most of the hotels in Tanah Rata are maps showing the main walks in the area. These vary from short, family-type rambles such as Walk 9 which goes to Robinson Falls or Walk 4 to Parit Falls, to longer and more strenuous ones. A good two-and-a-half hour walk covering a variety of terrain and plant life would be Walks 10 and 12 which, when combined, take you through lowland forest, the fast disappearing rain-

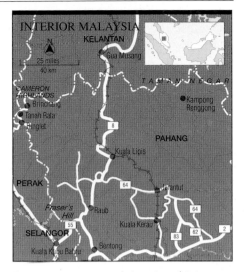

forest vegetation and then into higher terrain where the vegetation becomes typically stunted and where many pitcher plants, the carnivorous plants native to Malaysia, can be seen.

You should take care in these jungle walks and always let someone know which walk you intend to take. One famous incident is the disappearance of Jim Thompson, the wealthy ex-CIA man who took a walk on March 26, 1967 and was never found, despite a search by police and the *Orang Asli*, the local aborigines.

WHAT TO SEE

A visit to the tea plantations in the area is a fascinating experience. There are two **Boh plantations** in the Highlands as well as the and both welcome visitors and provide guided tours of the tea making process. The Boh plantation below Tanah Rata packs the tea as well as dries and ferments it, but the plantation above Brinchang is bigger. To get to it one has to travel through the barrack-like houses of the tea plantation workers. Tea gathering hasn't changed much since the British first began their tea plantations in India. It has become slightly easier on the workers now since they use a kind of hedge clipper to cut the new shoots rather than handpicking each shoot, but they still carry the baskets on their heads and handpick

The Golf Club, Cameron Highlands.

shoots from the less accessible parts of the bush. Most of the workers at this plantation are Tamils, descendants of the first wave of cheap labor brought over from Sri Lanka. You may notice that a very high proportion of the population in the Highlands is of Tamil or other ethnic Indian origin.

Another interesting sight is the **Cameron Highlands Butterfly Park** ((05) 491-0115 at 0–5 43rd mile Green Cow Kea Farm, 39100 Tanah Rata, where many butterflies live and breed. Unlike most such places where the butterflies are shipped in and die without breeding because the climate is too hot, these are furiously fertile and often cause damage to the many rare and unusual plants growing inside. There is a section here where some of the local carnivorous plants are struggling to stay alive and another section for the poisonous plants that these butterflies need to breed but which are too dangerous to have out in the main park. There are also many of the indigenous insects, some of which look like extras from a '50s science-fiction movie, and a gigantic python which gets fed a whole live chicken once a month and then sleeps it off till the next month. Try to persuade the owner, Mr. Patrick Chow, to give a guided tour. He knows a lot about the creatures he looks after. Also, look out for the green roses which flourish in here.

Other places to visit include the **Sam Poh Kong Temple,** about a kilometer (just over half-a mile) off the main road to Brinchang, a strawberry farm in Brinchang, and further up, beyond Brinchang, some vegetable farms which grow cabbage and cress on precarious ledges. These ledges have cables leading up to the road to carry the produce to the lorry which collects it all once a day. Rose lovers might also like to visit the rose garden.

WHERE TO STAY

Expensive

Accommodation covers the whole range of possibilities from self-catering apartments to luxury hotels. The poshest is **Ye Olde Smokehouse** ((05) 491-1214/5 FAX (05) 491-1214 By-the-golf-course, 39007 Cameron Highlands, Malaysia, P.O. Box 77, built in the thirties as a resthouse for weary planters and glowing with Ye Olde English kitsch. As

hotels go, it is very small and very exclusive, and will cheerfully turn you away if you don't look like the right sort. Foster, the man who built it, was a sort of colonial Basil Fawlty and thought nothing of sending the dogs out to chase away the curious. If you don't stay there you should go in for tea. Room rates start at $140. Each room is individual, very large and contains a huge four-poster bed. In the evenings they light log fires and residents sit about engaging in the gentle art of conversation.

When Foster got fed-up with the tourists he sold the Smokehouse and built another similarly-styled hotel known as the **Lakehouse** ((05) 495-6152 FAX (05) 495-6213, back down at Ringlet, which is probably the only reason you'd want to spend any time there.

Similar in style to the Smokehouse but with less kitsch, and its rates are slightly lower at $100 for a double. Bookings can be made at The Lakehouse, 30th mile, Ringlet, 39200 Cameron Highlands, Phang, Malaysia. If you don't mind package tourists and often noisy Singaporeans you might try Strawberry Park Resort at Jalan Kemunting, Tanah Rata ((05) 491-1166, which has horse riding, squash, tennis and good views. Doubles at $75, apartments from $88 to $144.

Moderate

More mundane but serviceable are the Merlin Inn Resort ((05) 491-1205 FAX (05) 491-1178, where rates for a double are $85.

In the medium price range there is the New Garden Inn ((05) 491-5170 FAX (05) 491-5169 at Tanah Rata, which has its own cinema, pool tables and a restaurant and where double rooms cost $40 including breakfast. Further up at Brinchang, there are several hotels, including the very neat Hill Garden Lodge ((05) 491-2988 FAX (05) 491-2226, 15–16 Jalan Besar, 39100 Brinchang, Cameron Highlands, Pahang, where rooms cost $23 for a double on weekdays. This is a pretty basic hotel with no restaurant. On the other side of the road is the Parkland Hotel ((05) 491-1299 FAX (05) 491-1803, at Lot 5, 39100 Brinchang, Cameron Highlands, which has a tendency toward Tudor beams and log fires, albeit artificial ones, and where

Ye Old Smokehouse. You can almost hear the planters' ice tinkling in their drinks as they relaxed after a hard day's work.

doubles are $28. This place has a restaurant and competes with several other restaurants in this strip to create the best and cheapest steamboat, a kind of fish, meat and vegetable fondue. This area, Brinchang, is a working town and the hotels look over the main road and wet market so there are no scenic views here.

Inexpensive

The most popular with travelers is run by the charismatic Bala himself, who also organizes cheap tours and bus tickets. Bala's Holiday Chalets ((05) 491-1660, is in Jalan Tanah Rata; turn onto the marked road two kilometers (1.2 miles) north of Tanah Rata town. Dormitory beds and rooms, with a double costing $17. Another popular place is The Orient ((05) 491-1633, at N38 Jalan Besar, 39000 Tanah Rata, Cameron Highlands, Pahang. Rates depend on the number of people, the season and how long you intend to stay, but a double room with bathroom should be in the area of $20. Like many of the smaller places, prices are fluid. Downstairs is a very popular Chinese restaurant and down the road they have a coffeehouse which does a good breakfast.

If you are really on a shoestring (like $4 a night) head for the Father's House, which is a collection of ex-British army Nissen huts around the local priest's house. Head toward the convent and you'll see the priest's house from there. Accommodation is a bed in a dormitory with cooking facilities.

There are also self catering places, many of which are advertised in shop windows, or you can call in at the local travel agent, C.S. Travel & Tours Sdn. Bhd ((05) 491-1200 FAX (05) 491-2390, N47 Jalan Besar, 39000 Tanah Rata, who manage several places for their owners. They also handle ticketing, tours of the area and hotel accommodation.

WHERE TO EAT

Eating out here is as expensive or unusual as you care to make it. The big hotels all have restaurants; at the Merlin, the **Rajah Brooke** serves Western and Chinese food at reasonable prices, the **Smokehouse** is quite pricey but does some dishes you won't find anywhere else, such as beef Wellington, which the local Sultan is pretty fond of, or steak and kidney pie for the homesick British. The **Lakehouse** also has a pricey Western restaurant. You can find reasonably priced Western food in Tanah Rata at the **Chop and Steak House**, on Main Road. There are two excellent banana leaf places serving *murtabaks* and *roti canai* as well as curries served on a banana leaf. One is the **Restoran Kumar**, and next door is the **Restoran Thanam**, the only place where I have ever seen a woman making the *roti*. The food stalls on Main Road have a good selection of curries and

noodle dishes, as well as Western food. Up at Brinchang you should really try the steamboat. These restaurants are in fierce competition to do the cheapest and best, but many Malaysian visitors opt for Parkland Hotel's version. At **Jasmine Restaurant** on the main road in Tanah Rata you'll find a four-course set meal for only $5. If you are eating on a shoestring, try the **Restoran Sentosa** at Brinchang which does Indian Muslim food at ridiculous prices. Very seedy looking but the food is good and there's lots of it.

ABOVE: English country flowers abound in the Cameron Highlands. OPPOSITE: A tea plantation where Indian workers still pick the that brought their ancestors here from southern India.

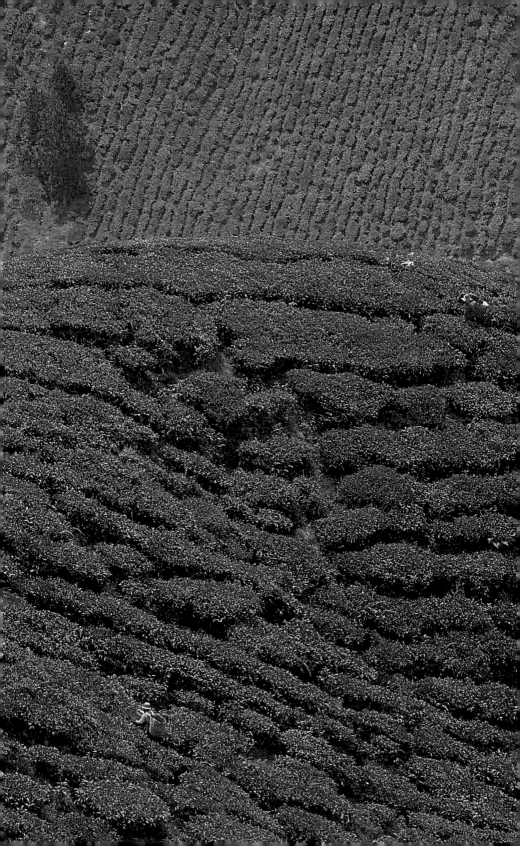

GETTING THERE

Getting to the Cameron Highlands can be difficult. Trains stop at Tapah Road, 20 minutes from the town of Tapah at the bottom of the hill, and you can arrange a taxi up to Tanah Rata from there. There are also hourly buses from Tapah to Tanah Rata. There are express buses from most major towns to the Highlands or a taxi can be hired. The easiest mode of transport is of course by car, which will make your stay at the Highlands easier since

FRASER'S HILL

Fraser's Hill is over 100 km (62 miles) from Kuala Lumpur, and the best way to get there is from the capital. Legend has it that a man called Louis James Fraser lived in the hills and ran mule trains of tin back to the nearest trading posts. In the early twentieth century he disappeared, and those who came looking for him found instead a perfect hill resort with a daytime temperature of around 24°C (75°F) and green hills to put up bungalows

the three villages are some miles apart and a car is a useful means of transport if you wish to visit tea plantations or the temple. If you intend to go from here to Thailand, the train from Ipoh connects with trains to Thailand, although you should check timetables.

The government has proposed building a highway linking Cameron Highlands with Fraser's Hill. Malaysian environmental groups have strongly urged the government to scrap such plans, pointing to a number of disastrous accidents caused by landslides near Genting Highlands and to the vital importance of retaining this mountainous forested region as a catchment area. One can only hope that the WWF and Malaysian Nature Society, among others, will win the battle.

for the colonialists needing a rest from the boiling temperatures of the Empire. The place soon attracted other colonials who wanted a second residence to escape from the humidity of the lowlands. Today Fraser's Hill is hardly the idyllic mountain retreat it was in the early part of this century, but it has many hotels and facilities like jungle walks, swimming, an open-to-the-public nine-hole golf course, tennis, fishing, boating and a sports complex with a heated swimming pool.

GENERAL INFORMATION

There is an information center just before the Merlin Hotel ((09) 32-2201, to help with the booking of rooms and providing of maps.

Because of its easy access and closeness to Kuala Lumpur, Fraser's Hill tends to get overcrowded on weekends, public holidays or school holidays (when the prices normally go up). At other times the place is quiet and relaxing with few organized activities, and even the jungle walks are underplayed.

WHERE TO STAY AND EAT

Outside the peak periods, accommodation is no problem. The **Fraser's Hill Development Corporation (** (09) 362-2044, or (03) 804-1026, has old colonial-era bungalows for around $32 but make sure you see what you are paying for, and don't expect any frills. An alternative is the functional **Merlin Resort** **(** (09) 362-2300, a good value at around $75 on weekdays, including American breakfast. It has good views, a coffeeshop and a bar where people hang out at night around the fire. Very definitely upmarket is the **Ye Olde Smoke House (** (09) 362-2266 FAX (09) 362-2035, not a place for children who could do untold damage to the multitudes of flower arrangements, busts of Henry VIII, and other bric-a-brac littering the place. It has 12 rooms, all individually designed with four posters and all the trimmings. Rooms go for various prices, from around $180. Lunch or dinner is available and the afternoon tea and strawberries are popular with local tourists who may be under the illusion that this is what life in Britain is like.

There is also the **Fraser's Pine Resort (** (03) 783-2577 FAX (03) 783-6108, which rents condominium-type accommodation. The apartments have two or three double bedrooms, a small kitchen and a balcony. It has a mediocre Chinese restaurant and at peak times is exceptionally noisy with little privacy. One unit can take up to 10 people and costs about $90. There are several smaller places in the area — the **Temerloh Bungalow**, for example, which has rather scruffy and basic rooms for $18. The best feature here is the attached steakhouse which offers decent meals at decent prices. Unless you have no choice, I do not recommend staying at the Puncak Inn **(** (09) 362-2201, where the rooms are basically unpleasant. At the bottom of the hill there is the old **Gap House** with more character and atmosphere than anywhere in Fraser's Hill itself. Rooms at around $12 and a restaurant make this place worth a night's stay on your way there or back.

GETTING THERE

You really need a car to get there in comfort. Along the main Kuala Lumpur to Ipoh road there is a turn-off at Kuala Kubu Bharu which leads to a one way system up the steep winding hill. From the Gap to Fraser's Hill, traffic goes uphill from 7 AM to 7:45 AM, and then every second hour until 7:40 PM. Downhill

traffic is on alternate hours starting at 8 AM. There is a proposal to put in a two-way road but this seems to be bogged down — literally. An alternative is to take up one of the many packages offered by tour operators in Kuala Lumpur and Singapore. There is a public bus to Kuala Kubu Bharu, but the connecting bus to Fraser's Hill only runs twice a day, at 8 AM and 12 noon, so it's more practical to charter a taxi up to Fraser's Hill for around $12.

TAMAN NEGARA

BACKGROUND

Just imagine over 4,000 sq km (1,544 sq miles) of primeval, virgin rainforest, situated between four and five degrees north of the equator, and protected by statute from loggers and others despoilers of the environ-

A pretty resort built in the heart of Taman Negara OPPOSITE gives visitors the opportunity to explore the virgin rainforest ABOVE.

ment. This is Taman Negara: Malaysia's greatest asset and one of the major natural wonders of planet Earth.

At a time when rainforests around the globe are being systematically logged Taman Negara has become even more precious, and a visit there is a unique experience. It is a place for anyone who appreciates nature, and whether you're six or 60, or somewhere in between, this is a place you can handle because the choice of activities is up to the individual. Around 300 *Orang Asli*, the original inhabitants of the Malay peninsula, still live a semi-nomadic existence within the borders of Taman Negara, some of them working as porters at the Park.

GENERAL INFORMATION

Between mid-November and mid-January the monsoon rains present a danger so the Park Headquarters are closed to visitors from November 15, until January 15, but at any other time of the year a little planning and preparation will ensure a rewarding and fascinating glimpse into the life of the tropical rainforest.

The accommodation of the park has been privatized (except for the fishing lodges and hides). There are two types of accommodation, the more upmarket **Taman Negara Resort ℂ** (03) 245-5585 FAX (03) 261-0615. and the less pricey **Nusa Camp ℂ** (03) 262-7682 FAX (03) 262-7682, which is further upriver (see WHERE TO STAY). You can turn up at the jetty without a reservation but of course there's no guarantee of a place. It really is worth making a phone call beforehand.

WHAT TO SEE

The medium is the message and, unless you fly in from Kuala Lumpur, the experience begins on the jetty at Kuala Tembeling. There are no roads in Taman Negara and access is by means of the eight-seater *perahu*, a wooden boat with an outboard motor. The journey will take around three hours depending on the time of the year. The 60-km (37-mile) boat trip up the Sengai Tembeling is a memorable and glorious journey. At first you'll see signs of *kampung* life along the banks, women washing their children or

their clothes and village buffaloes up to their necks in the water, but these give way to long stretches of inactivity when you're tempted to nod off and then wake with a shock as you gaze around. Occasionally a majestic flash of blue will signal one of the three types of kingfisher, or you'll spot a two meter long monitor lizard (*Varanus salvator*). Between April and July look out for the blue-throated bee-eater that will sweep across the water when disturbed by the sound of the motor.

By the time you reach the Park Headquarters the magic of the jungle should have started to play on your mind. Most nights a 16 mm film about Taman Negara is shown around 8 PM. Don't miss this (unless, of course, you happen to be staying at Nusa Camp). It's first-rate and concludes with a rallying call to get out of the Park Headquarters, get a sweat on, get tired, and experience Taman Negara. Spend your first afternoon relaxing by all means; purchase a copy of the excellent guide and plan your stay. For the active and fit, the trails are just waiting for you, but if you wish to stay overnight in one of the jungle hides or go on a river trip, you will need to book ahead, ensure you have sufficient food and fuel and collect the necessary bed linen and accessories like lanterns.

If you're staying at Park Headquarters, this is where you book in, collect keys, study the maps and acclimatize yourself. Check out the inconspicuous glass cabinet that contains artifacts for sale, all made by the *Orang Asli* — the native non-Malay inhabitants of the area. Items include aphrodisiacs culled from jungle roots.

There is sufficient variety in the types of trails to suit all tastes and staminas. From the edge of the forest near the restaurant there is an 800-m (874-yard) circuit path with points of interest marked and linked up with knowledgeable explanations in the guide book. Here's your chance to see, strangling figs, jungle epiphytes, giant termites' nests, the valuable merbau tree that has just about disappeared from other parts of Malaysia, 250-year-old tualang trees, rattan palms and lots more interesting flora.

In the midst of the jungle, Lata Berkoh is a refreshing place for a swim or even a chance to fish.

An even shorter walk leads to a *bumbun*, a wildlife observation post or hide that looks out upon a natural salt-lick. If you're lucky, and perhaps very patient, you might spot mouse-deer, barking-deer or sambar, or maybe even the Malayan tapir or civet or the large black gibbon. Other walks of one to two hours and longer will take you to other hides deeper in the jungle.

An attractive feature of the park is the availability of boat trips that allow you to cut down on the leg work. **Lata Berkoh**, for instance, is a rock-fall area that marks the limit

of navigability on one of the main river's tributaries. Trekking here will take you a healthy five hours but you can book a boat for the return journey or take a boat there and back. Either way, Lata Berkoh is a delightful resting place where you can swim or fish (rods can be hired from headquarters) or just relax and watch for those incredible hornbills that raucously announce their imminent arrival. A sight to behold.

Another river trip well worth booking ahead on the day you arrive is a journey upstream on the Sungei Tembeling to **Kuala Trenggan**. From here you can trek for 90 minutes to a Visitor's Hide and stay the night or just rest and watch birds. Unless the river is shallow at the time, you can expect fun on

the way back as the boat rides the numerous rapids.

Consider a night out in the jungle. Taking a few basics (torch, mosquito coils, matches, candles, food, a novel to read perhaps) you can book a four-seater boat which will take you close to a lodge or hide and bring you back the next morning. The boatmen will probably stay the night as well. As dark settles in, light a small campfire and sit back to enjoy the magical lights of the fireflies and the symphony of sounds. As you contemplate your insignificance in the black vastness that surrounds you, a primitive humility and awe will lull you to sleep. The light of morning will seem like one of nature's miracles.

Real enthusiasts may consider the eight-day round-trip to **Gunung Tahan**, the highest mountain in West Malaysia. Guides are compulsory and the whole thing is best arranged before coming to the Park. As the guide book says, "This is an arduous journey demanding physical fitness and mental determination, as well as good equipment, thorough preparations and sound leadership for large groups."

If you want to test your mental stamina I'd suggest a morning trip to **Gua Telinga**. This is a small but spectacular limestone cave you thread your way through by following a rope. Not for the claustrophobic but terrific if you like seeing thousands of roundleaf bats, giant toads, harmless whip spiders and black-striped frogs. A more difficult-to-reach cave is Gua Kepayang where you can move around freely and search for elephant droppings. Don't let any of this scare you. No one has ever been trampled to death in Taman Negara or bitten by a poisonous snake. You may have a small amount of blood taken from your system by leeches but this is harmless and painless. All part of the fun. And if you don't want anything hectic and physically demanding just stay around the Park Headquarters and relax. Go for short walks and return river trips. You'll see and learn a lot wherever you go.

WHERE TO STAY

You have a choice of accommodation at either the **Taman Negara Resort** ((09) 263-5000 FAX (09) 261-5000; sales office in Kuala

Lumpur ☏ (03) 245-5585 FAX (03) 261-0615, located at Park Headquarters, or further upriver at **Nusa Camp** ☏ (09) 263-5000 FAX (09) 261-5000 or at their sales office in Kuala Lumpur ☏ (03) 245-5585 FAX (03) 261-0615. Accommodation at Taman Negara Resort ranges from private air-conditioned chalets costing $70 to standard guest houses which cost $50 for a double and dormitory beds at $14. Nusa Camp, which runs the Nusa Riverbus from Kuala Tahan to the Camp, has everything from campsites (less than $1 per person) to hostel beds ($4), A-frame chalets ($18) up to Malay-style cottages and houses ($28 to $32). Book through the sales agent in Kuala Lumpur, SPKG Tours ☏ 03-262-7682, extension 112 FAX (03) 262-7682 whose office is located in the Malaysia Tourist Information Complex, 109 Jalan Ampang.

WHERE TO EAT

Park Headquarters has two restaurants; the **Tahan Restaurant** and the self-service **Teresek Restaurant**. At the Tahan an American breakfast is $7, a set lunch $10 and a buffet dinner $12. Packed lunches are around $8. At the Teresek restaurant a meal is about $5. Nusa Camp offers set meals ranging from $2.40 for breakfast up to $7 for dinner, as well as an à la carte menu.

COSTS

You not only have to pay 15 percent on all accommodation within the Park (the standard service charge and government tax) but all trips within the park are charged. Naturally, these vary on the duration of the trip and distance traveled by boat. Some examples are $20 for night fishing, $8 for a tour to an *Orang Asli* village, $10 for a trip to the Abai waterfall, and $18 to visit Gua Telinga.

GETTING THERE

If you are traveling from Singapore, catch the night train that departs at 10 PM and arrives at Tembeling Halt around 8 AM in the morning. The train will only be stopping for those visiting Taman Negara. From here you have to walk for half-an-hour to the jetty at Kuala Tembeling where boats leave at around

9 AM and 2 PM. Nusa Camp's agent, SPKG Tours, operates and air-conditioned van and bus shuttle from Kuala Lumpur to Kuala Tembeling, and have an express boat service which takes you from here up to Nusa Camp. The fare is $15 per person.

The easiest way to get from Kuala Lumpur to Jerantut, the jumping off point for Taman Negara, is to take a shared taxi from the Pudu Raya station. Alternatively, take the Oriental Bus Company bus from Perhentian Pekeliling on Jalan Tun Razak at 9 AM, 1:30 PM and 5:30 PM; the trip costs around $4 and takes three hours. Leaving the park means a boat down the river in the morning or after lunch. From the jetty you can walk to Tembeling Halt and catch the night train to Singapore (around 8 PM). This involves a long wait but you can drop in at the small village built on the river bank and find food there. You may feel a little uncertain as you wait on the platform in the dark, probably alone, wondering if the international express train really will stop just for you. I felt compelled to flag it down like a bus and was astounded when the train actually ground to a halt and the guard stepped down to politely inquire whether I was going to Singapore or not! It's more sensible to catch a bus or taxi to Jerantut from the jetty and spend the evening there waiting for the night train at a real station. The trains back to Singapore only have sleeping berths on certain nights of the week so check this beforehand. If you're traveling north you will have to spend the night in Jerantut and catch the train up the next morning.

Traveling from Kota Bharu means a long train journey with either a long wait at Gua Musang till 4 AM or going on to Kuala Lipis and spending a night there in order to catch a morning train to Tembeling Halt.

By road from Kuala Lumpur involves traveling along the main Kerak highway toward Kuantan and turning off at Temerloh for Jerantut. From here it is a 15-minute drive to the boat jetty where cars can be left in a compound. From the central Pudu Raya bus station in Kuala Lumpur a taxi could be hired for the three- to four-hour journey.

The *Orang Asli*, original inhabitants of the central Malaysia, are not often encountered these days.

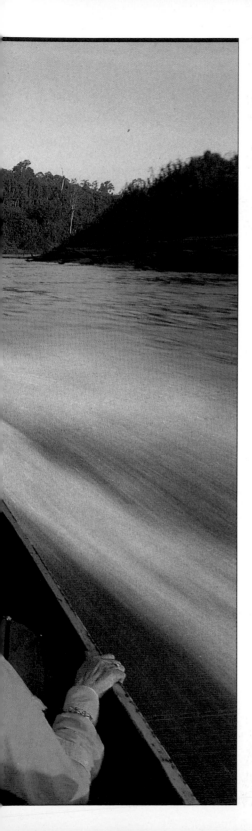

Sarawak

SARAWAK is at times the embodiment of Borneo, a land where rivers are often the only highways into the interior, and where Dyak tribes still live in huge communal longhouses (albeit with comforts such as like generators). The combination of extremely friendly people who retain the best of their traditions, and of some of Malaysia's most interesting national parks, including the remarkable Gunung Mulu with its network of caves, make Sarawak an unforgettable destination. Kuching, the capital, is one of Southeast Asia's most charming cities. The longhouses of the Bidayuh, once know as Land Dyaks, are an easy half-day trip from Kuching, while nearby Bako National Park is ideal for an overnight stay. Longhouse visits can be made The Rejang River, where the Iban tribe predominates, is a fascinating place to explore. In the north, in the upper reaches of the Baram River and up in the Kelabit Highlands, a grouping of tribes known as the Orang Ulu live in their distinctive longhouses. The prehistoric caves at Niah and Gunung Mulu National Park are both reached via Miri. Gunung Mulu is a place that no visitor to Sarawak should miss, offering some of the world's most striking caves, rich rainforest and the chance for adventure caving and trekking.

Traveling upriver by hired longboat as opposed to public express boat is expensive in Sarawak, for the locals as well as for visitors. Longhouse visits can be expensive also, and visitors should be aware that the chances of viewing wildlife and birds are far greater in neighboring Sabah. However, Sarawak has a unique charm that the adventurous tourist will long remember.

BACKGROUND

From the fifteenth century Sarawak was part of the Sultanate of Brunei. When antimony was discovered in the 1820s, the dependency began to attract attention. The Sultan's power was threatened by Malays and Bidayuh natives fighting for their independence. The Englishman James Brooke arrived at Sarawak in 1839 and was rewarded for his help in putting down the rebel revolt by being given the land around the Sarawak River in 1842. He became the first White Rajah of

Sarawak, and the Astana in Kuching became his residence and seat of government. When he died in 1868, his nephew, Charles Brooke took over the throne and ruled with an iron hand until his death in 1917. The Brooke era came to an abrupt end with the Japanese invasion in 1941. After the war, Sarawak became a British Crown Colony. Civil unrest simmered and reached a climax in 1949 when the governor was assassinated in Sibu.

The struggle against the British was associated with the Brooke heir apparent, Anthony Brooke, the nephew of the third

Rajah, Vyner Brooke, but in 1951 he publicly disassociated himself from the campaign.

In 1962 a revolt broke out in Brunei, and a plan to unite with Sarawak and Sabah was formed. The fighting spread to parts of Sarawak, and British troops helped crush the rebellion. When Malaya's independence was being negotiated, the idea of incorporating Sarawak and Sabah into a Malaysian Federation gained popularity with Malay politicians because it was seen as a way of reducing the numerically large Chinese element. In 1963, Malaysia became a political reality but was strongly contested by President Sukarno of Indonesia and an undeclared war — known as Confrontation — lasted until 1969.

Peace now reigns with Indonesia and Malaysia on friendly terms, and the state of Sarawak prospers from its rich logging and petroleum and gas industries, as well as vast palm oil plantations.

The highly ornate tribal dress OPPOSITE of the Orang Ulu, Sarawak and exotic hornbill ABOVE create an impressive tribal headdress.

VISITING LONGHOUSES

No visit to Sarawak is complete with a trip to a longhouse (see TOP SPOTS). Half-day trips to some of the Bidayuh longhouses near Kuching, such as Anna Rais, Benuk, Gaya and Mentu Tapu show a very different way of life to that of the Iban. The Bidayuh are rather shy people, renowned for their weaving of baskets and mats.

Some tour operators offer overnight trips to the Iban longhouses along the Skrang river.

are more easily accessible, or where they own their own resthouse next to a longhouse. This is not to say that the experience will not be rewarding, but do check the details carefully before you commit yourself. Ask to see photos of the longhouse and accommodation, and check its location on a map.

The most reputable operators, all of whom offer longhouse trips, are **Borneo Adventure** ((082) 410569 FAX (082) 422626, 55 Main Bazaar; **Ibanika Expedition** ((082) 424022 FAX (082) 424021, 411A 4th Floor, Wisma Saberkas; **Interworld Travel** ((082)

These have been visited for more than 20 years and consequently suffer from an overdose of tourists. Ask your tour operator for something further afield, such as the Lemanak and Batang Ai rivers which are reached via Kuching. However, interesting Iban longhouses on the Rajang can be found upriver from Sibu, in tributaries near Kanowit or Kapit, while many of the rivers around Bintulu (particularly the Kapuas and smaller rivers off the Kemena) have longhouses with a mixture of peoples, including Punan Bah. You have to go to the uppermost reaches of the Baram to find any relatively traditional Orang Ulu longhouses in the Miri district. Tour operators naturally have a vested interest in you going to places which

252344 FAX (082) 424515, 85 Jln Rambutan; **Singai Travel Service** ((082) 420918 FAX (082) 258320, 108 Jln Chan Chin Ann. A Kapit-based tour operator who can offer interesting longhouse trips in the Rajang area is **Tan Teck Chuan** (Ah Chuan), Kapit Adventure Tours ((084) 796352 FAX (084) 796655, 11 Jln Tan Sit Leong. Longhouse tours are not cheap, and the price depends to a large extent on the distance traveled. The price for one to two persons for a two-day/one-night trip is generally in the region of RM400–500 ($160 to $200), while three days/two nights is around RM800. If you go on your own, be sure to pay for your food in the longhouse, RM20 to RM30 a day is considered an acceptable rate.

NATIONAL PARKS

These are one of the major attractions of Sarawak. Although there are 10 existing Parks as well as a number of sanctuaries and nature reserves, most visitors explore only three. Permits are currently required to visit the Parks, to the inconvenience of travellers and tour operators. Although the situation at Gunung Mulu improved for a while, with permits given on arrival, it appears that it is once again essential to obtain the permit in

Niah National Park, two hours by road from Miri (there's a public bus which goes to Kampung Niah nearby), has a dramatic Great Cave where swifts built their edible nests high up in the gloomy recesses. Pottery and other prehistoric remains found at Niah indicate men were living here 25,000 to 35,000 years ago. The Painted Caves has 1,000-year-old paintings on the wall, but the old wooden coffins have been moved to the Sarawak Museum.

Gunung Mulu National Park, which can be reached by a 25-minute flight from Miri, is

advance. It's easiest to book accommodation and obtain permits at the relatively new Sarawak Tourism Board Information Centre next to the Museum or the information office in the Waterfront Park. Alternatively, book at the National Parks and Wildlife Office in Kuching ((082) 442180 or Miri (for Niah and Gunung Mulu) ((085) 434184, or ask your tour operator to handle this for you.

Bako National Park, the smallest and oldest park, is close to Kuching. Travel to Kampung Bako by road (there's even a public bus) and take a 25-minute boat ride to the Park. Bako is a good place to see pitcher plants, wild pig, macaques and occasional proboscis monkeys. Stay overnight in one of the chalets, and enjoy a swim from one of the beaches.

home to an enormous number of fascinating limestone caves, including the world's largest cave chamber. The rich flora and fauna, and the possibility for adventure caving and trekking, make Gunung Mulu a must for the adventurous.

Reliable tour agents are mentioned above, under VISITING LONGHOUSES, but if you are planning your trip from Kuala Lumpur the people to contact are Asian Overland Services ((03) 292-5622 FAX (03) 292-5209. They specialize in packages to the national parks and longhouses.

OPPOSITE: The farther afield, the more authentic a longhouse experience will be. ABOVE: Niah Caves National Park, Sarawak, brings you close to nature and to man's early history.

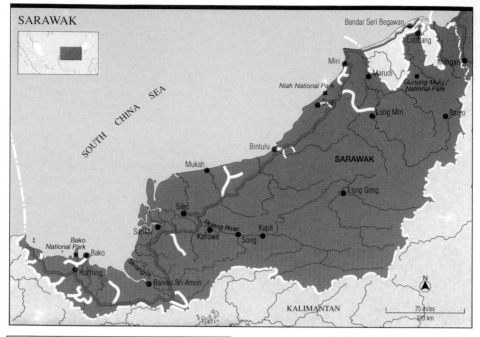

TRAVELING IN SARAWAK

Travel in Sarawak is quite different from travel in Peninsular Malaysia. In many areas, roads are of secondary importance to rivers and while it is seldom possible to make reservations for scheduled boat journeys, it is advisable to always plan ahead and have a general idea of how you intend spending your time in Sarawak. Plane journeys are sometimes necessary and should be booked ahead. For instance, if you are intending to travel from Kuching to Miri, or from Sibu to Miri, a plane is the best way to cover the distance. Although it is possible to travel by bus from Sibu to Miri on roads which are being continually improved, the journey involves six to seven hours of travel along a route of minimal interest. Malaysia Airlines has a good network of routes and the prices are reasonable, but if you don't have a reservation you may find yourself waiting around for hours or even days. And the key to a successful time in Sarawak is getting to where you want to go to with the minimum fuss. There is just no joy in hanging around in the towns waiting for connections. Decide on the places you want to visit and plan accordingly, making whatever flight arrangements are necessary. Bear in mind, too, that from July to October the dry season can sometimes make the upper reaches of the rivers difficult to navigate.

KUCHING

One hour by air from Singapore and 90 minutes from Kuala Lumpur will bring you to Kuching, a wonderfully laid-back town which has managed to accept the modern world without being overwhelmed by it. All the modern hotels and shopping complexes are not far from the Sarawak River, with the Main Bazaar and other streets of the old town retaining their identity and charm. The creation in 1994 of the Waterfront Park, which runs for almost one kilometer (just over half-a-mile) along the river in front of Main Bazaar, has revealed the beauty of the area, and the old houses and traditional lifestyles on the northern bank remain remarkably untouched. Kuching is a town not to be missed and a least a couple of days are needed here if the place is going to work its magic. More time is required if you want to visit the nearby Bako National Park.

GENERAL INFORMATION

The **Sarawak Tourism Board** ((082) 410944, maintains two information centers in

Kuching: one is located alongside the Padang just below the new wing of the Sarawak Museum, and the other next to the renovated Sarawak Steamship Building in the Waterfront Park opposite Main Bazaar. **Sarawak Plaza** Sarawak Plaza was Kuching's first modern shopping complex next to the Holiday Inn and here you will find shops selling native artifacts and handicrafts. The newer complex next to Riverside Majestic Hotel includes a large department store and supermarket, as well as a number of speciality shops. Tour operators are listed under Visit-

WHAT TO SEE

Kuching suffered remarkably little damage from the ravages of the Second World War and a number of old colonial relics are well preserved and all conveniently located within easy walking distance of the river. The **Court House**, erected in 1847, housed the Brooke administration and its Romanesque style somehow blends in comfortably with the sleepy Asian setting. Around the corner in Jalan Tun Abang Haji Openg is the **Post**

ing Longhouses. Golf and a variety of water sports can be enjoyed at Damai Beach, 40 minutes away from Kuching. Exercise can also be had by joining the **Hash House Harriers** ((082) 421133, on their weekly runs. For reading material visit the book shop in the Holiday Inn, the Curio Shoppe in the Hilton or the souvenir shop inside the Sarawak Museum. If you are traveling upriver consider purchasing here the 1:50,000 scale map of Sarawak, or the Periplus Travel Map of Sarawak.

Traveling around Sarawak is very likely to involve flights, and **Malaysia Airlines** ((082) 246622, makes reservations at their office in Song Thian Cheok Road, not far from the Holiday Inn.

Office, and its mighty Corinthian columns seem equally at ease with their surroundings. A real treat is **Fort Margherita** on the other side of the river and not the least of its attractions is the journey there. There are a couple of departure points for the *tambang* ferries along Waterfront Park, where the ferryman will use oars to maneuver the boat out into the river and then speed across by engine. Passengers casually toss 20 *sen* onto the prow of the boat to pay for the crossing. Just follow their example. The fort, completed in 1879 by the second rajah, Charles Brooke, and named after his wife, is perfectly preserved for two reasons: it was strategically

Fort Margherita Museum is well worth the trip to the other side of the Sarawak River.

located to repel troublesome natives but trouble never came, and secondly, because of faulty marksmanship, the attacking Japanese dropped their bombs in the river instead of their intended target. The Fort now houses a **Police Museum**. The fort's watchtower is now home to six laughing skulls, collected in battle many years ago, but reported to have been heard laughing since then. The **Astana** is also on this side of the river but the original home of the White Rajahs is now the official home of the state governor and is not open to the public.

the museum, and these should be seen if you are planning to visit the caves themselves.

It is easy to spend a half day strolling the old parts of Kuching. Upriver slightly from **Main Bazaar** and not far from the big mosque, Jalan Datuk Abijah Abol has some lovely wooden *kampung* houses, particularly 504 and 507. Take time to wander the streets of Chinatown, starting in Jalan Carpenter which runs parallel with Main Bazaar towards the colorful **Tua Pek Kong** temple, built in 1876. Artisans still work in many of the shops in this area, and the coffeeshops offer some

One place that cannot be missed on any trip to Kuching is the **Sarawak Museum**, conceived during the reign of the second Rajah. The nineteenth-century naturalist, Alfred Russell Wallace, who conceived independently of Darwin the theory of natural selection, played a vital role in the museum's establishment. It now houses a fascinating collection of natural and anthropological exhibits that could well convince you of the need to take a trip into the interior. The museum shop is equally well stocked. The two wings of the museum are joined by a bridge over the busy road and are open daily, except Friday, from 9 AM to 6 PM. Admission is free. The 1,200-year-old funeral boats discovered in the Niah Caves are on display in

excellent food. You can even eat at food stalls set up in front of a *wayang* stage where Chinese operas were performed opposite an old Chinese temple. Main Bazaar is full of antique and curio shops where woodcarvings, basketware, mats, antique beads and a host of other fascinating items are sold. Many of the goods are reproductions from Kalimantan, so if you want to be sure you're buying a genuine antique, go to a well known dealer such as Nelson Tan (shop 84) or Jimmy Teo of Arts of Asia (shop 68). The Waterfront Park is a good spot to watch the locals relaxing, to read a little of the history of Kuching on the plaques set into the walkway, to visit the Chinese History Museum and perhaps to enjoy a cold drink and a *popiah*, a fresh spring roll, at the Riverside Café nearby (open from 3 PM until midnight). On Saturday night and Sunday there is a busy and interesting market on Jalan Satok.

OUT OF TOWN

Out at Damai beach, between the Holiday Inn Damai Beach and the Damai Lagoon Resort, is the **Sarawak Cultural Village** ((082) 416777. It takes up nearly eight hectares (17 acres) displaying the lifestyles of the various ethnic groups that make Sarawak

than going on some of the longhouse trips up the Skrang river. A taxi from town will cost $10, but the N° 2B bus or the shuttle service operating from Holiday Inn Kuching to Holiday Inn Damai will also take you there for considerably less. Santubong is the name of the nearby fishing village and during the evening you can eat at one of the many seafood restaurants or stalls in the area.

If you are not visiting the **Sepilok Orang-Utan Rehabilitation Centre** near Sandakan in Sabah, you might like to see Kuching's

such an exciting place. Longhouses from the Bidayuh, Iban and Orang Ulu have been reconstructed, all very different in their architecture, as well as a Penan hut where blow pipe making is demonstrated. Demonstrations of arts and crafts are on hand as well as a small theater showing different dances. Allow a whole morning or afternoon to see the place and catch one of the regular tours and cultural shows. Admission is RM45 for non-Malaysians, expensive but well worth while. Like all such exhibitions, the place may seem too studied for some, but as an introduction to Sarawak's cultural diversity and a spur to visit the interior, this cultural village serves a purpose. Quite honestly, I would say a visit here is a better use of time

equivalent at the **Semenggok Wildlife Rehabilitation Centre** about 22 km (14 miles) out of town. Here you can see orangutans, honey bears, hornbills and monkeys after a half-hour walk from the road to the entrance. Unfortunately, most of the animals are in cages and it's usually difficult to see the wild orangutans close up. Permits are available from the Tourist Information Centre but if you arrange a visit through a tour operator this will be handled for you. Go in the morning to catch the feeding time.

OPPOSITE: Kuching, the most Conradian town in the whole of Malaysia, is a cozy cluster of old shophouses nestled on the banks of the Sarawak. ABOVE: Sarawak's Cultural Village celebrates the indigenous culture of Borneo.

An interesting half-day trip can be made to the old gold-mining town of **Bau**. Nearby is **Fairy Cave** situated about 30 m (100 ft) or 200 steps above the ground; the cave is quite easy to explore with a guide, once you reach it. You can usually see birds' nests which are gathered in caves near Bau being painstakingly cleaned in one of the old shops in nearby Siniawan Bazaar. An organized trip which includes a visit to a local pottery, costs around $60 for two people.

Bako National Park

When the park was gazetted in 1957 it was announced that "Bako was picked… as both the flora and bird life of Bako are of exceptional interest, the scenery beautiful and there are numerous bathing beaches." The simple truth still holds today, and while not spectacular Bako has the virtue of being easily accessible. What I like most is the fact that you can set off on a jungle trek, work up an almighty sweat, but then collapse in joy when you discover a beautiful beach that marks one of the trails' destinations. It was in Bako that I first saw pitcher plants with their cups suspended from the leaf-tips to trap and digest insects. A memorable experience that can be guaranteed on the Lintan trail that takes you up onto an open and barren plateau, quite un-Bornean until you realize the pitcher plants are all around you.

There are 16 clearly marked trails in the park and they range from a one-hour return trip to a seven-hour trek that requires overnight camping. Accommodation at the Park Headquarters includes nine four-room chalets, three hostels and a campsite. Prices range from $4 for a hostel bed to $17 for a double resthouse room to $34 for a chalet. Bedding and self-catering facilities are provided, including a 'fridge, and although there is a canteen at the park it is better to bring your own basic provisions.

Getting to Bako is not as difficult as tour companies might suggest. Bus N° 6 leaves regularly every morning from the bus station near Kuching's open market and takes you to Kampung Bako (Bako village). The bus ride is followed by a short ferry crossing, the whole journey taking two hours. From Kampung Bako you must travel by longboat into the park. When you make your book-

ing the official park boat will have a place reserved for you. You can book at the through the Sarawak Tourism Board information centres in the Waterfront Park opposite Main Bazaar or next to the Museum. It's so easy to travel independently that it's scarcely worth going to the expense of booking a tour; you can expect to pay at least $170 per person for a two day/one night package with transfers, all fees and an English speaking guide.

WHERE TO STAY

Expensive

At the moment there are three top quality hotels, and because of competition, you can usually obtain a discount merely by asking when you check in. For serenity and sedateness stay at the **Kuching Hilton** ((082) 248200 FAX (082) 428984, in Jalan Tunku Abdul Rahman, and be sure to ask for a room overlooking the river if you want that Conradian view early in the morning. Rooms start at around $75. Next door, the **Riverside Majestic** ((082) 247777 FAX (082) 425858, which is twinned with the Damai Lagoon Resort, offers similar rates to the Kuching Hilton, though the view has been obliterated by a highrise apartment block right on the waterfront. The **Holiday Inn Kuching**, just a stone's throw away along the same road, is the first of the major hotels in town and despite a relatively recent renovation, lacks the grandeur of its newer competitors. Rooms start at about $75, and for $10 more there's a river view room ((082) 423111 FAX (082) 426169. There are a couple of luxurious resorts at Damai Beach, about 40 minutes from Kuching. Oldest is the **Holiday Inn Damai Beach** ((082) 411777 FAX (082) 428911, with rooms that start at $80. The rooms and suites in the hilltop extension have stunning views and a separate swimming pool and are the nicest accommodation in all of Damai. Next door and also with a beach frontage is the **Damai Lagoon Resort** ((082) 846900 FAX (082) 846901, with rooms and chalets starting at $68.

Moderate

A more moderately priced three-star resort at Damai, **Santubong Kuching Resort** ((082) 846888 FAX (082) 846777 has rooms from $40.

Close to the Damai Beach Resort is **Damai Rainforest Lodge** (previously known as Camp Permai) ℂ (082) 416777 FAX (082) 244585, where air-conditioned tree houses are available for $60 and log cabins for $76. The rates increase at weekends and lots of organized student groups invade the place then and during school holidays. Not a bad idea for families though, because there are lots of organized recreational activities. Unfortunately, Damai Rainforest Lodge lost its beachfront to the Damai Lagoon Resort, but is still a pleasant place to stay.

If you want to stay in the modern part of Kuching, a short walk from the Holiday Inn will bring you to an older hotel in the same area, the **City Inn** ℂ (082) 414866, in Jalan Abell ($20). There is an open-air seafood restaurant next door as well. In the old part of town in McDougall Road is the **Fata Hotel** ℂ (082) 248111 FAX (082) 428987, charging $26 for double rooms with a 'fridge, less for smaller rooms. Good value can be had at the **Borneo Hotel** ℂ (082) 244122 FAX (082) 254848, just across the road from the Fata Hotel. This is a good tourist hotel with rooms from around $30. The modern **Telang Usan Hotel** ℂ (082) 415588 FAX (082) 425316, is on Ban Hock Road, P.O. Box 1579, 93732 Kuching, with rooms around $35.

Inexpensive

Not far from the Sarawak Plaza and the Holiday Inn, on Jalan Padungan, is the **Kapit Hotel** ℂ (082) 244179, with pokey air-conditioned rooms for $15. The conveniently located **Green Mountain**, One Green Hill ℂ (082) 232828 has air-conditioned rooms from $16. Next door to the Borneo Hotel, the **B & B Inn** offers bed and breakfast from $6–20 ℂ 237366 FAX (082) 238398.

WHERE TO EAT

Naturally, the major hotels offer a variety of Asian cuisines (usually Chinese, Northern Indian and a few Malaysian dishes) and Western food, but you didn't come all the way to Borneo to eat what you can at home. Be sure to try the famous Sarawak *laksa*, a noodle dish with spicy coconut-milk gravy, chicken and egg, sold only in the mornings in many of the coffeeshops. Many Kuching-ites swear it's best at **Marie Café**, in Jalan Ban Hock, not far from the Liwah Hotel and a short walk from Main Bazaar. Some of the best seafood in town is sold nightly at **Benson Seafood**; to get there, walk about 75 m (82 yds) downriver from the Holiday Inn. Don't stop at the first a brightly lit open air seafood restaurant, but continue on through a gap in a high corrugated iron wall and there you are. The fresh fish and vegetables are arranged market style; choose what you want and specify how you'd like it cooked. And don't forget their excellent

Foochow noodles. Another cheaper seafood option is **See Good**, a casual, mostly open-air restaurant in Jalan Bukit Mata (behind Malaysia Airlines). Ask the owners, Mr. or Mrs. Kong, to recommend the specialties. The food stalls near the bridge in Satok Road (you'll need to take a taxi to get there) specialize in Malay and Indian food in the evenings. Good Indian vegetarian food is available at **Green Vegetarian Café**, 16 Main Bazaar. Thompson Corner, on the corner of Jalan Nanas and Palm Road, is well known for its good food stalls: a N° 6 town bus will take you there.

This superb Chinese temple overlooks the mighty Rejang River.

GETTING THERE

From Singapore, Malaysia Airlines flies twice daily to Kuching, and Singapore Airlines has flights twice a week. There are also flights from Hong Kong, Seoul, Tokyo and Bandar Seri Begawan (Brunei). Malaysia Airlines has numerous flights from Kuala Lumpur and Johor Bahru. Flying from Johor Bahru is significantly cheaper than from Singapore, and Malaysia Airlines has a coach that runs from the Novotel Orchid Inn in Bukit Timah Road

in Singapore to the airport in Johor Bahru. Cheaper still would be to purchase the ticket in Johor Bahru paying in Malaysian *ringgit* rather than Singapore currency. Sarawak has its own immigration control, so your passport will get stamped again when you arrive in Kuching from Kuala Lumpur or Johor Bahru.

SIBU

If you're visiting longhouses along the Rejang River, you have to pass by Sibu. The town itself has decent hotels and is well known in Sarawak for its Foochow cuisine. There is no tourist office, and the major tourist attraction, apart from a couple of potteries on the outskirts of town, is the lovely seven-story Chinese pagoda which at night provides an atmospheric view of the mighty Rejang River. It is advisable to have your travel plans made before arriving in Sibu because it isn't really the most interesting place to hang around. If you are staying overnight, however, don't miss the atmospheric night market and the

great snack food sold there. There two local tour companies worth considering. The first is under the charge of Mr. Johnny **Wong** ((084) 326972 FAX (084) 323399. A three-hour tour of Sibu would cost $40 for two people and a complete three-day/two-night trip staying one night in Sibu and another in an Iban longhouse would cost around $320 for two people. Frankie Ting of **Sazhong Travel Service**, 4 Central Road ((084) 338031 FAX (084) 338031, offers a range of upriver tours and will also arrange for exploration of the seldom-visited Mukah district, with its Melanau people and sago culture.

BACKGROUND

Situated some 128 km (80 miles) from the sea, Sibu has an interesting history. It was only in 1900 that a Mr. Wong Nai Siong came exploring the Rejang basin looking for land suitable for development, returning a year later with about 70 farmers, all Foochows from southern China. More followed and today the vast majority of Chinese in Sibu are descendants of these pioneers. Apart from the Chinese, who dominate Sarawak's second largest town, the population consists mostly of Ibans and Malays.

WHERE TO STAY

The best hotel is appropriately named the **Premier** ((084) 323222 FAX (084) 323399, and it is located on Jalan Kampung Nyabor. Published room rates range from $80 to $100 but any independent traveler should expect a 20 percent discount. The location is a central one, near the night market and within walking distance of the wharf where the boats depart. The **Tanahmas** ((084) 333188 FAX (084) 333288, is on the same road, and has a pool; a standard double is around $65. The **Centrepoint Inn** is in the Jing Hwa Building off Central Road ((084) 320222 FAX (084) 320496, and with room rates around $20 this is a good value for a clean and modern room with television and video, especially if you are just staying overnight and leaving on a boat early in the morning. Another place, the **Hotel Bahagia**, also on Central Road ((084) 320303, is an even better value. Get in touch with the Bahagia by fax through its sister hotel, the **Capitol** Hotel FAX (084) 311706; at $10 for a double. There is also a coffeehouse here, unlike the Centrepoint. There are plenty of other hotels to choose from in the central town but beware of the cheaper-looking ones: they charge by the hour.

An honorable exception is the **Methodist Guest House**, Hoover House, next to the church on Jalan Pulau. No air conditioning but a fan and an attached bathroom, and at $5 that seems quite reasonable.

WHERE TO EAT

Sibu not surprisingly offers the best *kang muan*, Foochow noodles in Sarawak, available in most coffeeshops. The oldest and some say the best Foochow food is available at **Hock Choo Lau** restaurant in Jalan Blacksmith; try the Hangchow duck, bean curd soup and special fried noodles. Good Malay food can be found at the **Muslim Gerai** (food stalls) between the Tanahmas Hotel and Sibu Municipal Council, and at the **Gerai Makanan Muslim** near the express boat wharf for Kapit.

GETTING THERE

The best way of reaching Sibu is to fly with MAS from Kuching; the fare is currently $29. The flight gives good views of the coastline and the network of rivers that define the topography of Sarawak. In Sibu the Malaysia Airlines office ((084) 326166 is at 61 Jalan Tuanku Osman.

From Kuching the express boat trip takes from three and a half to five hours and costs $12 upwards. Check the newspapers in Kuching for advertisements or ring **Concorde Marine** ((082) 412551; **Ekspres Bahagia** ((082) 421948; or Ekspres Pertama ((082) 414735. There are buses from Sibu to Bintulu and Miri; although the ride to Bintulu is tolerable, traveling on directly to Miri is not recommended, as the ride is long and not particularly interesting; the plane fare is well worth it.

UPRIVER FROM SIBU

From the waterfront in Sibu, boats depart for Kuching and upriver to Kapit and Belaga. At the time of writing, non-Malaysians are banned from traveling on to Belaga, owing to the construction of the controversial Bakun Dam further upriver. Do not try to break the ban; you will only be turned around by police when you arrive in Belaga. If you don't intend getting off at Song or Kanowit, take the express to Kapit. It will take around three hours in a fast steel-bottomed launch that speeds through the water at more than 30 kph (20 mph), generating a noise that drowns out conversation. If you are lucky it will also drown out the voices coming from the non-stop videos that are an obligatory part of the

journey. Non-express boats will stop briefly at **Kanowit** which is 64 km (40 miles) from Sibu. Kanowit was where Charles Brooke built a fort to use as a base in his campaigns to suppress headhunting. But this is all there is to see and it hardly justifies stopping off unless you wish to continue up the Kanowit River to one of the many interesting longhouses in the region. About two hours from Sibu will bring you to **Song** where, during the Second World War, the Ibans were given permission to renew headhunting, against the Japanese that is. Song is a typical river settlement where Ibans come to sell their produce and buy provisions. There are no good restaurants or hotels but at 6 Ling Hak Seng ((084) 777228, there is a local guide and tour operator who could arrange a visit to Iban longhouses for a lot less than the agents in Sibu. Costs could be negotiated and they will depend on how far you wanted to travel

OPPOSITE: A ferryman carries travelers across the river at Kuching. ABOVE: Upcountry Sarawak, rivers replace roads as the major transport arteries.

and for how long. Expect to pay around $200 for two people staying two nights with full board.

Kapit is the last outpost along the Rejang. It has a wooden fort that dates back to the time of Charles Brooke, and like the much smaller Song, the town itself attracts tribespeople from the interior who come here to buy and sell. Many Iban longhouses grow pepper and rubber which they sell to the Chinese merchants who monopolize the trade. **Malaysia Airlines** ticketing is handled by the **Hua Chiong Company** ((084) 796988,

Sibu leave fairly regularly throughout the day until about 3 PM and you can take your pick.

If you have come this far consider going further upstream along either the Rejang or the Baleh river. Unfortunately, is no longer possible to travel on to **Belaga**, although the luxurious and sensitively designed **Pelagus Rapids Resort** ((082) 238033 FAX (082) 238050, situated at the start of the infamous Pelagus Rapids along the Rejang, offers an idyllic spot to stay for a night or two, with a visit to a nearby Iban longhouse arranged if you like. Double river-facing rooms cost $52.

Jalan Temenggong Koh, just opposite the jetty. It is easy to arrange visits to longhouses in the immediate vicinity but they are urbanized and well used to visitors. If you want to go further afield, contact **Tan Teck Chuan** (Ah Chuan), Kapit Adventure Tours, 11 Jalan Tan Sit Leong ((084) 796352 FAX (084) 796655.

The best hotel in town is the centrally located **Meligai** ((084) 796611, at Jalan Airport. A double room costs around $28. Another clean, comfortable and moderately priced alternative is the **Greenland Hotel** ((084) 796388 FAX (084) 706708, Lot 463-464 Jln Teo Chow Beng, with rooms from $20. The pleasant **New Rejang**, just around the corner from the Greenland Hotel, offers double rooms from $15. The boats back to

The **Pelagus Rapids** form the traditional boundary between the fierce Iban and the less aggressive Orang Ulu tribes (mostly Kenyah and Kayan) who retreated upriver to escape the head-hunting Iban.

A trip up the **Baleh River** takes you past countless Iban longhouses, most of which have modernized although the welcome is still traditional, and the women still weave superb *ikat* fabric, especially at **Nanga Entawau**.

Officially, you are supposed to have a permit for travel beyond Kapit and this can be arranged at the State Government Complex in Kapit. In practice, however, it is a waste of time collecting them because they will never be asked for.

Bintulu itself has little of interest for tourists, although there are a number of traditional longhouses up rivers an hour or so from Bintulu, such as the Sungei Kakus and the Kemena. If you are traveling from Sibu and don't wish to explore any of these longhouses, consider instead heading straight for Miri from where the Niah Caves are just as accessible.

MIRI

Miri serves as a base for visiting some of the most interesting places in Sarawak. If you were short of time, Kuching and Miri are the only two towns you need visit in order to see much of what is best in Sarawak. Kuching accesses the Batang Ai, Lemanak and other rivers with worthwhile longhouses and the Bako National Park, while Miri opens up the Niah and Gunung Mulu National Parks, as well as the delightful settlement of Bareo up in the highlands near the border with Indonesia's Kalimantan. From Miri you could also make a quick visit to **Brunei Darussalam**, an independent country ruled by a sultan who is reputedly the richest man in the world.

GENERAL INFORMATION

Miri is a fast growing town with new commercial centers springing up. The older part of town is where you'll find the MAS office ((085) 414144, a number of good hotels and a supermarket. The top hotels are located a short taxi ride out of town, along the beach, but a number of moderately priced and budget hotels all within easy walking distance downtown. So too is the bus station, beside the Wisma Pelita tower block. In this block you will find book shops and a couple of mediocre handicraft shops and on the fourth floor the government map department where you can purchase the detailed 1:50,000 scale maps of Sarawak. There is a **tourism information office** located next to the bus station, where you can arrange for National Park permits and accommodation. Not far from here is the fascinating native produce market, the **Tamu Muhibbah**, which you should visit if you have some time to kill. Watch out for the wriggling sago grubs, which are often eaten *au naturel*.

There are several experienced and reliable tour companies in Miri offering more or less the same services and packages. One of the best known is **Tropical Adventure** ((085) 414503 FAX (085) 414503, is at Lot 228, First floor, Jalan Maju, Beautiful Jade Centre, P.O. Box 1433. As well as basic trips to Niah, Mulu and Bareo, they have the expertise to design a one-off tour for anyone with special requests, including adventure caving. Another recommended company is **Borneo Overland Services** ((085) 30255 FAX (085) 416424, at 37, Ground floor, Raghavan Building, Jalan Brooke, P.O. Box 1509, next to the Plaza Regency Hotel. **Borneo Adventure** ((085) 414935, 9th floor, Wisma Pelita Tuanku, also maintains an office in Miri. All these companies offer excellent packages to Gunung Mulu National Park.

WHERE TO STAY

Expensive
There are two luxury hotels located along the beach just five minutes from downtown Miri. The **Holiday Inn Miri** ((085) 418888 FAX (085) 419999, Jln Temenggong Datuk Oyong, has rooms from around $100. You may get a better deal if you're going to the Royal Mulu Resort in Gunung Mulu National Park if you stay at the Miri hotel managed by the same company. This is the **Rihga Royal Hotel** ((085) 421121 FAX (085) 421099, located next to the Holiday Inn; rooms are listed from around $95; the most striking feature of this luxurious hotel is its vast free-form swimming pool.

Moderate
Miri has a large number of hotels in this category, catering largely to Bruneians who come here to live it up on weekends and enjoy a drink of two (alcohol is banned in Brunei). The **Gloria Hotel** ((085) 416699 FAX (085) 418866, is on Brooke Road, P.O. Box 1293, and their doubles start at $39. Across from the MAS office on South Yu Seng Road there are a few middle range hotels all offering clean, modern rooms at around $25. Typical of these is the **Million Inn** ((085) 415077

OPPOSITE: Miri is a bustling little boom town but many of its Malay communities still live beside the river.

FAX (085) 415085, but my first choice would be the **Today Inn** which is tucked behind the Maxim restaurant. There is no coffeehouse but the rooms are a good value for the money and their rates for overseas calls are very reasonable.

Inexpensive

One of the best deals in Sarawak is the friendly **Brooke Inn** ((085) 412881 FAX (085) 420899, 14 Jalan Brooke. The hotel is within walking distance of the bus station and a couple of shopping centres and there is excellent Malay food at Taman Seroja nearby. The air-conditioned rooms with attached bathroom and television cost only $18 a double. Other hotels in this category are mostly in Jalan China and the surrounding streets. The only problem is that Jalan China also has its fair share of brothels and there is no way of telling the difference just by looking at them from the pavement. The **Tai Tong Lodging House** ((085) 411498, at 26, opposite the Chinese temple at the bottom of the road, is the cheapest at $15, but I persuaded myself to pay an extra $3 and stay at the **Thai Foh Inn** ((085) 418395, at Nº19. This is fine if you arrive late and plan to leave early. Nearby at 7 Kingsway is the **Sarawak Lodging House** ((085) 413233, often full but with clean rooms at $14. There is also a money changer here, open long after the banks have closed.

WHERE TO EAT

If you want to eat at a luxury hotel, try the **Holiday Inn** or **Rihga Royal**; both have Chinese restaurants, while Rihga Royal also offers Japanese cuisine. Western food is available in their coffeeshops. Near the Gloria Hotel the **Café de Hamburg** serves a set dinner for $10 but two people could eat à la carte for $20, not including wine. Next to the Tropical Adventure office, on Jalan Maju, there is an Islamic café serving Indian Muslim food and around the corner near the Bank Simpanan National there is the **Restoran Jashimah** with a similar menu. For a good Chinese breakfast of *mien* noodles or *laksa* (rice-noodle soup) try the **Toto Café** opposite the Kentucky Fried Chicken outlet. A breakfast and coffee will cost only RM3 to 4. The **Maxim**, on South Yu Seng Road, is very

good indeed, serving tasty curries and Chinese dishes at reasonable prices. Many locals consider it the best restaurant in town. **Tanjong Seaview Restaurant**, opposite the Holiday Inn, has excellent seafood and is a pleasant place to eat at night. Delicious Malay food is available at **Taman Seroja**, next to Brooke Inn in Jalan Brooke.

NIAH NATIONAL PARK

This park is most famous for its caves in which, some 40 years ago, archaeologists found a treasure-trove of human and cultural remains which were thought to indicate that the caves were inhabited some 40,000 years ago. Later research, however, tends to re-date the cave dwelling to about 25,000 years ago. The excavations have come to an end and all the finds, save one, have been removed to the Sarawak Museum in Kuching. What they couldn't remove from the caves were the hematite rock paintings of coffin ships and skirted dancing figures in what is called the Painted Cave. These are believed to date back a thousand years and although they have faded the shapes are quite distinguishable.

Speleologically speaking, the caves themselves cannot be compared with the splendor of the Mulu Caves although the Great Cave is impressive. But apart from the wall paintings there is another reason for visiting the caves; the present-day humans who daily risk their lives to earn a living collecting birds' nests from every available nook and cranny. They balance themselves on bamboo crossbars 60 m (200 ft) above the ground, no safety nets here, and dislodge the nests with 10-m (30 ft) poles with torch lights attached to their ends. The nests contain solidified bird saliva which is highly regarded by the Chinese as a medicinal cure-all. The collectors will sell the nests for $225 to $1,400 per kilo ($100 to $636 per pound). Make no mistake, this is fatally dangerous work and over a recent three-year period over 40 collectors are said to have fallen to their death. The collecting of the nests is supposed to be limited to certain times of the year but owing to over-exploitation, the National Parks put a total ban

OPPOSOITE TOP: Reaching Niah caves is half the fun. BOTTOM: A detail of the prehistoric cave paintings to be seen at Niah.

on collecting in 1996. New agreements with the harvesters were signed and harvesting was permitted to recommence with strict control enforced in mid-1997. As well as giving way to the nest collectors as you walk along the three-kilometer (two mile) walkway to the cave entrance, you are also likely to encounter locals carrying huge bags of guano on their backs. Guano is bat and bird excrement which is sold as a rich fertilizer particularly popular with pepper farmers.

Where to Stay

The National Park has its own accommodation center at the entrance to the park with chalets costing $48 a night and a room for half that. Cooking facilities are provided so you can bring own supplies if you don't want to eat at the canteen. If you go during the week during local school term time, there will always be room available. At weekends it is best to make a booking at the Miri tourism information center or through the Miri office of **National Parks** ((085) 434184, or from Kuching ((082) 248088. In Kampung Niah, where the buses stop, there are three unimpressive hotels. The **Yung Hua Hotel** ((085) 737736, is the best at $13 or an air-conditioned double room. I am not sure why you would stay in town rather than at the park headquarters, because the town has nothing to recommend it. There is a supermarket in Kampung Niah where you could buy food and drink if you wish to do your own catering at the Park.

Getting There

The Niah National Park is located some 120 km (75 miles) and around two hours southwest of Miri and it is easy to board a bus from Miri that will take you to Kampung Niah. From there it is a RM10 boat ride or a 10–15 minute walk to the park entrance. The problem is that the last bus back to Miri leaves town at 1 PM and that turns a one-day trip into a mad rush as it is a good 30-minute walk from the Park Headquarters to the cave entrance. However you have the option of staying a night at the park or hiring a taxi for your return journey. From Miri a taxi will cost $7 straight to the Park entrance but for the return journey you need to ask the park office to phone for a taxi. Alternatively, you

can walk or take the boat service back to Niah town where there are plenty of taxis. Be warned that the taxis try to charge as much as double the normal price if you're going back to Miri late in the day — it's what's known as a seller's market.

Another alternative is to take a tour from one of the Miri tour operators. This makes sense if you only have one day, but if you have time to stay overnight then a tour trip is not necessary. If you are going on your own, do bring a torch with you. The caves are dark and the torch will help you see the tiny figures of the nest collectors perilously perched above you. It is also possible to take a bus from Bintulu to Niah; a taxi for the three-hour journey costs around $10 per person.

MULU NATIONAL PARK

The Niah Caves are world famous and yet, archaeology apart, they pale in comparison to the **Gunung Mulu Caves**. Indeed, if time is at a premium I would suggest jettisoning plans to spend a day or two at Niah and devote the time to Mulu instead.

Physically the caves are stupendous. **Sarawak Chamber**, the world's largest natural cave chamber, is capable of holding forty 747 jumbo jets lined nose to tail. **Gunung Mulu** itself, only 2,376 m (7,795 ft), is, like the rest of the park, a naturalist's paradise, although it was first climbed only in 1932 and the National Park opened only in 1985. In the park may be found 170 different orchids, 10 different pitcher plants and 262 species of

birds including all eight types of hornbills found in Borneo.

Beyond the Park Headquarters, the Melinau River appears to stop at the face of limestone cliffs. The river, in fact, flows underground through the cave system, exiting from **Clearwater Cave**. Over 60 km (37 miles) in length, only a small part of the cave network is open to visitors as yet, but this is enough to make the trip worthwhile, especially if you have a knowledgeable guide. There are four "show" caves open to the public, all with good boardwalks and adequate lighting. Deer Cave is two kilometers (one-and-a-quarter miles) in length and less

Visitors to the Deer Cave will be amazed by the multitudes of bats that fly out of it at dusk.

than 100 m (328 ft) high. Next to this is the beautiful **Lang's Cave**, with intricate stalactites and stalagmites. Both of these two caves are open in the afternoon only, and after viewing them, wait near the entrance of Deer Cave to catch the wonderful sight of thousands and thousands of bats spiralling out at dusk on their hunting expeditions. **Wind Cave** is named after the cool breeze which always flows through the cave. Visit here in the morning and then follow the cliff-hugging boardwalk to the impressive Clearwater Cave. Most tour operators arrange for a picnic lunch in the pavilions set at the side of the unbelievably clear river which flows out of the cave; be sure to bring your swimming gear so you can swim among the clearly visible fish.

If you are interested in **adventure caving**, make this clear well in advance with your tour operator; although some of the park guides are specialized cavers, caving helmets and other equipment are rarely available through the National Parks. An excellent passage taking about five hours underground can be done from Wind Cave through to Clearwater Cave, the last part wading through the icy waters of the Clearwater River.

Where to Stay

If you are part of an organized trip, the tour company will have arranged accommodation for you. Many operators maintain private resthouses just outside the boundaries of the park. However, if you're looking for luxury, stay at the attractively designed **Royal Mulu Resort**, which you can book via your tour operator or through the Rihga Royal Hotel in Miri ((085) 421122 FAX (085) 421088. If you are managing your own way there, you must make arrangements at the National Park Office in Miri to stay in one of their resthouses. Bottled gas cookers are available but you need to bring your own food unless you want to eat in the park's canteen. Don't forget to bring a good torch.

Getting There

You must have a permit before arriving at the park; this is obtainable via your tour operator. Alternatively, apply at the new tourism information office in Miri or the **National**

Park Office ((085) 434184, Section Forest Office, 98000 Miri. This is the same office that handles Niah Park.

An alternative, well worth considering, is a package trip through one of the tour operators in Kuching, Miri or Kuala Lumpur. They will arrange all travel from Miri to Mulu, accommodation, food, guiding and park fees; a typical three-day, two-night tour is around $350 per person, more if you wish to stay at the upmarket Royal Mulu Resort.

Getting to Gunung Mulu used to be a real hassle, involving a bus ride from Miri to Kuala Baram, an express boat ride from there to the town of Marudi, another express boat to Long Panai and then a longboat from there into the park. This all-day trip (which gives sad evidence of erosion of the river banks and deforestation) is no longer necessary, as there are four daily flights from Miri to Mulu Airport, just a five-minute drive from the Royal Mulu Lodge and park headquarters. The 25-minute flight usually provides excellent views; you can tell when you're passing over Brunei, as this is the only totally unlogged forest you'll see until you enter the park. If the weather is good and your pilot cooperative, he may fly you over the **Pinnacles**, the stunning grey stone pillars which thrust up through Mulu's forest.

BAREO AND THE KELABIT HIGHLANDS

Bareo, sometimes spelled Bario, is home to a Kelabit community set high on a valley floor in one of the highest inhabited parts of Borneo — the 1,127-m (3,700-ft)-high Kelabit Highlands. While Kelabits are the main inhabitants of Bareo, there are also a number of Muruts as well as semi-nomadic Punan and Penan.

Bareo is different from anywhere else in Sarawak. It is flat and cool and the paddy fields of this agricultural community are spread out in a way that is more reminiscent of Bali than Borneo. The land is especially rich and Bareo has maintained its reputation for producing the best rice in the country. In

TOP: All manner of people, goods and animals pass through Bareo airstrip in a day. BOTTOM: These express boats hurtle through the water dodging log barges, river debris — and each other.

the morning, before the daily MAS flight arrives, you will see sacks of the rice piled up next to the airfield waiting to be taken down to Lawas and Miri. Vegetables and fruit are also grown for the Miri market, and in the past, salt was a valuable produce because of the salt springs in the region. Salt is still collected and an hour's walk to the main salt spring is one way of spending a morning around here. Bareo is very much a self-sufficient community and villagers still organize hunting trips into the forest for fresh meat. In the morning, groups of Penan hunt-

ers, tattooed and easily recognizable by their basin haircuts and loincloths, bring in wild boar meat to sell. If you stay here and have a meal you can be sure of the most organic ingredients because the farmers use no chemical fertilizers or sprays, and the meat will be fresh from the jungle.

If you do come to Bareo, and I highly recommend it, do try to plan for it by bringing with you a copy of Tom Harrison's *The World Within*. Toward the end of the Second World War, Tom Harrison and seven other men were dropped in here by the Australian air force, their mission being to organize local resistance to the Japanese. Harrison was intensely interested in the culture of the Kelabits and his book is a unique mixture of

military memoirs and anthropology. He was able to observe and study the Kelabits before their whole lifestyle was transformed by the Christian missionaries who felt obliged to disapprove of so many of their traditions, beliefs and practices. Harrison lived in Bareo for some time (the airfield you land on was built by his team) and was deeply respected by the people. I witnessed this myself when visiting a longhouse near the salt spring, for pinned to the wall was an old black-and-white photograph of Harrison, next to a color print of the Blessed Virgin. The Kelabits are now nearly all Christians, although some of the older folk still have stretched earlobes and tattoos.

Another noticeable feature about Bareo is the presence of the Malaysian army. They have a camp on the other side of the airfield and the odd group of soldiers moving around, with and without their weapons, is a common enough sight. This goes back to the early 1960s when Indonesia was vigorously pursuing its claim to Sarawak, and British and Gurkha troops were stationed in the Highlands. This threat is now a thing of the past and the soldiers are basically acting as border guards, although one wonders if the army is more concerned with the protest movement against the logging of the forests. A fascinating book is available, *The Battle for Sarawak's Forests*, that records in words and pictures the struggle of the native people who depend on the forest for their food and shelter.

WHAT TO SEE

First and foremost Bareo is a place to unwind and relax, taking strolls around the countryside and observing the way of life of the farmer villagers. There are a number of treks available. A three-hour trek takes you to **Pa'Berang**, a Penan settlement where accommodation could be arranged at a longhouse. Walking to the salt spring has already been mentioned and this trek could take in the Batu Narit rock carving at **Pa'Umor**. **Pa Lungan** is another interesting four-hour trip. Nearby hills can be climbed without too much effort and they afford terrific views of the countryside around Bareo.

The longer treks offer fascinating possibilities. Two days would bring you to the Indonesian border with Kalimantan. Officially, non-Malaysians are not permitted to enter Indonesia here without a visa, but the reality is that if you offer the Indonesian immigration officials some "coffee money" you will be permitted to cross into **Long Bawan**, home of the Lun Bawang tribe. A night could be spent in there before returning to Malaysia. From Bareo you could also set out to climb **Gunung Murud**, 2,422 m (7,946 ft), first climbed in 1922 by Mjoberg with a team of 70 porters. This would take about a week, as would the return trip to Batu Lawi, 2,043 m (6,703 ft), not a climb for the inexperienced. Full details, again, in the Briggs book. What is within anyone's capabilities, though it might sound audacious, is to organize a four-day trip into Pa Tik and spend the time with the semi-nomadic Penan people. All you would need to bring with you is a spirit of adventure and cans of food and dried soup. Many travelers like to fly from Miri directly to the lovely village of **Ba Kelalan**, in the south of the Kelabit Highlands. The airport is an all-weather one (Bareo airport is often closed by bad weather) and there is more untouched forest in the environs.

Reliable guides for any of the treks just mentioned can be arranged through the tour companies in Miri or directly through Peter Matu (Kelabit Highlands, 98050 Baram, Bareo, East Malaysia) in Bareo. Guides cost about $15 a day and accommodation would be in longhouses along the way. Not just an adventure but an education too. John Terawes, owner of the resthouse in Bareo, can also arrange trips and guides.

WHERE TO STAY

In Bareo itself there is only one official resthouse, the **Bareo Airtel Lodge**, just next to the airstrip. A three-bed, room is $6 regardless of the number of people using it and meals are available at $2. The visitors' book makes for interesting reading and could give you a few ideas on how to spend your time. Many travelers prefer to stay at the lodge run by John and Karen Terawes. At the actual airstrip there is a coffeeshop serving drinks and simple food. All other accommodation will be at longhouses, either Kelabit or Penan, and you should think of paying $5–8 a night for your lodging and breakfast. In Ba Kelalan, the **Green Valley Inn** is the popular place to stay.

GETTING THERE

Getting there is indeed half the fun. Bareo is only accessible by air on the rural service offered by Malaysia Airlines. Twin Otters fly in daily from Miri and from Lawas in northern Sarawak, just south of Sabah, returning the same day. The flight from Miri takes 40 minutes, and for the first half of the journey all you will see, trickling through the forest canopy below, is a network of pathways created by the logging companies for their lorries as they systematically cut down the trees.

Until the new all-weather Bareo airstrip is completed, there can be a problem with the existing airstrip which prohibits landing if there is low cloud or continuous rain. Flights can be canceled and the 19-seater Twin Otter can easily fill up. So make reservations as far in advance as possible. I was once caught in Bareo this way, and there were two alternatives: trek for two full days to Ba Kelalan where the daily flights to Miri are rarely canceled, or negotiate a place with one of the private air charter companies that fly produce in and out of Bareo. They charged me the same rate as MAS.

Permits are required for any visit to Bareo and the Highlands and these are available from the Resident's Office in Miri.

OPPOSITE: One of the most tranquil and pristine areas of Malaysia, the Mulu National Park is a wonderhouse of natural beauty.

Sabah

LAND BELOW THE WIND

Sabah, which occupies the northern tip of Borneo, is the second largest state in Malaysia after neighboring Sarawak. Known to bygone sailors as the "Land Below the Wind", Sabah it is just south of the destructive path cut by typhoons sweeping through the Philippines each year. With a coastline of almost 1,500 km (940 miles), coral-fringed islands, rugged mountains culminating in **Mount Kinabalu** — at 4,101 m (13,455 ft), the highest peak between the Himalayas and New Guinea — and rainforests rich in flora and fauna, Sabah is the perfect place for the nature lover and for the adventurous.

For those interested in wildlife, there's nowhere better in all Malaysia than Sabah's East Coast, where wildlife experiences are virtually guaranteed. Top of most visitor's list is the orangutan sanctuary at **Sepilok** near Sandakan; there's also the **Turtle Islands Park**, where marine turtles come ashore to lay their eggs, and a huge rainforest conservation area with the international-standard Borneo Rainforest Lodge at **Danum Valley**. The unique proboscis monkey, magnificent birds and other wildlife are found near **Sukau** on the Kinabatang river, while the marine life and coral reefs at **Pulau Sipadan** are internationally renowned among scuba divers.

Unfortunately, accommodation, car hire and taxis invariably cost more in Sabah than elsewhere in Malaysia, and because of the rugged nature of the land, it is preferable to travel to the East Coast by plane rather than road. However, Sabah offers many unique experiences which make any visit well worth the expense.

BACKGROUND

Sabah was nominally under the control of the Sultan of Brunei until colonial expansion led to the bizarre situation of the land being leased to an American, who later sold his rights to a British business consortium which set up the British North Borneo Chartered Company in 1881.

The Sultan of Sulu (in the southern Philippines) traded with settlements on Sabah's East Coast around Sandakan for centuries, and held considerable influence over the region. When Malaysia was established in 1963, Sabah and neighboring Sarawak both joined the Federation on the condition that they retain a certain number of privileges, including control over immigration. The Philippines and Indonesia initially objected to the inclusion of Sabah in the Federation, but are now cooperating within a newly established trade region, BIMP-EAGA, which includes Sabah, Sarawak, Brunei, Kalimantan and the southern Philippines.

Sabah's population of around 1.7 million is made up of over 30 different ethnic communities, the largest being the Kadazan/Dusun group. Although the majority of the indigenous people are Christian, the coastal Bajau, Suluk, Illanun and other groups who originally came from the Philippines are Muslim. Adding to Sabah's cultural potpourri are Chinese and Indonesians who migrated during the nineteenth and early twentieth century, frequently intermarrying with the indigenous people.

OPPOSITE TOP and BOTTOM: Giant rainforest trees form a dense cover on the slopes of Mount Kinabalu. ABOVE: An orangutan, released from captivity, learns jungle survival techniques from a ranger at Sepilok Orangutan Sanctuary.

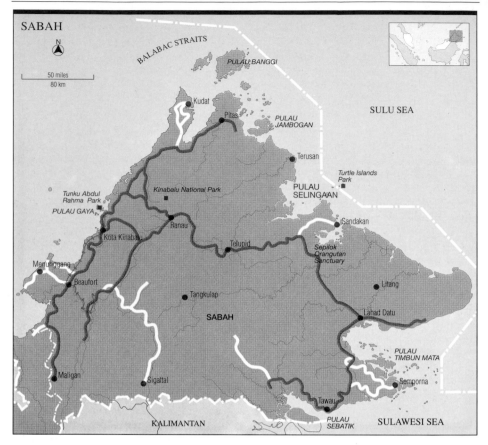

The large number of illegal immigrants from the Philippines and Indonesia who have flooded in Sabah since the 1970s poses considerable social problems for the state which are yet to be resolved.

KOTA KINABALU

Sabah's capital, Kota Kinabalu, is located on the west coast. There are excellent international air links with Hong Kong, Taiwan, Japan, Korea, the Philippines and Singapore, as well as a large number of regional flights to Brunei, Sarawak, Kalimantan and Peninsular Malaysia.

Kota Kinabalu is an ideal base for exploration of the west coast, for day trips to Kinabalu Park and some of the attractions of the Interior, the region just across the rugged Crocker Range. White-water rafting, scuba diving, mountain biking and exploration of nearby stilt villages can all be done from Kota Kinabalu.

GENERAL INFORMATION

Sabah Tourism Promotion Corporation ((088) 219310 maintains an office near the arrival halls at the airport; their main office is in a lovely white restored colonial building at 51 Gaya Street. Service is very friendly and information on accommodation, transport, festivals etc. available.

Bookings for accommodation at **Kinabalu Park** should be made in advance at Sabah Parks ((088) 211881, Jalan Tun Fuad Stephens, opposite the ramshackle collection of stalls known as the Filipino market and nearby the huge Central Market. Advance reservations are strongly recommended in February, April, July, August and December. Write to PO Box 10626, 88806 Kota Kinabalu, Sabah, Malaysia.

Specialized tour operators include **Borneo Adventure** ((088) 238731, for personalized culture, nature and adventure tours in both Sabah and Sarawak; **Borneo**

Divers ((088) 222226, for scuba training, diving trips to Pulau Sipadan and diving around Kota Kinabalu; **Borneo Eco Tours** ((088) 234009, for tours focusing on Sabah's natural environment; **Borneo Expeditions** ((088) for white-water rafting, kayaking and mountain biking and **Wildlife Expeditions** ((088) 24600, for visits to Sepilok, Turtle Islands and Danum Valley.

Long-distance taxis which can be shared or chartered are a comfortable way to travel on the west coast and to Tenom. Minibuses are a quick and inexpensive way to reach Kinabalu Park, while an alternative to flying to Sandakan is to take an air-conditioned bus. All these forms of transport depart from near the town *Padang* or green (anyone will be able to tell you where this is).

WHAT TO SEE

Kota Kinabalu is perfectly located at the edge of a bay, with a backdrop of mountains and a scattering of islands nearby. Unfortunately, the town was totally destroyed by bombing at the end of the Second World War and rebuilt with little concern for aesthetics. The current flurry of new construction is doing little to improve the appearance of Kota Kinabalu, which holds few attractions for the visitor apart from the lively **Central Market** and the souvenirs available at the **Filipino Market** (take care of your belongings and be sure to bargain).

It's worth making a visit to the **Sabah State Museum** (closed Friday), primarily to look at the life-sized traditional houses on the hillside near the carpark. The museum is a RM5 taxi ride from downtown or from Tanjung Aru.

For a good range of books on Borneo, try Borneo Craft on the ground floor of **Wisma Merdeka**, in Jalan Tun Razak in the heart of downtown Kota Kinabalu. This shopping complex, like the newer **Centrepoint** (which has a branch of the Yaohan departmental stores), offers a wide range of shops with souvenirs, photographic equipment, money changers and restaurants.

The five islands making up the **Tunku Abdul Rahman Park** are everyone's dream of a tropical island: exquisite warm clear waters, white sandy beaches backed by shade trees and trails over the forest-covered hills. The islands can be reached in about 20 minutes by speedboat from the waterfront near the Hyatt Hotel; bargain and pay only on the return trip if you decide to spend a few hours on an island. The price is as little as RM10 per head to most islands, though around twice that to the more remote Police Beach, an idyllic spot (except during the northeast monsoon, from December through March) on Pulau Gaya. Tour operators organize barbecue lunches at Pulau Sapi, which is becoming rather

crowded. Pack your own picnic lunch and go to pretty little Pulau Mamutik instead. If you want to stay overnight on a tropical island, book one of the chalets on Pulau Manukan, which has a restaurant, swimming pool and other facilities, at Sabah Parks.

If you're interested in seeing a traditional Bajau fishing village perched on stilts above the water, ask your tour operator to arrange a visit to **Kampung Penambawan**, reached via Surusup just north of Tuaran. Don't let them take you to ghastly Mengkabong, which is closer to Kota Kinabalu.

Houses built on stilts teeter precariously over the sea at Pulau Gaya.

WHERE TO STAY

The top hotel is the luxurious Shangri-La's **Tanjung Aru Resort** ((088) 225800 FAX (088) 217155, mid-way between the airport and downtown Kota Kinabalu. The wide range of activities, especially sea sports, make this a firm favorite. Room prices currently begin at $136. A sister hotel, Shangri-La's **Rasa Ria Resort** ((088) 792888 FAX (088) 792000, is located about 45 minutes from the airport on its own private beach at Pantai Dalit and

offers an 18-hole golf course as well as countless other activities. Rates are slightly less than those at Tanjung Aru.

The **Promenade Hotel** ((088) 265555 FAX (088) 246666, with rooms from around $110, is the first of the new-wave quality hotels in downtown Kota Kinabalu, offering an attractive alternative to the **Hyatt Kinabalu Hotel** ((088) 219888 FAX (088) 225972, which suffers from a rather insalubrious location. The Renaissance and the Pan Pacific will be managing new five-star hotels due to open by early 1998 and with increased competition, prices are all major hotels should be negotiable. Businessmen often opt for the "small is beautiful" boutique hotel, The **Jesselton** ((088) 223333 FAX (088) 240401, at the edge of Kota Kinabalu's banking and commercial district. Prices from $100.

Moderate

Moderately priced hotels ($60–80) include the **Berjaya Palace Hotel** ((088) 211911 FAX (088) 211600 and the **Hotel Shangri-la** ((088) 0212800 FAX (088) 212078, both on the

edge of town. The cheaper **Hotel Holiday** ($32) ((088) 213116 FAX (088) 215576, is opposite the main Post Office.

Inexpensive

The fan-cooled **Backpacker Lodge** ((088) 261494, is near the old central Police Station and costs $7. Families invariably enjoy the unpretentious, friendly **Seaside Travellers Inn** ((088) 750555 FAX (088) 223399, on Kinarut Beach about 20 minutes south of Kota Kinabalu. Rates from $8 for a dormitory bed to $40 for a comfortable double room, including breakfast.

WHERE TO EAT

Although hotel restaurants offer a selection of local and Western food, it's worth trying some of the many restaurants in town. Seafood is good and inexpensive by international standards. Expect to pay around $15-20 per head for a lavish meal at **Port View** ((088) 221753, very popular with tour groups at night; locals generally prefer the slightly cheaper **Ocean Seafood**, a casual open-air restaurant in the Asia City complex, or **Beach Seafood** stalls set up at Tanjung Aru Beach, just five minutes' walk from Shangri-La's Tanjung Aru Resort, where a meal is in the region of $4–8 per person.

Excellent and inexpensive Northern Indian food is available at **Rana Sahib's**, in Asia City (around $12 for two excluding drinks). Opposite, in Api Api complex (near Centrepoint), **Tam Nak Thai** offers Thai cuisine (expect to pay $25–30 for two). The best place to go Japanese is **Azuma**, on the 2nd floor of Wisma Merdeka; like all Japanese restaurants, it is not cheap.

Moderately priced local and Western favorites can be enjoyed at the comfortable **Wishbone Café**, on the ground floor of the Jesselton, just 50 m (164 ft) from the Sabah Tourism Promotion Corporation office. Inside the same building is the more expensive **Gardenia** restaurant, offering very ordinary Continental cuisine and prime rib roast at the weekends.

The basement of **Centrepoint** complex offers a wide range of inexpensive local food (as little as RM3 or a bit more than $1 for a plate of *nasi campur*, rice with meat, fish and vegetables) as well as international fast food. Not far from Centrepoint, in Block 2 of Api Api Centre, **Bon Appétit** offers a mixture of Western and local food at affordable prices. If you have to go to the Malaysia Airlines office in Kompleks Karamunsing, look for **Bistretto** where moderately priced Western food, ice creams and pancakes are available.

GETTING THERE

Malaysia Airlines ((088) 213555, has direct flights from Kuala Lumpur and Johor Bahru in Peninsular Malaysia, as well as flights from Kuching, Bintulu, Sibu and Miri in Sarawak, and from Brunei. **Transmile** ((03) 243022, and **AirAsia** ((03)202-7777 or ((088) 257100 offer tickets from Kuala Lumpur to Kota Kinabalu for less than MAS. If departing Singapore for Sabah, it's much cheaper to leave from Johor Bahru than Singapore's Changi Airport; check with MAS when booking your ticket and arrange to take the bus departing Singapore's Novotel Orchid Inn for the Johor Bahru airport.

International flights link Kota Kinabalu with Davao, Hong Kong, Kaoshiung, Taipeh, Tokyo, Seoul, Singapore Manila and Brunei. As competitively priced Royal Brunei continues to increase its international airlinks and positions Brunei as the regional air hub, it is worth considering flying directly to Brunei and transferring to a flight to Kota Kinabalu.

On arrival at Kota Kinabalu Airport, purchase a taxi coupon to ensure you don't pay more than the normal price for the ride to your hotel. Check the Sabah Tourism office if you need information; several hotels also maintain information booths at the airport. The airport is about 10 minutes (and a $5-ride) from the centre of town.

BEAUFORT AND TENOM

Borneo's only railway line runs from Kota Kinabalu to the interior town of Tenom. Forget the first stage of the journey from Kota Kinabalu to Beaufort (it involves a very slow old train which goes along an uninteresting route), but do consider taking the charming little railcar which hurtles along the **Padas Gorge** between Beaufort (reached by mini-

bus for only RM5) and Tenom. There's not much of compelling interest in Beaufort itself; most visitors come en route for a day's **white-water rafting** on the Padas River. Book with a tour operator, who will organize bus transfers to Beaufort, the railcar ride upriver and the exciting ride down through the rapids to a resthouse where showers, cool drinks and a barbecue await.

An interesting round trip can be made by road from Kota Kinabalu across the forest-covered mountains of the Crocker Range via Tambunan to Tenom, returning after an over-

night stay via railcar to Beaufort, and then taking a minibus to Kota Kinabalu. Just across the top of the Crocker Range, the **Rafflesia Information Centre** offers information on the world's largest flower and advises where any flowers might be blooming within the Reserve, which is set in beautiful lower montane rainforest. **Tambunan** is an attractive rice-growing area, home to the indigenous Dusun people. From here it's less than a couple of hours to **Tenom**, set in a fertile valley. The main attraction here is the **Sabah Agricultural Park**, a recreational and educational facility which should be fully opened

OPPOSITE: Following fashion, a Muslim elder favors sports a dyed beard. ABOVE: Boy in traditional Malay costume, east Malaysia.

by 1999. The nucleus of the Park is the **Orchid Centre**, established in 1981, which houses Borneo's biggest collection of native orchids, and the fascinating **Crop Museum**; both these are within the Agricultural Research Station about 17 km (11 miles) from Tenom.

WHERE TO STAY

Stay overnight in Tenom at the three-star **Hotel Perkasa** ((087) 737952, perched on a hilltop. Rooms are from $30 and they'll pick you up from the train station if you call. A cheaper alternative is the **Antanom Hotel** ((087) 736381, in the main street, where doubles go for around $15–18. **Chi Hin** coffeeshop in town has excellent freshwater fish and other Chinese cuisine at night.

KUDAT

Sabah's most traditional people, the Rungus, still live in their distinctive communal longhouses in the Kudat district just three hours north of Kota Kinabalu. A couple of wood and thatch longhouses built in traditional style but with added amenities for tourists (such as mattresses, mosquitoes nets and proper toilet and showering facilities) are found in **Kampung Bavanggazo**. Spend a night in the longhouse, enjoying the local rice wine with dinner and watch a cultural performance, then visit some of the interesting villages located in this region and have a swim at a stunning deserted beach such as **Terongkongan**. Best organize this trip with a tour operator, especially if you don't speak Malay.

KINABALU PARK

Kinabalu Park's vast terrain (754 sq km or 287 sq miles) ranges from lower montane forest up to alpine vegetation. It is reputed to have the greatest range of plants of any park in the world, including 1,200 species of orchid, insect-eating pitcher plants, rhododendrons and the world's largest flower, the evil-smelling Rafflesia, whose blooms can grow up to one meter in diameter.

Many visitors go to Kinabalu Park on a day trip, enjoying some of the easy trails around **Park Headquarters** (at 1,500 m or

5,000 ft) and visiting the interesting **Mountain Garden**. It's worth traveling another hour to **Poring Hot Springs**, on the eastern side of Kinabalu Park (but never on a Sunday, when it's too crowded), where there's a canopy walkway above the rainforest, a butterfly park, hot sulfur baths and a cool freshwater pool.

WHERE TO STAY

The beautiful environment within the **Kinabalu Park** makes it the ideal place to

stay. Top of the range are the two-bedroom Nepenthes Chalets ($100 per night); like other chalets here, these have kitchens and fireplaces. There's something to suit all budgets within the Park, from twin-bed cabins to rooms in the Administration Building and hostels, the latter costing only $4 per bed. Two restaurants are located within the Park. Book in advance at Sabah Park's Kota Kinabalu office, especially during weekends and in February, April, July, August and December.

About 10 minutes away from Park Headquarters, in the vegetable-growing district of Kundasang, there are a number of hotels, few of them worth even considering. **Kinabalu Pine Resort** ((088) 889388, with 16 chalets, is currently one of the exceptions. Chalets cost $95 and sleep six. There is also the moderately priced **Hotel Perkasa** ((088) 889511, with a good view of the mountain; rooms from $40.

WHERE TO EAT

The **Kinabalu Balsam Restaurant** just inside the entrance to Park Headquarters is recommended at lunchtime, especially if you don't want to get ignored in favor of the tour groups who congregate at the Mount Kinabalu

get fit in advance. Be sure to bring a warm jacket (the temperature can drop below freezing), a waterproof jacket or poncho, gloves for using on the ropes on the summit plateau and a torch. Water is available at rest stops on the way to Panar Laban, but buy a bottle of mineral water at Laban Rata Resthouse for the climb beyond here. Headache tablets help with the headaches often caused by the altitude.

The eight-kilometer (five-mile) trail to the summit begins at Timpohon Gate, near the Power Station reached by road from Park

Restaurant within the Administration Building further down hill. At Poring Hot Springs, there is a pleasant restaurant located near the baths. Those climbing to the summit of Mount Kinabalu can bring their own food or eat at the restaurant at Laban Rata Resthouse. It's a good idea to stock up on snacks such as biscuits and chocolates at the store inside Kinabalu Balsam Restaurant; supplies at Laban Rata can be unreliable.

CLIMBING MOUNT KINABALU

No mountaineering experience is needed to reach the summit of 4,101 m (13,455 ft) Mount Kinabalu, but the ascent is demanding on the legs, heart and lungs so it helps to

Headquarters. From here (altitude 1,830 m or 6,000 ft), the well-maintained trail leads relentlessly up through beautiful lower montane forest with oaks, beeches and rhododendrons, on through bamboos, tree ferns and mossy cloud forest to the region where pitcher plants are found. At around 3,000 m, (10,000 ft) the vegetation becomes stunted and the plants (including ground orchids) cling tenaciously to tiny pockets of soil.

At Panar Laban (altitude 3,300 m or 10,800 ft) there are a couple of basic moun-

OPPOSITE: Porters carry the night's food up to the resthouse on Mount Kinabalu. ABOVE: The view from St. John's peak, best seen at dawn when the sun rises on a landscape of wind whipped rock.

tain huts as well as the Laban Rata Resthouse and the Gunting Lagadan Hostel, all crouching on the rocks just below the granite wall where the trail leads on up towards the summit. It's possible to rent sleeping bags for the huts and hostel; the heated resthouse has everything provided, including a restaurant (those staying in the huts and hostel can also eat here if they don't want to cook their own food).

There are seven rest stops with shelters, toilets and water en route from the start of the trail up to Panar Laban, where most visi-

literally breathtaking view, wave after wave of mountains rolling away at your feet as you gaze out over north Borneo and across to the South China Sea.

GETTING THERE

Minibuses (RM10) start leaving the Padang for Ranau around 7 AM; if you can, travel early in the day when it's cooler. The trip takes under two hours, and the driver will let you off at the Park entrance, 19 km (12 miles) before Ranau. Alternatively, a taxi

tors spend the evening. The normal pattern is to get up at some ungodly hour the following morning to struggle through the dark, following the ropes leading up a granite face and on to the summit. The often icy wind ensures that by the time dawn arrives, climbers awaiting the sunrise are freezing cold and the tiny summit peak crowded. It's much better to leave Panar Laban at 5 AM, scaling the granite face around dawn when you can see what you're doing, arriving at the summit after the crowds have left. The often spectacular sunrise looks just as good a few hundred meters down the mountain.

No matter how you time it, if you are lucky with the weather you'll be rewarded with a

can be chartered for around $80 for a day trip to Park Headquarters and on to Poring Hot Springs. This gives you the flexibility to stop anywhere to take photos and to explore the interesting market at Nabalu, about 20 minutes before the Park. Tour operators offer package trips including lunch.

SANDAKAN

BACKGROUND

Sandakan, located on a huge bay on Sabah's East Coast, was the capital of North Borneo until 1946, when it was shifted to Kota Kinabalu (then Jesselton) owing to the total destruction of Sandakan during the final days of the Second World War. During the heyday of logging, in the 1960s and 1970s, Sandakan was reputed to have more millionaires than any other city in the world. Oil palm plantations have largely replaced the logging industry, and Sandakan seems somewhat of a backwater these days. In terms of tourism, however, Sandakan is uniquely poised with the **Turtle Islands Marine Park**, **Sepilok Orang-Utan Rehabilitation Centre**, **Gomantang** bird's nest caves and **Kinabatangan** region with its

one of the Turtle Islands, and some tour operators have already built private accommodation on islands just outside the Park.

Best known tour operator for the East Coast is **Wildlife Expeditions**, located in Sandakan Renaissance Hotel ((089) 219616 as well as in Kota Kinabalu on the ground floor of Shangri-La's Tanjung Aru Resort ((088) 246000. Alternatively, try **SI Tours** ((089) 213503 or (010) 826631. Both maintain lodges at Sukau on the Kinabatangan for viewing proboscis monkeys, as do another three Kota Kinabalu-based tour companies.

proboscis monkeys and rich birdlife all less than a couple of hours away.

GENERAL INFORMATION

Most travelers opt to fly in and out of Sandakan from Kota Kinabalu. The Malaysia Airlines office can be contacted on ((089) 273962. Independent travelers wishing to arrange for transport and an overnight stay at Turtle Islands must either write in advance to **East Coast Parks**, PO Box 768, Sandakan, or go to the **Regional Office East Coast Parks** ((089) 273453, 9th floor, Wisma Khoo Saik Chew, Jalan Buli Sim Sim, Sandakan. There is talk of closing the accommodation (which holds only a total of 26 persons) on Pulau Selingan,

WHERE TO STAY

Sandakan Renaissance Hotel ((089) 213299 FAX (089) 271271, is a very pleasant four-star hotel complete with swimming pool, Rates from $80. More competitive in terms of price is **Sanbay Hotel** ((089) 275000 FAX (089) 275575, (rooms from $48), a friendly place with small bar/restaurant in Jalan Leila just a short taxi ride from the town centre. If you want to be right downtown, try the **Hotel City View** ((089) 271122 FAX (089) 273115; rooms from

OPPOSITE: Giant insectivorous pitcher plants LEFT abound on the slopes of Mount Kinabalu; the turtle's long crawl ashore RIGHT ends as her eggs are carefully collected. ABOVE: Snorkeling LEFT off the coast of Sandakan, Sabah; a young inhabitant RIGHT of Pulau Gaya.

Sabah

$42. Budget travellers wanting to stay right in town usually opt for **Hung Wing Hotel** ((089) 218855, Jalan Tiga, rooms from $13. **Uncle Tan's Bed & Breakfast** ((089) 531917 FAX (089) 531639, a basic place at Mile 17 ½, Tawau Road (near Sepilok) not only offers cheap accommodation ($8 bed and breakfast) but arranges in-depth tours to Turtle Islands and to their rustic lodge on the Kinabatangan River. Just off the road to the Sepilok Orang-Utan Sanctuary are two places well worth considering in terms of price, beauty of surroundings and proximity to the Orang-Utan

Sanctuary and the Rainforest Interpretation Centre. The **Wildlife Lodge** ((089) 533031 FAX (089) 533029, part of **Sepilok Jungle Resort**, has a wide range of accommodation in an idyllic setting, with prices ranging from RM20 for a bed in a four-bed dormitory, up to RM75 for a double air-conditioned bedroom; prices include breakfast. The smaller **Sepilok B & B** offers clean, fan-cooled rooms plus breakfast for RM25 per person.

For lack of business, almost all hotels in Sandakan will reduce their prices if asked.

WHERE TO EAT

Sandakan's seafood is legendary, and there's nowhere better to eat it during the evening than **Golden Palace**, on the hilltop at Trig Hill with a stunning view of the bay. It's just five-minutes drive from the Renaissance; it's best to take a taxi and ask the driver to wait (around $5 to 6). An alternative seafood place is **Pasir Puteh**, once again a short taxi ride from the center of town. Enjoy Sabah's best value-for-money breakfast at **Fairwood**

Restaurant, on the main street of Jalan Tiga opposite Kentucky Fried Chicken.

Sandakan's oldest restaurant is the unpretentious **Kedai Kopi Sin Cheong Loong** in Jalan Tiga opposite Hock Hua Bank; highly regarded chicken rice and steamed fish, which are available for lunch only.

SEPILOK ORANG-UTAN REHABILITATION CENTRE

Now an endangered species because of the destruction of its natural habitat, orangutan captured in logging camps or kept illegally as pets are brought to the sanctuary for rehabilitation. Since its foundation in 1964, over 100 apes have been released back into the forest.

A visit to the sanctuary is a memorable experience and quite different from viewing them in a zoo. Adult males weigh up to 100 kg (220 lb), stand about a meter (just over three feet) tall, and despite their dangling arms they bear an uncanny resemblance to humans. Their faces display personality and there are many stories of their gentle and playful ways. Many female orangutan who have spent some time at the center return to the sanctuary from the forest when about to give birth.

The sanctuary is 30 minutes by car from Sandakan. In town, the best place for taxis, and the occasional bus that goes there, is around the waterfront near the fruit and vegetable market. Package trips can be organized from Kota Kinabalu or in Sandakan. You should plan to visit the sanctuary to catch the feeding sessions at 10 AM or 2:30 PM. There is an interesting information center and a mini-theater where a well-made video on the orangutan is shown after the feeding. The restaurant offers cold drinks and light meals.

RAINFOREST INTERPRETATION CENTRE

A visit to this beautifully laid out center, part of the Forest Research Centre adjacent to the Orang-Utan Rehabilitation Centre, is a must for understanding the rainforest environment. There is an 800-m (half-a-mile) trail walk around a lake, with many of the plants identified, and a small but well laid out information centre which covers all aspects of the rainforest. The display of various forms of seeds, the samples of different types of wood found in Sabah's forests and the feature showing traditional usages of forest plants are particularly interesting. The center is open from 8:15 AM to 12:15 PM, 2 PM to 4 PM Monday to Thursday; 8:15 AM to 11:35 AM and 2 PM to 4 PM Friday; 8:15 AM to 12:15 PM Saturday.

TURTLE ISLANDS PARK

The park is made up of three islands located some 40 km (25 miles) north of Sandakan and close to the Philippines, whose islands can

the return trip. If you are lucky, a boat will be going anyway, and an extra place can be arranged for around $40. A package trip, arranged in Kota Kinabalu or Sandakan, reflects this level of pricing. The only consolation is that perhaps the price of getting there actually helps to keep the turtles relatively undisturbed. The creatures are very sensitive and the slightest noise can cause them to negotiate a cumbersome u-turn on the sand before returning to the sea. It is no surprise that they are fast disappearing from Peninsular Malaysia's East Coast.

be seen in the distance (see TOP SPOTS). A visit to the park is a wonderful experience not just for the opportunity of seeing the turtles lumbering ashore and laying their eggs, but also for the equally magical sight of tiny turtles hatching from the protected eggs and later being released into the sea.

Accommodation is currently available on Pulau Selingan in comfortable chalets for $10 a night, and there is a small restaurant serving meals. These three chalets may be closed in the near future and tour operators are already taking visitors to accommodation on nearby Libaran Island or even returning to Sandakan after the turtle viewing. Reaching the island now takes less than an hour in a 100-hp speedboat, but the price is high for

SUKAU

The swamp forests around Sabah's longest river, the Kinabatangan, are home to a rich variety of birds and some remarkable wildlife, most notably the long-nosed, potbellied proboscis monkey found only in Borneo. Near the village of Sukau (about two hours by road from Sandakan), a tributary of the Kinabatangan, the Menanggol River, is an excellent spot for viewing the monkeys as they crowd the riverside trees in the late afternoon. Tours to Sukau usually pause en route

OPPOSITE: Bajau tribesmen are known for their horse-riding skills. Protected shores ABOVE in the Abdul Rahman National Park.

at the interesting **Gomantong Caves**, where valuable edible birds' nests are harvested twice a year. Several tour operators maintain lodges near Sukau, providing dinner and breakfast, the river tour, overnight accommodation and, if time permits, another early morning river trip before returning to Sandakan. **Wildlife Expeditions (** (088) 246000, offer a two-day/one-night package to Sukau for $230, including return airfare, transportation, food and accommodation, and visits to Gomantong Caves, the Menaggol river and the oxbow lakes off the Kinabatangan.

SI Tours ((089) 213503 in Sandakan and major tour operators in Kota Kinabalu all offer trips to Sukau.

DANUM VALLEY

Reached after a two-hour drive from the town of Lahad Datu (40 minutes by air from Kota Kinabalu), **Borneo Rainforest Lodge** is the perfect base for exploring the rainforest of the huge Danum Valley Conservation Area. This international-standard lodge is an environmentally sensitive and thoroughly delightful place from which one can discover the magnificent flora and fauna of virgin Borneo rainforest. All of Sabah's mammals, including the rare rhinoceros, elephant and orangutan live within this area, as well as some 250 species of birds, including eight varieties of hornbill.

A canopy walkway high above the forest floor offers a superb view of the forest — you may catch sight of a flying lizard going just above your head, or virtually be dive-bombed by hornbills) while night drives

usually reveal nocturnal species. Remember that sightings of mammals are not guaranteed. The rainforest is a totally different environment to the open plains of Africa or the grasslands of southern Nepal. Trail walks reveal the complex environment of rainforest plants and glimpses of birds and other wildlife, and also lead to jungle pools just made for a refreshing swim, and to ancient cave burial sites used by the *Orang Sungei* who once inhabited this region.

Borneo Rainforest Lodge offers return transport from Lahad Datu ($40 per person) plus all food, accommodation and guided tours at $140 per person per day. Guided tours are given in the forest around the lodge and also, if you wish, to the **Danum Field Centre (** (088) 244100 FAX (088) 243244, where research projects are ongoing, as well as to various plots where reforestation is being studied. Call the Centre for bookings.

SIPADAN ISLAND

Sipadan, Malaysia's only oceanic island, is a 12-hectare (30-acre) dot rising up 600 m (2,000 ft) from the floor of the Celebes Sea, reached by boat from the small East Coast town of Semporna. In less than a decade, it has gone from being an isolated gem where one dive operator maintained a few simple huts to become one of the world's top scuba diving locations where lack of government control has resulted in its being over run with both dive lodges and divers. Nonetheless, the dramatic wall dives, varied corals, underwater caves and stunning variety of marine life make Sipadan a must for any scuba diver. Contact the original and still the most professional operator, **Borneo Divers & Sea Sports (** (088) 222226 FAX (088) 221550; they offer dive packages from Kota Kinabalu, which start at S$725 for transport, unlimited diving for three days/two nights.

ABOVE: Putting Borneo on the map, the start of the Borneo Safari. Away from the coast, Sabah's rich topography RIGHT rises gently to the summit of Southeast Asia's highest peak — the 4,101 m (13,454 ft) Mt. Kinabalu.

Singapore

BACKGROUND

The Malay word for this island, comes from the Sanskrit words meaning Lion City. Not that lions ever inhabited Southeast Asia, and when the Englishman Raffles landed here in 1819 the island was home to only a few Malay fisherman. Raffles, however, saw the potential of the deep and well-sheltered harbor, and he pulled a fast one by exploiting a local dispute about ownership of the island. Raffles set up a sultan of Johore who was more than willing to let the East India Company establish a trading post in return for an annual payoff. Immigrants were welcomed and within decades Singapore was a thriving port gaining the kind of reputation that ensured commercial success. Such a reputation has continued up to the present day, as will be immediately noticeable the moment you arrive at the city's airport. The impact is not quite so dramatic if you arrive by train or coach across the causeway from Malaysia, but it won't be long before you notice the difference.

GENERAL INFORMATION

For tourist information, Singapore is one of the most efficient spots in the world. The hotels abound with free leaflets and magazines which carry useful information about the city. *This Week Singapore*, a free guide, is well worth picking up; the Singapore Tourist Promotion Board, the STPB, also publishes the *Official Guide Singapore*, with monthly updates on what's going on. The Singapore Tourist Promotion Board ℂ 1-800-831-3311, has a 24-hour, toll-free line providing tourist information in English, Japanese, German and Mandarin. You can ask for information and advice at the board's two information centers: one is located at Tourist Court ℂ (65) 736-6622, One Orchard Spring Lane, which is next to Trader's Hotel just off Tanglin Road. The other office is at 02-34, Raffles Hotel Arcade, 328 North Bridge Road ℂ (65) 334-1336. The Airport also has many racks of leaflets for you to pick up on your way through, as well as a free hotel booking service. Most of the big hotels have agents handling city tours and short trips to Johor Bahru and the Indonesian islands of Batam

and Bintan. Travel agents are ubiquitous in the Orchard Road area and many maintain desks in the major hotels.

See the TELEPHONES section in TRAVELERS' TIPS for useful Singapore numbers.

WHAT TO SEE

Much of Singapore was built in the last 25 years. However, a few places of interest have survived the ravages of modernization and more recently places in the last stages of decay have been saved due to conservation

efforts. Nearly all the districts mentioned below have countless eating possibilities, so check the WHERE TO EAT section if you are going to combine your sightseeing with a meal in the same area.

CHINATOWN

Much reduced in size but holding its own, Chinatown finally came to the attention of the government as a major potential tourist attraction and now what remains is safe from the developers, if not from the merchants of kitsch. It has undergone a massive cleanup

OPPOSITE: Sir Stamford Raffles broods over the city that he founded. ABOVE: A shophouse in Singapore's Chinatown.

in recent years but the essential nature of the area is intact in a few streets and back lanes. The men who make lion heads for lion dances still sit out on the street in the cool of the evening, fortune tellers still make a living along South Bridge Road and temple shops keep up with the times by selling paper VCRs and washing machines to be burnt and so sent up to the heavens for one's ancestors.

What follows is a suggested walk taking you through the most authentic and interesting part of Chinatown, although it is by no means an exhaustive tour.

Start from the Furama Hotel and walk up New Bridge Road toward the People's Park Complex. At the corner of Cross Street is the old Customs Building built in the thirties which is quite an imposing sight. Opposite is the old Great Southern Hotel, the first hotel in Singapore to have an elevator and to hold cabarets in the tea garden on the roof. Next door is the Majestic Theatre, originally built to house Cantonese operas but later converted to the cinema it is today. Continuing along New Bridge Road, take the next left turn, Mosque Street. Here you may still see the amazing ability of plants in the region to find a sprouting place absolutely anywhere. One gets the feeling with some of these buildings that if the plants were taken down the structures that support them would crumble away to nothing. At the end of Mosque Street turn right into South Bridge Road where you will come across the Jamae Mosque, built in the 1830s. If you would like to go in, please remember to remove your shoes first.

Further along is Pagoda Street, a one-time haunt of opium smokers, many of whom were coolies, near slave laborers, brought into Singapore to work unloading the cargo boats which came up the river. Further along is the Sri Mariammam Temple, open until 8 PM, where the name of the first Indian immigrant to Singapore in 1819 has been recorded in stone. Continue along South Bridge Road to Smith Street on which, it is said, 25 brothels operated in 1901. Cross South Bridge Road and go up Ann Siang Road where you will find a shop making Lion Dance heads and, opposite that, a temple shop selling all the paraphernalia one's newly departed relatives might need in the afterlife, all made out of paper. Walk back down South Bridge Road and to Smith Street where, when in season, the pervasive aroma of durians will greet you. If you're feeling daring you could even buy one and try it. It is reputed to be a very powerful aphrodisiac. This road will bring you back to Eu Tong Street where in the evening you can have your fortune told.

TANJONG PAGAR

The area of Tanjong Pagar includes Neil Road, Tanjong Pagar Road, and the smaller roads between them. At one time this whole area was a huge nutmeg plantation but later became a major road from the docks at the top of the road to the warehouses along the Singapore River. On the corner of Neil and Tanjong Pagar roads is the old Rickshaw Station, which once had 10,000 rickshaws and their human beasts of burden hanging about round it; it has, like almost all the buildings in the region, been renovated and is currently a restaurant. Walk up Tanjong Pagar Road and take in the vista of the beautifully renovated shop houses. Go back through Duxton Road and browse around the many craft and artifact shops here. Genteel pubs and restaurants are easy to find in an area that, as recently as the 1950s, housed opium dens and gangsters. Well worth visiting is the Tea Chapter at 9A–9B Neil Road, a tea shop serving Chinese tea in the traditional style in a pleasant atmosphere.

SERANGOON ROAD (LITTLE INDIA)

On a busy night, the chaos of New Dehli or Bombay is almost palpable, although the cleanliness of the area owes everything to Singapore. Crowds gather around the temples or on street corners while fortune tellers and their parrots linger and garland makers hawk wares used for religious services, weddings and festivals. Shops also have catalogues of photographs from which to choose garlands, and prices for these braids of *margosas* and jasmines run into hundreds of dollars. From the temples along the road a great cacophony of sound emerges. Shops sell everything from gold jewelry to garish sari material to clay oil lamps and huge boxes

duce, spices and cooked food are sold o ground floor, while the upper-levels stan sell standard Singaporean clothes or cloth. Opposite is a converted group of shophouses known as **Little India Arcade**, with lots of small stalls, shops and good food to be found within. There are many interesting shops and restaurants on the streets running off Serangoon Road. The shops along Serangoon Road itself have undergone gentrification and are too expensive for the original spice merchants and grocers, many of whom now cluster in Buffalo Road, Dunlop Street and

of spices. The many luggage shops along the road cater mostly to visitors from India who buy things here which would be expensive or unavailable in their own country. This area is best seen either early morning when you can enjoy a wonderful South Indian breakfast, or later in the evening when the area becomes crowded and the temples are busy.

You should start your visit to **Serangoon Road**, nicknamed **Little India**, at its junction with Bukit Timah Road. Buses that will take you here are N° 64, N° 65, N° 92, N° 111 or N° 139. Zhu Jiao Centre, the market at the top of the road, is still referred to by the locals as Tek Kar, the name of the original spacious market once located opposite this functional, crowded, but interesting market. Fresh pro-

Upper Dickson Road. **Racecourse Road** has a string of tasty and inexpensive restaurants, while Komala Vilas vegetarian restaurant on Serangoon Road is almost legendary.

A little further down Serangoon Road is **Sri Srinvasa Perumal Temple**. The site for this temple was acquired in the nineteenth century but most of the exuberant exterior was built after 1960. The temple is dedicated to the Hindu god, Vishnu. Inside, worshipers buy offerings of coconuts or bananas which

OPPOSITE: Still handmade in Chinatown, dragons are very much a part of the Chinese New Year celebrations. ABOVE LEFT: Souvenirs at prices to suit all pockets color the streets in Chinatown. ABOVE RIGHT: Celebrating the Chinese New Year in Chinatown.

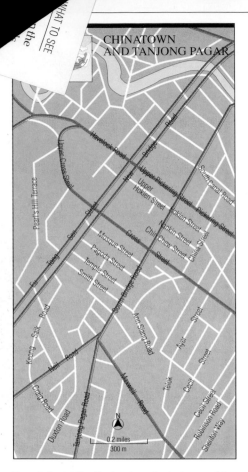

CHINATOWN
AND TANJONG PAGAR

Further down Serangoon Road is **Desker Road**, a well established red light area frequented by locals. Sightseers and interested parties should peer down the alley that runs down the back. Further down Serangoon Road still is the **Veeramaknaliamman Temple** dedicated to Shiva, another manifestation of the Hindu godhead. It is from this temple that the annual **Thaipusam** festival begins, where penitent sinners skewer themselves with steel rods and carry enormously heavy decorated weights which are attached to their body with more skewers (see TOP SPOTS).

You should time your trip to Serangoon Road to coincide with a meal time. Great Indian food can be found in Singapore and much of it is in and around Serangoon Road.

SENTOSA

During the colonial era an island military base, Sentosa is now marketed as a leisure center ("Singapore's Discovery Island") and is home to a couple of five-star resorts. A bridge provides a link with the mainland, but the island can also be reached by ferry from the World Trade Centre or by cable car from **Mount Faber**, which is nearby. Sentosa can certainly offer a day off from the traffic and noise of the city. On weekdays in particular, Sentosa is a little haven of peace and good taste and a positive heaven for nature lovers. Corridors of vegetation are being carefully preserved across the island and several areas are kept undeveloped, assuring visitors an enormous range of bird-life visible, with some patience, from any of the paths or exhibitions there. The Nature Walk will reveal to the visitor two species of carnivorous pitcher plants and secondary rainforest plants. There are also small areas of mangrove swamp with the associated wildlife.

If nature isn't your cup of tea, there is still much to see there, including the **Underwater World**, a $40 million water theme park known as Fantasy Island (a top favorite with the kids), **Volcano Land**, an exciting virtual reality theater called **Cinemania**, an exhibition of boats, a butterfly park, a **coralarium**, a roller skating rink, a lagoon with water sports, and some well presented remains of

they take to the Brahmin priest at one of the smaller sanctums inside, who then blesses the devotee with ash, and red dye. The fruit represents *vasanas*, the desires of man and its offering symbolizes an attempt to divest oneself of desire, thus taking an essential step toward self-fulfillment. Vishnu followers are given a V-shaped mark on their forehead rather than the more usual red spot. After having their offerings accepted the worshiper circumambulates within Indian temples, and this one particularly, are very unlike a place of worship that western tourists might be accustomed to. They are noisy and seemingly irreverent places, with children running around, cars parked in the precincts, lounging Brahmins, and an odd mix of erotic and outlandish deities. A digital clock is suspended above an elephant-headed, many armed figure; the Brahmin, in a white sarong and with long hair, smokes a surreptitious cigarette while waiting for the next devotee.

the military fortifications of The Second World War. After the sun sets spotlights play over the dancing fountains. The new 37-m (121-ft) Merlion, which belches smoke and zaps laser beams from its eyes, is a monument to bad taste. However, if you take the elevator to the 10th floor and then climb another couple of floors, you'll be rewarded with a panorama of Singapore and the nearby Indonesian islands of Batam and Bintan. Sentosa offers a wide range of places to eat, including a Mississippi river boat and food stalls, or alternatively there's the World Trade Centre itself or the Food Centre across the road near the bus station. The basic admission to Sentosa is S$5 for adults, S$3 for children. Admission to the various attractions can be expensive (eg S$16 for **Fantasy Island** for adults, S$10 for children). Transportation around the island by bus or monorail is included in the price of the entry ticket, or you can hire bicycles from the ferry terminal or the lagoon. Inside the World Trade Centre opposite Sentosa, there are a number of shops, money changing offices, food outlets and the *Guinness Book of Records* **Exhibition**.

Jurong Bird Park

Many birds of the region can be seen here, some completely free, others in cages, and some in a gigantic walk-in aviary. It's worth taking a scenic rail ride for an overview of the whole park. There are a number of shows: **Birds of Prey** can be seen at 10 AM and 4 PM; the **All Stars Bird Show** is at 11 AM and 3 PM, and **lory feeding** times at 9:30 AM and 3:30 PM. The price per adult is S$10.30, S$4.12 for children, there is also a special family admission package for two adults and three children under 12 priced at S$20.60.

To get there, take the MRT to Boon Lay station and then a cab or bus Nº 194 or 251. A sunny day at the bird park can be a hot and debilitating experience, so make full use of the open air buses traveling around the park and plan your visit around the shows. There are plenty of places in the park for snacks and drinks. Near the park is a crocodile farm where terribly unhappy crocodiles languish in concrete pits.

Haw Par Villa

Situated on Pasir Panjang Road, a 20-minute car journey from Orchard Road, is **Haw Par Villa**, which has existed in one form or another for almost 100 years. Once a private residence of the makers of Tiger Balm ointment, it is now a theme park focusing on Chinese mythology. Its major attraction is the Wrath of the Water Gods Flume, for which you may have to queue patiently for the pleasure of a stomach churning ride. Not for the

squeamish, there is the Tales of China boat ride, a five-minute exploration of the myriad ways in which wrongdoers are punished in hell. If you don't like the sound of either of these, laser and film shows on Chinese mythology, a puppet show, and a very realistic mechanical old man who tells stories are alternatives. Owing to declining popularity of Haw Par Villa, entry price was slashed in mid-1997 to only S$5 for adults, S$3.50 for children and all rides, shows, etc., are free. It would be a good idea to telephone first to ensure the park is still running ((65) 774-0300. The nearest MRT stop is Buona Vista from where you can take the SBS service Nº 200 or get a cab.

Exploring the River and Harbor

The Singapore River has undergone many changes since Stamford Raffles sailed up it in 1819. He saw dense mangroves, crocodiles,

Part of the Irish contribution to the Singapore skyline — the Supreme Court building was designed by George Coleman in 1826.

virgin jungle and envisioned a vital trading post, a link between Europe, India and the East. A couple of decades ago, the riverside was a furious chaos of coolies, *tongkangs* and sampans, godowns and lorries and unlicensed hawker stalls. Now the only vessels on it are the tourist bumboats. Two major restoration cum development projects have taken place along the river, with a third (Robertson Quay) underway. The first area to be developed (and the liveliest) is **Boat Quay**, on the south side of the river just off South Bridge road. This really comes alive

at night, with cafés, jazz bars and pubs, and an array of restaurants serving everything from Italian cuisine to Balinese satay. Boat Quay draws a predominantly yuppy crowd, including young expatriates, who throng the tables set up along the riverside.

Clarke Quay, on the other bank and bit further upriver, is aimed more at families and is full of shops, amusement areas, pushcarts selling all kinds of bric-a-brac and souvenirs, stilt walkers, a Disney-style Adventure Ride, outdoor eating areas and a range of restaurants, including one set on an old *tongkang* moored at the riverside.

To explore the area along the river, start at the **North Boat Quay**, where a statue of Raffles gazes at his achievements. This is the

spot where he first disembarked. The attorney general's chambers are nearby, as is Parliament House, designed by the Irishman George Coleman in 1826. It was originally a private house, built for John Maxwell and has been added to many times since the original construction was undertaken. Most of it dates back to 1875. **Empress Place** used to be the immigration department where people queued daily and waited, scrambled and sweated in the crumbling, boxed-in cubicles with tired old fans failing to disturb the air and government regulation linoleum crumbling gently beneath their feet. It was boarded up in the mid-eighties and several years later there emerged the magnificent new Empress Place restored and in pristine condition. It was used as an exhibition center for some years but is once again undergoing renovation and will open in the year 2000 as the **Asian Cultural Museum II**, focusing on Southeast Asian and Indian culture.

Walk along the other bank of the river, crossing it via **Cavanagh Bridge** built in Glasgow in 1869 and shipped out here. It was named after Sir Orfeur Cavanagh, a former governor of the colony. Beside it is a tax office, once the General Post Office and at various other times the Singapore Club and a hostel for female British prisoners of war. The steps leading down into the river from the side of the building date back to the construction of Boat Quay in 1842.

You might like to take one of the half-hour bumboat rides which offer a trip up the river, showing the beautiful renovated buildings of Boat and Clarke Quay and then back down to the river mouth itself and into Marina Bay with a view of the Merlion fountain.

If you're in a nautical mood, a trip out into **Marina Bay** and beyond is a fascinating experience. There are several organizations which arrange trips out into the bay, including Watertours ((65) 533-9811, which has an authentic-looking Chinese junk and an excellent tour guide. There are several different trips to choose from but the best is the twilight cruise which includes a good buffet meal, an informative talk by the guide, and great sunsets, all at a decent price. Tours leave from Clifford Pier at 6 PM or 6:30 PM, or from the World Trade Centre, returning at 9 PM.

THE COLONIAL HEART

The colonial heart of Singapore, where the original government administration offices and a number of churches were located, is centered around the north side of the river and around the wide open green spaces of what is known as **the Padang**.

Cricket was first played here in the 1820s in front of the imposing **Singapore Cricket Club**. The Padang itself has witnessed some of the less happy moments of Singapore's

Victorian building where Lord Louis Mountbatten accepted the surrender of the Japanese forces in 1945, while opposite the Cricket Club is **Singapore Recreation Club**, started by Eurasians who were once banned from the toffy-nosed colonial Cricket Cub.

Set in an expanse of green shaded by vast trees and bounded by St. Andrew's Road, Stamford Road and North Bridge Road, the pretty white **St. Andrew's Cathedral** is an historic haven of peace and tranquillity in the heart of the city.

history, such as the day in February 1915 when a match was interrupted by the news that an armed uprising was taking place. The Fifth Light Infantry of the British Indian army, the only unit stationed on the island, mutinied after having heard a rumor that they would be battling fellow Muslims in Turkey. Another historic event occurred on February 17, 1942, when the defeated British were lined up here, before being marched off to Changi prison. Cricket wasn't played here again until the Japanese prisoners of war cleared the area of shell craters in 1945. Now the green is once again the site of cricket matches and the annual celebration of Singapore's independence. On one side of the Padang is **City Hall**, a

Further up North Bridge Road, bounded on one side by Bras Basah Road, you'll find one of Singapore's latest restoration areas, **CHIJMES**. Once the site of the Convent of the Holy Infant Jesus, this has five fine neo-Gothic buildings including a church with beautiful stained glass windows and Caldwell House, the only remaining house designed by the important early architect, Coleman. Set around a series of courtyards, gardens and fountains linked by lovely colonnaded walkways covered with terracotta tiles, CHIJMES is home to a wide range of

OPPOSITE: The Victoria Theatre, a showpiece of colonial architecture. ABOVE: City Hall and the Supreme Court, behind, line the Padang.

restaurants and boutiques. The most interesting tenants here include the restaurant, **Stars**, where famed California chef Jeremiah Towers has created a signature East-West menu, and **Bonne Santé,** currently the most highly regarded wine bar in Singapore with a excellent selection of wines ranging from the moderately priced to the very expensive.

Museums and Galleries

Also on Bras Basah Road is another beautiful historic building, **St. Joseph's Institution**, the first part of which was completed in 1867. The school, run by the La Salle Brothers, was relocated in 1990 and the magnificent building converted to house the **Singapore Art Museum**. This is one of the best art museums in the region, not just because of the building which houses it but because of the excellent displays and the interactive multimedia programs on art in Singapore and the wider Southeast Asian region. The Art Museum is open Tuesday to Sunday from 9 AM to 5:30 PM. It's well worth while taking the free guided tour, which is at 11 AM from Tuesday to Friday, with an additional afternoon tour at 2:30 PM on Saturdays and Sundays. The Dome Café adjoining the Art Museum is a delightful place to relax over a coffee or a meal after your visit.

The cultural scene in Singapore received the seal of government approval a few years ago and the National Heritage Board was set up. This recommended restructuring the old National Museum to become the **Singapore History Museum**, due to open in about 2000, with two new Asian Civilization museums to be created. The **National Museum** in Stamford Road is in a state of transition, and the only gallery really worth visiting at the moment is the Rumah Baba, a recreated Peranakan house complete with furnishings and displays of clothing, jewelry, porcelain and other items.

The first **Asian Civilization Museum** opened in mid-1997 in the old Tao Nan School in Armenian Street, off Stamford Road not far from the National Library. This historic building, which began life as a school in 1907, has been beautifully refurbished and now houses a truly superb museum with a small but excellently displayed collection tracing the development of Chinese civilization. If you have time to visit only one museum in Singapore, this should be it. The monochrome porcelain wares are some of the finest you'll see outside Taipei's National Palace Museum, and the ceramics section shows the making of ceramics and traces their historical development. Another particularly fine gallery is devoted to classical Chinese furniture, while some of the stone Buddhas here are breathtaking. The museum, open from Tuesday to Sunday from 9 AM to 5:30 PM, has guided tours at 11 AM Tuesday to Friday, with an additional afternoon tour at 2:30 PM on Saturdays and Sundays. Recover and refuel at the small but popular Café Les Amis adjoining the museum.

FORT CANNING PARK

Archaeological evidence has been found on this site proving the existence of a civilization four hundred years before this area became the site of Singapore's first Government House. There was an old Christian cemetery here whose gates still remain, although some of the tombstones have been moved to the sides, and others taken elsewhere. This ground has been a holy place for many cultures and turning left out of the cemetery gates you will come to the Iskandar Shah Shrine, a Muslim place of worship where the body of the last ruler of ancient Singapura is said to be interred. The park itself makes a pleasant evening walk above the bustle of the city and offers some splendid views. The hill was also the scene of some of the historic moments of the Second World War. The headquarters of the British military command were here in underground rooms which are still intact. **Fort Canning Centre** is now a venue for the Arts, and the lawns on the hillside sometimes used for outdoor performances.

THE BOTANIC GARDENS

Situated just beyond the Orchard Road area at the junction of Holland and Cluny Roads are the **Botanic Gardens** which offer the interested visitor a great introduction to the flora of the tropical regions. It was in these gardens that the first rubber trees were planted in the Far East by the Irishman "Mad" Ridley. It was from these plants that the huge rubber plantations of Malaysia began. A plaque marks the spot where the first tree was planted. The park also contains an area of primary rainforest complete with macaques, Singapore's only surviving wild monkey. The park has many attractions including a very informative **orchid garden** where you can buy cuttings. The trees are all labeled with their common name as well as botanical name and place of origin. Opposite the main gates of the park in Cluny Road is one of my favorite hawker centers, where you can get such delicacies as *roti*

the hill on Bukit Timah Road, it is easy to miss the start of the road which goes into the reserve's car park and all the way to the top of the hill. In addition to this road (closed to public vehicles beyond the car park), there are many other pathways to explore. The macaque monkeys are abundant, particularly at the top of the hill. The best times to visit are very early morning, or early evening, when birds are around, due to the large numbers of insects. One particularly spectacular bird is the racket-tailed drongo with enormous streamers trailing out behind it.

John (Singaporean version of French toast) or *tahu goreng*, fried tofu, possibly the best in Singapore.

At the bottom of the hill is a small information hut which sells a fascinating booklet about the nature reserve.

BUKIT TIMAH NATURE RESERVE

While Singapore appears to many people to be entirely urbanized, there are a few areas which have not yet spawned the inevitable blocks of flats. One of these is **Bukit Timah Hill**. Although this is surrounded by secondary rainforest, the central portion is virgin forest which has never been disturbed. At the lower parts of the hill you can still see trees remaining from the time when this area was planted with nutmeg and rubber trees. Owing to a flurry of building at the base of

SINGAPORE ZOOLOGICAL GARDENS AND NIGHT SAFARI

Having had some of life's most depressing experiences in zoos — neurotic and sickly tigers at Jaipur, enfeebled penguins hunched together in communal misery at Warsaw, or frost-bitten parrots keeping up a brave face in the depths of a Regents Park winter — I can cheerfully recommend **Singapore Zoo** as an idyllic setting to both voluntary visi-

The Botanic Gardens — a haven from the rush of Orchard Road.

tors and to residents of the zoo. Set in one of Singapore's pockets of countryside it offers its visitors user-friendly information about the animals and natural barriers such as lakes or pits rather than cages. There are daily animal shows (10:30 AM, 11:30 AM, 2:30 PM and 3:30 PM) featuring trained elephants, apes and seals as well as a children's petting zoo. On the road leading in to the zoo you will find the **Mandai Orchid Gardens** which will send cut orchids grown here all around the world. Get to the Zoo by taking the MRT to Ang Mo Kio station (on the Northern line) and transfer to bus N° 138, which drops you at the entrance.

Adjacent to the Zoo, the Night Safari is the only place of its kind in the world (see TOP SPOTS, page 18). This is a chance to see animals (and particularly the nocturnal feeders) really come to life during the cool evening hours. Starting from the wonderful Madagascan lemurs leaping about their trees on an island at the entrance, the place is non-stop enchantment. Take the walking trails and also ride on the special tram which traverses a region where you can came face-to-face with the rare one-horned rhino. If your time in Singapore is limited, make this your priority. The Night Safari is open from 7:30 PM until midnight, and you can eat at the restaurant or fast food outlets near the entrance, or facing the lake in front of the hill where the giraffes roam. To reach the Night Safari, take the same transport here as you would to reach the Zoo.

EMERALD HILL

At the bottom of the road where it joins Orchard Road is **Peranakan Place**, a collection of interesting restaurants (many with outdoor tables at night) and popular bars. The term Peranakan refers to the descendants of the early Chinese immigrants to the Straits Settlements of Melaka, Penang and Singapore who intermarried with local women. A **museum** ((65) 732-6966 situated in an original Peranakan house is well worth a visit; unfortunately, it opens for a guided tour only once a day from Monday to Friday, at 3 PM, for a minimum of four visitors. A museum guide will start your tour on the doorstep of the house and you can spot the place easily

enough by walking up the right side of Emerald Hill Road, past the street tables, until you see a house flanked by two large white lanterns which are embellished with red Chinese characters that spell out the family name.

The terraced houses on **Emerald Hill Road** are good examples of Peranakan architecture, sometimes referred to as Chinese Baroque. The cowboy saloon bar-looking doors on the front of these houses are called *pintu pagar*, made to provide ventilation while at the same time offering privacy to the family.

Take a walk all the way up Emerald Hill Road, pausing at N° 12 where you can observe the peep hole in the ceiling that allowed a *Nonya* to see who was at the front door without revealing herself. N° 14 has a ghost-busting hexagonal mirror above the door, known as a *pakwa*. *Pa* is Chinese for the lucky number eight and *kwa* stands for the elements like fire and water. Keeping on the left side, you come to a crossing, and facing the junction on the right side of Emerald Hill Road is a house with the most unfortunate *feng shui* (the art of geomancy as it relates to the positioning of buildings and sometimes even furniture so as to ward off evil spirits and attract good ones). Because it faces an open road the spirits had a clear runway for a speedy entrance and pity the poor householder who didn't take sensible precautions. If you peep in at the door you'll see how the owners have placed a temple directly in the

OPPOSITE: Some of the happiest animals in the world fascinate hundreds of people daily at the Singapore Zoo. ABOVE: Exotic denizen of the Jurong Bird Park.

line of any advancing nasties. A temple in your front room might not be convenient but it certainly beats having an uninvited ghost. Coming back down the road look for the lozenge-shaped small side windows. They are in the shape of a bat, the Chinese word for which, *fu*, has the same sound as another word meaning good luck and prosperity.

ARAB STREET

Although it was originally settled by Arabs, the area along North Bridge Road and **Arab**

us again, transvestites and all. It is open 24 hours and offers beer gardens, hawker food, a *pasar malam*, shows and much more.

WHERE TO STAY

EXPENSIVE

Most of the mega-hotel chains are represented in Singapore, offering their paying guests every luxury imaginable.

The legendary **Raffles (** (65) 337-1866 FAX (65) 339-7650 was closed for three years

Street down to Beach Road now reflects the Indian Muslim presence in Singapore. The **Sultan Mosque**, built in the 1920s, represents a bizarre blend of architectural influences from Persia, Turkey and North Africa. Remove your shoes before entering. Along Arab Street, the parallel **Bussorah Street** and **North Bridge Road** are many interesting shops selling perfumes, batik, cane items and the like. Also very close by is the resurrected Bugis Street hawker center. Many of those who remember the original Bugis Street sigh with sadness at its parting because of its unique atmosphere and impromptu shows by the transvestites. But now, shifted slightly to the left, a resurrected Bugis Street and the air-conditioned **Bugis Street Village** are with

for major renovation but reopened in 1991 (SEE LIVING IT UP in YOUR CHOICE). If you don't stay here then at least call in for a drink and a bit of nostalgia. First built in 1886 by the Sarkie brothers, Armenians in origin, it was originally a tiffin room and boarding house. By the mid-twentieth century it had collected its string of famous names: Coward, Chaplin, Fairbanks and Maugham and had become a rallying place for colonialists where they could be sure of not running into any riff-raff. In more recent times Raffles opened its doors to one and all but now, sadly, its renovation has again rendered it beyond the

One of the world's greatest hotels, the legendary Raffles, now restored to its original luxurious splendor.

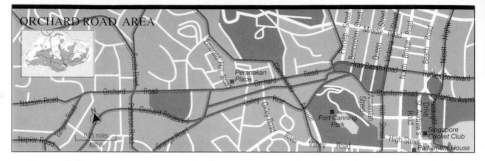

pockets of the average tourist. The least expensive doubles are $400.

Another hotel steeped in history is the **Goodwood Park** ((65) 737-7411 FAX (65) 732-8558, at 22 Scotts Road. Originally the Teutonic Club, it opened in 1900 to entertain the German community in Singapore. Taken as a spoil of war during the First World War it became a club for the British colonialists in the 1920s. It assumed its present identity in 1929 and rivaled Raffles as a haunt for Europeans, including British royalty. During and after the Japanese invasion the hotel became a residence of army officers and witnessed war crimes trials after Singapore's liberation. The hotel boomed in the fifties and sixties and attracted the glitterati of those years — Cliff Richard, Acker Bilk, Shirley Bassey, Matt Monroe and many others. A double room here costs $293.

Many of the other hotels in Singapore saw their birth in the 1970s and 1980s. **The Hilton** ((65) 737-2233 FAX (65) 732-2917, at 581 Orchard Road, underwent major renovations in the 1980s and offers all the luxuries including the highest pool in Singapore. Compared to the other big chains it is a restrained and quiet hotel with good restaurants and an excellent lounge bar in the lobby. The lobby leads into a mall of designer shops. A double room here costs $240.

Still in the Orchard Road area and in the same price range is the **Royal Holiday Inn Crowne Plaza** ((65) 737-7966 FAX (65) 737-6646, at 25 Scotts Road. Owned by the Sultan of Brunei, the hotel has a special entrance for the Sultan to use when he is in town which leads directly to his gold-plated suite. The interior of the hotel has been brought up to the standards befitting a place patronized by the man reputed to be the richest in the world. Doubles from $227.

Nearby is the **Singapore Marriot** ((65) 735-5800 FAX (65) 735-9800, on the corner of Scotts and Orchard Road, which was previously known as the Dynasty. Standard doubles cost $162. The hotel's open-fronted café is acknowledged as the best spot in Singapore for watching the passing parade, and because it's not air-conditioned, unrepentant smokers can puff away while they eat.

Located on a hilltop just off Orchard Road, the **Shangri-La** Singapore ((65) 737-3644 FAX (65) 737-7220, at 22 Orange Grove Road, has been regarded as one of Singapore's top hotels since it opened in 1971. Its luxuriant gardens are legendary, and the service exemplary. Double rooms are priced at $338.

The **Four Seasons** ((65) 734-1110 FAX (65) 733-0682, 190 Orchard Boulevard, is one of the newest (and many say the best) hotels in Singapore. Everything here speaks of refined good taste; the rooms even have laser video and CD players and some of the four tennis courts are air-conditioned — the last word in tropical luxury. Doubles from $272. A little further down Orchard Road, and with an incredible array of restaurants, bars and discos, is the twin-towered **Mandarin Hotel** ((65) 737-4411 FAX (65) 732-2361, at 333 Orchard Road. Big and impersonal, but centrally located, its restaurants and facilities are top class. A standard double is $262.

The newest hotel the Marina Square area is the swanky **Ritz-Carlton Millennia** ((65) 337-8888 FAX (65) 338-0001, (see LIVING IT UP in YOUR CHOICE), opened in 1996. Located at 7 Raffles Avenue, the huge rooms offer stunning views even from your bed or bathtub. Rates start at $310. In the same area is **The Oriental** ((65) 338-0066 FAX (65) 339-9537, 6 Raffles Boulevard. A business hotel with style it has great views from the rooms and its atrium bar is a treat. Doubles here are $248.

There are also excellent hotels outside the main Orchard Road area. In Chinatown, **The Furama** ((65) 533-3888 FAX (65) 534-1489, is at 60 Eu Tong Sen Street. It has an excellent Cantonese restaurant which serves delicacies such as bear's paws, snake, deep fried duck tongue and more on request. A double room costs $115.

MODERATE

Most of these hotels are out of the main Orchard Road area; the closer they get to the center the higher the room rate. At the top end of Orchard Road, near the Shangri-La, you will find the **Ladyhill Hotel** ((65) 737-2111 FAX (65) 737-4606, at One Ladyhill Road. This low rise hotel occupies quite a large area. It is ideal for families and has a nice pool, a good coffeeshop and Singapore's only Swiss restaurant. Doubles are $131.

One of the most popular hotels with businessmen and travelers looking for a moderately priced, well-located and unpretentious hotel with the facilities of a first-class property is the **Traders Hotel** ((65) 738-2222 FAX (65) 831-4314, opened by the Shangri-La group in 1996. Billed as a "value-for-money" hotel, Traders is at 1A Cuscaden Road. The hotel, where doubles start at $182, is just off Tanglin Road and strategically located between the offices of the Singapore Tourist Promotion Board and the Tanglin Mall shopping complex. Quite close to Orchard Road is the **RELC Hotel** ((65) 737-9044 FAX (65) 733-9976, at 30 Orange Grove Road, a conference centre frequently used for seminars and where the rooms are located on the upper floors. A double with breakfast is $69. It has a convenient location close to the center, but with limited restaurant facilities and no pool, though the rooms are still very good.

Ideally located about one minute off Orchard Road, the **Hotel Grand Central** ((65) 737-9944 FAX (65) 733-3175, at 22 Cavenagh Road, offers reasonably priced rooms and a perennially popular Sichuan restaurant, the Omei, as well as other restaurants and a pool. Standard doubles cost $96. The **YMCA** ((65) 337-3444 FAX (65) 337-3140, is probably the best deal in Singapore at this price range. Close to the center at One Orchard Road, rooms cost $90. You can even

get room service from the McDonald's downstairs.

The **Strand Hotel** ((65) 338-1866 FAX (65) 336-3149, 25 Bencoolen Street, has decent rooms at $65. Also in this area is the **Hotel Bencoolen** ((65) 336-0822 FAX (65) 336-4384, 47 Bencoolen Street, at $57 a room.

INEXPENSIVE

Places that can be called inexpensive are growing rarer in Singapore as the older buildings get razed or renovated. Near Chinatown there are two hotels worth considering. The **Air View Hotel** ((65) 225-7788, 10 Peck Seah Street, has air-conditioned rooms with bathroom for $41. Almost next door, at Two Peck Seah Street, is the **New Asia Hotel** ((65) 221-1861, with rooms costing much the same as the Air View. The **New Mayfair** ((65) 337-5405, 40–44 Armenian Street, has rooms at $50 and is opposite the new Asian Civilizations Museum while the **New Seventh Storey** ((65) 337-0251, 229 Rochor Road, has similar rooms for $51. The Singapore Tourist Promotion Board publishes a brochure, *Budget Hotels*, that is worth looking for.

WHERE TO EAT

If choosing one from the many top-class hotels in Singapore is difficult, deciding which of the thousands of eating places to go to is impossible. All the cuisines of the Far East in their myriad forms are amply represented here, as are those of the West and even the Middle East. What follows is based on novelty value, quality, and just plain prejudice. Smokers should be aware that smoking is banned in all air-conditioned restaurants; they may, however, puff away at open-air food stalls and fan-cooled coffeeshops. A number of fancy restaurants have an outdoor terrace with tables especially for smokers.

EXPENSIVE

It is not always easy to categorize Chinese restaurants in terms of price, because certain dishes such as shark's fin or bird's nest soup will jack up the price of your meal enormously. There are a number of stunning Chinese restaurants, one of the most elegant being the **Hai Tien Lo** ((65) 336-8111, on the 37th floor of the Pan Pacific Singapore at 6 Raffles Boulevard. Everything is exquisitely refined, including the Cantonese specialties. The ultimate dish here is Monk Jumps Over the Wall, but if you feel that S$100 per head is too much to pay for a bowl of dried abalone, dried scallops, ham, shark's fin and chicken, you can always settle for the scallops stuffed with minced prawns or beef fillet fried with black pepper and oyster sauce.

Pine Court ((65) 737-4411, is one of the few restaurants specializing in Peking food,

including the famous Peking duck, melt-in-the-mouth baked tench (a freshwater fish) and fried dried scallops. The attractive and spacious Pine Court is in the Mandarin Hotel in Orchard Road.

Northern Indian food in refined surroundings, complete with lotus pond and Indian musicians adding atmosphere at night, is what you'll find at the **Tandoor** ((65) 733-8333 in the Holiday Inn Park View. You can actually see your *tandoori* leg of lamb (one of the best offerings on the menu) being baked in the clay oven set behind a glass screen.

There are literally dozens of Japanese restaurants in Singapore, but my favorite is the discreet and beautifully located **Nadaman** ((65) 737-3644, which offers a great view of

Singapore from the 24th floor of the Shangri-La Singapore. Apart from the usual *sushi, sashimi, teppanyaki* and *tempura*, the chef does an exquisite *kaiseki*, tiny dishes which form part of a banquet. Try the green tea ice cream for a surprising modern Japanese dessert.

The **Latour** ((65) 737-3644, inside the Shangri-La Singapore, has maintained its popularity over the years despite the constant arrival of other European restaurants on the Singapore food scene. The speciality here is creative French food, not the *nouvelle cuisine* which reigned supreme during the 1980s and concentrated more on appearance than flavor, but light, irresistible dishes such as warm goose liver salad, rack of lamb with herb and morello sauce and slivers of marinated raw beef.

MODERATE

The restaurants listed above are appropriate for special occasions. Slightly less extravagant but nonetheless excellent food can be had at a price range of about $30 to $50 for two people, excluding drinks. In Orchard Road the **Long Jiang Sichuan restaurant** ((65) 734-1111, in the Crown Prince Hotel has good food and service. Specializing in Sichuan cooking, the restaurant serves an enormous range of Chinese dishes, including many Cantonese dishes as well as Sichuan specialties. Their "all you can eat" buffet is excellent value.

For a most unusual dining experience, don't miss the **Imperial Herbal Restaurant** ((65) 337-0491, in the Métropole Hotel at 41 Seah Street, just around the corner from the Raffles. Dozens of strange ingredients fill the pharmacy at the restaurant entrance, and the kitchen is supervised by a herbalist rather than a conventional chef. You can rest assured that what you eat here will be as good for you as it is delicious. Eel fried with garlic, egg white with scallops and herbs and eggplant with pine nuts are all remarkably tasty. Nothing bland about this health food.

Another exceptionally popular restaurant is the **Wah Lok Cantonese Restaurant** ((65) 330-3588, at the Carlton Hotel. Reservations are always necessary.

Teochew food is becoming increasingly popular and more and more small restaurants are opening up. One of the best of these is **Teochew City** ((65) 532-3622, a branch of which is on Battery Road in the city. Teochew food (known in Hong Kong as Chiu Chow cuisine) is quite homely in style and subdued by Singaporean standards, and is regarded as healthy as it is more likely to be steamed or simmered than fried.

The original **Thanying** ((65) 222-4688, restaurant at the Amara Hotel in Tanjong Pagar Road, which specializes in palace-style Thai cuisine, proved so popular with Singaporeans that a second restaurant has been

Coleman Street, **Annalakshmi** ((65) 339-9990, is an ultra-vegetarian restaurant run by an interesting group of people dedicated to the propagation of Indian culture. All the staff are volunteers. No alcohol is served here and prices are high by Indian vegetarian standards. Every lunchtime and on Saturday evenings, there is a buffet which will astound you with the variety of flavor. The menu alters, depending on who is volunteering to cook that day.

Another style of cooking you'll want to try is Vietnamese food, or at least its Singa-

opened along the Singapore river at Clarke Quay, Thanying ((65) 336-1821. Both restaurants are justifiably very popular and booking is strongly recommended.

Aziza's ((65) 235-1130, for years located on Emerald Hill Road but now moved to 02-15 Albert Court, 180 Albert Street, is one of the few elegant Malay restaurants in Singapore. The restaurant is full every night so reservations are quite necessary. The food here is spicy and based around the typical herbs and spices of the Malay *kampung*, coconut, chilli, and lemon grass. Wine is also served at this restaurant. Reservations are strongly recommended.

Tucked away on the first floor of the Excelsior Hotel and shopping complex in

porean variant. The **Saigon** restaurant in Cairnhill Place just off Orchard Road is probably the best of the bunch. It is pleasantly unpretentious with a kitchen-style look about the place, cane chairs and pink tablecloths. No one actually speaks any Vietnamese and the clientele is 50 percent Singaporean and 25 percent Japanese. The food is good and quite inexpensive. Most unusual are the starters, for example *chao tom*, minced prawns cooked on a piece of sugar cane which you can bite into, or *cha goi ton thit*, a spring roll wrapped in lettuce with fresh raw herbs. Reservations are not necessary here.

LEFT: A songbird fancier's café. ABOVE: Alfresco or indoors, Singapore seafood is an amazing experience.

Japanese food, especially *sushi*, is found everywhere in Singapore. A good place to start looking is in **Ngee Ann City**; in Cold Storage supermarket in the basement of the huge Takashimaya shopping center you'll find freshly made *sushi*, while more inexpensive Japanese food (and other cuisines too) is found at the food stalls facing the supermarket entrance. Other Japanese restaurants are found elsewhere in this shopping complex, including the **Nogawa** on Level 4.

Perhaps the most unusual and certainly one of the least expensive places to enjoy Singapore's much vaunted seafood is the **Palm Beach Seafood Restaurant**, located in a complex known as Leisure Park next to the National Stadium. There's no point in calling as reservations are not accepted in this vast and always packed restaurant, where the supervisor communicates with the kitchen by VHF radio. Best dishes include chilli crab, prawns fried in butter and milk or served in black sauce and *yu char kway*, a deep-fried cruller stuffed with squid mousse and served with a fragrant black sauce. Popular with families, noisy and highly informal.

The **Long Beach Seafood Restaurant** ((65) 445-8833, was once right on the beach at Bedok, but has since moved to 1018 East Coast Parkway, next to the Singapore Tennis Centre. A typical Singaporean dish to try, if you're not an animal liberationist, is drunken prawns, which are drowned in brandy before being boiled. Other dishes to try are chilli crab and barbecued fish. Their black pepper crabs (from Sri Lanka) are to die for.

grandeur. An evening visit here is an event, particularly if you decide to try the Indonesian *rijstaffel* served by a long train of gorgeous ladies. The food, Singaporeans would say, is *okay lah* (meaning nothing special) but the place makes up for that. It is a little out of town, and it is best to get a taxi or use the free Alkaff Trolley, which picks up passengers at the DFS Millennia in Tanglin Road, and Hilton and Paragon Shopping Centre in Orchard Road for both lunch and dinner.

Among the many restaurants offering French, Continental or Mediterranean cuisine, arguably the most attractive is **Bastiani's** ((65) 433-0156, located along the river at Clarke Quay. The food — Mediterranean with a Californian accent — is great too, and the wine cellar, which offers some 4,000 bottles, probably the most extensive in Singapore. Casually elegant rather than stuffy, Bastiani's offers a good deal at lunchtime, but is more expensive in the evenings.

One of the most popular Italian restaurants in town is **Prego** ((65) 278-6979. on the ground floor of the Westin Plaza. Airy, informal, Prego offers a large range of Italian favorites at surprisingly reasonable prices. Pity wine in Singapore has to be so expensive!

One of the most popular eateries along the Orchard Road area (certainly with the locals) is **Planet Hollywood**, 541 Orchard Road in Liat Towers, where fake palm trees outside the covered entrance strike an incongruous note with the real thing right in front. The combination of Hollywood hype, a souvenir shop, dozens of television screens playing Hollywood movies, over-the-top decor and "Hollywood food" (a touch of Italian, Tex Mex and American burgers and sandwiches) draws the crowds, mostly children with their parents or teenagers wanting to appear hip.

There's a collection of open-sided seafood restaurants (all of which were relocated here from further up the East Coast by the Urban Renewal Authority) along the East Coast Parkway. Romantically known as the **UDMC Seafood Centre**, the eight restaurants have similar offerings of seafood and noodles. Casual and the food is usually good.

In terms of entertainment value the best place in this price range has to be **Alkaff Mansion** ((65) 278-6979. Built in the late nineteenth century this is one of the four houses lived in by the Alkaff family, wealthy merchants who began their life in Singapore as traders in coffee, spices and sugar. Abandoned in the twenties, the house was spotted just as it was about to disappear into the lianas and at some cost was brought back to its original

INEXPENSIVE

Just because the food is cheap, it doesn't mean it's not good. Many small stalls inside coffeeshops specialize in one or two dishes which are as good as they are inexpensive, and Indian vegetarian restaurants are excellent value. And then, of course, there are the

Alkaff Mansion with the city skyline behind.

food centers with their astonishing variety and surprisingly low prices. No two Singaporeans will agree on the best hawker food even though they spend much time discussing the topic.

Many locals rate the hawker stalls at **Taman Serasi** by the main entrance to the Botanic Gardens, very highly for Malay food. You'll get the best *tahu goreng* (fried tofu in peanut sauce) in town and wonderful *roti John*, a peculiarly Singaporean dish which is a local interpretation of what the British soldiers used to enjoy: bread roll stuffed with fried onions and egg, slathered with tomato sauce. There is also a *roti prata* stall at Taman Serasi.

A great place to eat if the heat outside gets you down is at one of the air-conditioned food courts along Orchard Road. The one that started the trend toward upmarket food centers where you pay just a few cents more is **Picnic**, in the basement of Scotts Shopping Centre in Scotts Road, next to the Singapore Marriot. Another good one is **Food Court** in the basement of the Orchard Emerald, almost opposite the Mandarin Singapore.

Marina South is a really good hawker center, even if a little difficult to get reach by public transport. You can get there by cab, about S$8 from town, or by the N° 400 bus. Nearby **Marina Village** organizes evening buses from most major hotels, and you can then walk along the waterfront for about 10 minutes to the hawker center. The hawker center is very clean and relatively new. Stalls include a Japanese steamboat stall, a Thai stall (but check portion sizes), as well as the more regular places. Nearby is a bowling alley that caters to children, and up the road is Marina Village which has live music most nights. If you don't sit down the music is free. If you do sit down you get to pay high prices for drinks. There are many shops selling tourist goodies and particularly kites which you can fly on the beach. Tourist literature promotes the Newton Circus hawker center but this place is not recommended. Coach loads of tourists arrive by the hour and prices have inflated accordingly. The food is no better than the places just mentioned.

Serangoon Road is a wonderful place for inexpensive Indian food. There are a number of interesting food stalls inside the **Little**

India Centre opposite Zhu Jiao market, while **Komala Vilas**, at 76 Serangoon Road is fantastic for both atmosphere and southern Indian vegetarian food. Sit downstairs if you want a meal of *dosay* (rice and lentil pancakes with spicy dips) or *idli* (steamed rice dumplings); go upstairs for a banana leaf spread with rice and a number of spiced vegetable dishes, or for excellent Indian breads such as *puri*. Similar food in slightly more upmarket surroundings is available at **Madras New Woodlands**, just around the corner in Upper Dickson Road. **Racecourse Road**, which runs

parallel with Serangoon Road, has half a dozen air-conditioned restaurants selling Indian cuisine, such as Delhi, for northern favorites, and **Banana Leaf Apollo**, 56 Racecourse Road, where the star dish is Singapore's unique fish head curry.

Along Orchard Road and Scotts Road are a number of sidewalk cafés, some selling just one or two snack items such as ice creams or hot dogs, others, such as **Delifrance**'s popular Le Café outside Picnic in Scotts Road, offering a menu of light and moderately priced food.

SHOPPING

This section basically covers Orchard Road though you'll find shopping complexes just about everywhere in Singapore. Most of what you want will be found in **Orchard Road**, with one or two exceptions. If you are inter-

OPPOSITE TOP and BOTTOM: Shopping in the extensive malls and arcades is a favorite pastime in Singapore. ABOVE: A young spectator enjoying one of Singapore's many street fairs.

ested in computers and software the place to go is the **Funan Centre** near the Peninsula Hotel, and if you are shopping for artifacts I would recommend **Holland Village** (see below). The **People's Park Complex** in Chinatown has a few interesting stores for souvenirs, but for high-quality gifts visit the **Raffles Hotel** shopping arcade. This is near a number of hotels including, of course, the Raffles, as well as the Westin, Pan Pacific, Marina Mandarin, Oriental and Ritz Carlton.

Just around the corner from the top end of Orchard Road, Tanglin Shopping Centre is on Tanglin Road. Tailors and antique shops are here, as well as regular souvenir shops.

For real designer items visit the **Delfi Orchard** (Etienne Aigner, Givenchy and Waterford Wedgewood) and the **Hilton Hotel's** shopping gallery (Louis Vuitton, Bulgari, Loewe, Montana, Ferrer, Armani, Maud Frizon, Gucci, Jaeger *et alia*). The swanky **Palais Renaissance**, next to the much older Orchard Towers, houses a number of top designers including Prada and DKNY.

The blue-glassed **Forum**, next to the Hilton, has Toys 'R' Us and Electric City. Just past the Hilton is the **Far East Shopping Centre**, more interesting for the sculpture of Mother and Child that stands outside it than for anything you'll find inside.

Tang's department store is not bad for a little bit of everything at fixed prices. The highly popular **Lucky Plaza**, next to Tang's, has a good mix of shops selling electronic stuff like cameras plus lots of jewelry stores. Many of the shops here do not have fixed prices and bargaining is necessary. If possible, try to establish the fixed price in a department store or, for electronic items, in a place like a **Cost Plus** in Scotts Shopping Centre in Scotts Road. Scotts has a number of interesting shops, mostly selling fashion, as well as the very popular **Picnic** food stalls in the basement. Almost opposite, on the corner of Scotts and Orchard, is the large Lido cinema complex and an **Isetan** department store, as well as a number of smaller outlets and restaurants.

The dazzling blue building opposite Lucky Plaza is **Wisma Atria** and there is a mix of designer stores here plus four floors of the **Isetan** department store.

Next to Wisma Atria and Singapore's largest shopping area is the impressive **Ngee Ann City**, with its wide paved area and sculpture setting it apart. Anchor tenant here is the large **Takashimaya** Department Store, but there are a number of luxurious boutiques as well as fashion chains such as Guess, the Australian Country Road, East India Company and so on. You could probably get just about everything you needed at Ngee Ann City.

At Centrepoint further down Orchard Road you'll find a large Cold Storage supermarket and **Body Shop** in the basement, as well as British chains such as **Mothercare** and **Marks and Spencer**. **Robinsons** department store, the oldest in Singapore, is the biggest outlet here and it's pricey but the clothes are good. Hidden away are some good boutiques and cut price factory outlet stores which might appeal, although generally Singaporean clothes tend to be a little bit too frilly for Western tastes. **Times book shop** on the fourth floor of Centrepoint is one of the best places in town to look for books and magazines. If you are interested in art — Chinese calligraphy, paintings, artifacts — visit **The Orchard Point** 160 Orchard Road (just past Centrepoint and on the same side), near the Park View Holiday Inn and diagonally opposite Somerset MRT station. There are over eighty galleries here. Toward the end of Orchard Road is the flat roofed **Plaza Singapura**. Japanese based Yaohan has a large department store here offering a good mix of everything at affordable prices, and the Plaza also has some good shops selling Chinese rosewood furniture.

For an excellent selection of books as well as a whole floor devoted to music (mostly CDs), head for **MPH** in Stamford Road, just down from the National Library.

NIGHTLIFE

Singapore's night life has been, like the rest of the republic, cleaned up in recent years. However, there is a profusion of trendy pubs (Irish ones are the current rage), wine bars, discos and jazz bars. One of the more "respectable" nightclubs with floor shows and

The Singapore River, one a sleepy trading post, is now the site of a glittering array of sky-piercing high rise office blocks.

hostesses is at the **Kasbah**, in the Mandarin Hotel in Orchard Road. There are many discos, some with live music, others with DJs playing disks. All are noisy. Current favorites include the sophisticated **Celebrities**, in Orchard Towers; **Chinoiserie**, a yuppy hangout in the Hyatt Hotel and **Studebakers**, another yuppy scene in the penthouse of Pacific Plaza in Scotts Road. **Caesars**, in Orchard Towers, is a disco with a Roman theme, the waitresses wearing mini-togas. Old favorites such as **Top Ten**, a converted mini-theater also in Orchard Towers, and the Shangri-La's **Xanadu** (a place of technical wizardry where the scenery changes from Wild West to South Pacific tropical with the flick of a few switches) still draw the crowds.

If you want live music, without dancing, one of the best places in town is **Anywhere** ((65) 734-8233, at Tanglin Shopping Centre. It's small, windowless, dark, a bit scruffy and very crowded, but it's a great relief from squeaky-clean discos and bars which characterize too much of the tourist's Singapore. The resident band partly owns the premises and there's terrific rapport with the audience. A good spot for jazz, calypso or whatever happens to be playing, is the **Saxophone** bar and restaurant ((65) 235-8385, in Cuppage Terrace. Terrace. The music goes on till midnight. Jazz music is always available at the **Somerset** bar in the Westin Hotel. The atmosphere is a little sanitized for jazz but good bands are brought in from around the world. Other spots for jazz include the **Crazy Elephant** at Traders Market, Clarke Quay; **Harry's Quayside** at 28 Boat Quay and JJ Mahoney at 58 Duxton Road.

The pub scene is improving a lot in Singapore and there are quite a few places worth patronizing. **Brannigans**, at the Hyatt Regency Hotel in Scotts Road, has long been the favorite haunt of young and not-so-young night owls, and **The Bar** at the Holiday Inn across the road is famous for its Burton Bass beer imported from England. **The Hard Rock Café** ((65) 235-5232, in Cuscaden Road is within strolling distance of Orchard Towers.

Cultural nightlife is experiencing a little renaissance of its own in Singapore and the best way to find out what is on is by checking the daily newspaper which contains a current listings of film, theater and music.

SHOPPING AND DINING OUT OF THE CENTER OF TOWN

HOLLAND ROAD

If you only have a couple of days in Singapore and you want to buy lots of electrical items, silks, artifacts or other tourist goodies, **Holland Village** is where you should go. A taxi or the N° 106 or N° 7 bus from Somerset, Grange Road or Orchard Boulevard, will bring you to a little haven of good taste, good prices and an amazing array of good food.

Starting in the **Holland Road Shopping Centre**, 02-01 to 03 is the wonderful **Lim's**, which sells many arts and crafts at good fixed prices. It has an enormous range of Chinese table linen, happy coats, Thai and Chinese porcelain, Balinese bric-a-brac, Korean furniture and medicine chests and some pieces from Thailand such as faked old tables and chairs and carved wooden flowers. Ask for some discount if not paying by card. Lim's is on the same floor as several other treasure houses with whom you can bargain a little. There are a number of other art and antique shops, selling everything from benevolent Buddhas to fierce Balinese masks, on the second and third levels of the shopping center. Most of these shops deal regularly with people sending goods abroad so they will reliably handle any necessary shipping.

Holland Road Shopping Centre has several dress shops which have batik and other dresses from the region. There are embroidered blouses from China, beaded jumpers and blouses, as well as quilted Chinese and Thai silk jackets. Again, a polite request for a discount should have a beneficial effect but hard bargaining is not expected. There are several shops here which will make dresses or suits from a pattern or from a garment you already own.

There are also some fabric shops which sell mostly European style home furnishing fabric but also have embroidered and woven clothes from India. On the third floor is **J&A**, a carpet shop specializing in carpets from Pakistan, Afghanistan, Iran, Turkey, Kash-

Chinese opera singer.

mir and China. It is part of a bigger organization with a shop in Far East Plaza, so expect to bargain. **Rasha Collection** on the same floor has some excellent cushion covers, dhurries and other choice items from India.

Incidentally, if you run out of cash, there's a money changer inside the stamp shop at Nº 03–40.

If you're looking for electronic goods and gadgets, go round the corner to **Paris Silk Store** ((65) 466-6002, in Lorong Liput, and ask for their prices. Good things to buy here are multisystem televisions which work in

In Lorong Mambong there are several cane and pottery shops selling lots of pottery as well as domestic items and furniture. They will pack, ship and insure your purchases.

Having shopped till you've dropped in true Singaporean tradition, there are plenty of places to rest and eat, and enjoy the rest of the day. **Delifrance** has an outlet here which serves meals and wine by the glass as well as the usual light snacks and cakes. It is called **Le Bistrot** and is relaxed, informal and fairly cheap.

the USA, Europe, Australia and New Zealand and dual-voltage items which can be used in any country. Very few of their customers are tourists; most of their business is from expatriates who like to keep shopping time to a painless minimum. Don't expect a lot of sales chat at Paris Silk. They expect you to know what you want and don't allow much time for explanations or comparisons.

Near Paris Silk Store, on the corner of Lorong Liput, **Export Fashion** sells a wide range of seconds at bargain prices. Opposite, at 25B Lorong Liput (and also on the third level of the Holland Road Shopping Centre) is **Esteh Studio**, with a superb collection of old furniture and other collectibles from around the region.

A good cheap place to eat is **Shariff** restaurant, an Indian Muslim food place, 29, Lorong Liput, which has the usual assortment of Muslim food. Best is probably the *murtabak*. It's not as crunchily wonderful as the ones at Arab Street but it's filling, tasty and inexpensive.

Lorong Mambong and Lorong Liput abound with small food outlets and restaurants, with everything from take-away *sushi* to Italian *gelato*, North Indian cuisine to Tex Mex.

El Filipe's Cantina, 34 Lorong Mambong, serves Tex Mex rather than genuine Mexican food. The Wild Chicken (El Pollo Loco) is another great place for Tex Mex cuisine. For North Indian (and expensive), food, try the beautifully decorated **Hazaar** in Lorong Mambong. You could also try the Yee Cheong Yue Noodle Restaurant, or any one of the many food outlets in this very popular location.

Alternatively you can climb to the roof of the shopping center and eat alfresco at **Chao Phaya Thai Seafood Restaurant**. Foam deities adorn the walls of the air-conditioned section or you can choose your fish outside from a refrigerated market stall. At very reasonable prices you can enjoy typical Thai seafood. After eating, the place to be seen at

is **Java Jive** ((65) 468-4155, 17D Lorong Liput. It is a karaoke joint where the songs are sung by everybody.

GETTING THERE

See GETTING THERE in TRAVELERS' TIPS for information about getting to Singapore by air, train and bus from outside the region and from Thailand. Travel between Malaysia and Singapore is possible by a variety of means. There are many flights each day between Kuala Lumpur and Singapore, including a cheaper shuttle service where you just turn up and wait for an available seat. There is also an afternoon and night train service between the two cities and which takes about

eight hours. If you want to travel across to Johor Bahru, you can use the local shuttle train service which departs Singapore at 8:20 AM, 11:45 AM, 5:35 PM and 8:15 PM daily, costing only $2 one way.

Long-distance buses run from Kuala Lumpur, Penang, Melaka and other major destinations in Malaysia to and from Singapore. The *Straits Times* newspaper has a travel advertisement page daily and there you will find numbers of reputable travel agents who handle bus tickets. The local bus for Johor Bahru, the N° 170, leaves from the Queen Street station, and buses to Melaka and some other parts of Malaysia depart from the station at the junction of Lavender Street and Kallang Bahru ((65) 293-5915.

Instead of taking a taxi from Malaysia into Singapore it is easier to arrange, faster and more economical to travel by bus as far as Johor Bahru and then get the shuttle train or the N° 170 bus across to Singapore. The same applies for travel in the opposite direction, although there is a taxi company in Singapore that will pick you up and drive to any destination in Malaysia. The **Kuala Lumpur Taxi Service** ((65) 223-1889, is at 191 New Bridge Road.

There is a boat service to and from **Tioman** that departs at 8:30 AM daily and costs S$140 return; Call ((65) 733-5488 for information. This service does not run between mid-October and the first week of March owing to the northeast monsoon. There is also a ferry from Changi to Tanjong Belungkor in Johore, at 8:15 AM, 11:15 AM, 2:15 AM and 5:15 PM, which connects with road transport to Desaru. Contact **Ferrylink** ((65) 545-3600. Return fare is $24.

Singapore's major industry: shipping.

Travelers' Tips

GETTING THERE

BY AIR

Malaysia Airlines (MAS) and Singapore Airlines (SIA) have established routes to and from Europe, the USA, Australia, New Zealand and other parts of Asia. Singapore's **Changi Airport** is regularly noted as one of the world's most popular airports. Singapore Airlines and MAS offer very good service, and most other major international airlines serve Malaysia and Singapore as well. The least expensive flights usually involve several stopovers and roundabout routes. You get what you pay for, so if you are contemplating a cheaper flight check out the details carefully and try to establish a comfortable balance between convenience and finance.

At Malaysia's **Subang Airport**, outside Kuala Lumpur, (due to be replaced by the new international airport at Sepang by the end of 1998) there is a system for purchasing taxi coupons for the trip into town. The prices are fixed according to the distance, so be wary of entrepreneurs establishing their own prices. At Changi airport, however, you will be amazed at the efficiency with which you and your luggage are comfortably settled in your cab for a smooth ride into town.

BY TRAIN

From Thailand, an inexpensive and comfortable way to reach Malaysia or Singapore is by train. Departure from Bangkok is in the afternoon, arriving at Butterworth the following midday. Two hours later, an express leaves for the capital and reaches Kuala Lumpur at 8:20 PM that night. Changing platforms and waiting till 10 PM allows a connection with the night mail to Singapore which pulls in at 7 AM the following morning. Sleeping berths are available.

From Singapore there are various trains to Kuala Lumpur, including an early morning express and a night train that leaves at 10 PM and arrives at Kuala Lumpur at 7 AM. A first class air-conditioned berth is well worth the extra money if you fancy a wee bit of luxury. There is also a shuttle train service between Johor Bahru and Singapore.

BY BUS

The only reason for contemplating a bus journey into Malaysia from Thailand would be the unavailability of trains on a specific day. While bus and coach travel is fine within Malaysia and Singapore, there are few advantages to traveling by bus instead of train.

USEFUL ADDRESSES

MALAYSIAN TOURIST BOARDS OVERSEAS

United States
Tourism Malaysia ((213) 689-9702 FAX (213) 689-1530, N° 818 West 7th Street, Suite 804, Los Angeles, CA 90017; ((212) 754-1113/4/5/7 FAX (212) 754-1116, 595 Madison Avenue, Suite 1800, New York, NY 10022.

Britain
Tourism Malaysia ((0171) 930-7932 FAX (0171) 930-9015, N° 57 Trafalgar Square, London WC2N.

Germany
Tourism Malaysia ((069) 283-782 FAX (069) 282-215, Rossmarkt 11, 6000 Frankfurt am-Main.

France
Office National du Tourisme de Malaysie (01 42 97 41 71 FAX 01 42 97 41 69, N° 29 Rue Des Pyramides, 75001 Paris.

Australia
Tourism Malaysia ((02) 9299-4441/2/3 FAX (02) 9262-2026, Ground Floor, N° 65 York Street, Sydney, NSW 2000; ((90) 481-0400 FAX (09) 321-1421, 56 William Street, Perth, WA 6000.

Singapore
Tourism Malaysia ((65) 532-6351 FAX (65) 535-6650, N° 10 Collyer Quay, 01–03 Ocean Building, Singapore 0104.

SINGAPORE TOURIST BOARDS OVERSEAS

United States
Singapore Tourist Promotion Board ((213) 852-1901 FAX (213) 852-01289, 8484 Wilshire

Kapitan Mosque, Georgetown, Penang.

Boulevard, Suite 510, Beverley Hills, CA 90211; ((212) 302-4861 FAX (212) 302-4801, 590 Fifth Avenue, NBR 12th Floor, New York, NY 10036; ((312) 938-1888 FAX (312) 938-0086, Two Prudential Plaza, 180 North Stetson Avenue, Suite 1450, Chicago, IL 60601.

Britain

Singapore Tourist Promotion Board ((0171) 437-0033 FAX (0171) 734-2191, First Floor, Carrington House, N° 126–130 Regent Street, London W1R 5FE.

France

L'Office National du Tourisme de Singapour (01 42 97 16 16 FAX 01 42 97 16 17, Centre d'Affaires Le Louvre, Two Place du Palais-Royal, 75004 Paris Cedex 01.

Germany

Fremdenverkehrsburo von Singapur ((069) 920-7700 FAX (069) 297-8922, Hochstrasse 35–37, 6th floor, 60313 Frankfurt/Main 1.

Switzerland

Singapore Tourist Promotion Board ((01) 252-5454 FAX (01) 252-5303, Fremdenver-kehrsburo von Singapur, Hochstrasse 48, CH-8044 Zurich.

Australia

Singapore Tourist Promotion Board ((09) 325-8578 FAX (09) 221-3864, 8th Floor, St. Georges Court, 16 St. Georges Terrace, Perth WA 6000; ((02) 9241-3771 FAX (02) 9252-3586, Suite 1202, Level 12 Westpace Plaza, 60 Margaret Street, Sydney NSW 2000.

TOUR OPERATORS

Regarding specialist tours of Malaysia it is well worth writing directly to Asian Overland Services ((03) 292-5622. FAX (02) 292-5209, N° 33-M Jalan Dewan Sultan Sulaiman Sulu, 50300 Kuala Lumpur, Malaysia. They have good contacts throughout Malaysia and are recommended for reliability. In England a well-established travel company that handles small group exploratory holidays is Explore ((0252) 333031 FAX (0252) 343170, N° 1 Frederick Street, Aldershot Hampshire GU11 1LQ. Trailfinders ((0171) 938-3366 FAX (0171)

937-9294, 42–50 Earls Court Road, Kensington London W8 6EJ, is another well-known company that specializes in Southeast Asia and prides itself on offering the lowest fares as well as giving expert advice and discounts on hotels, car rental and local tours. For details of other operators you should contact any of the above offices of the Malaysian Tourist Board. They will provide details of recommended tour operators and charter flights.

See GENERAL INFORMATION in each chapter for details of tourist information centers within Malaysia and Singapore.

TRAVEL DOCUMENTS

MALAYSIA

American, British and Commonwealth and most European citizens do not require a visa. A passport valid for the next six months will ensure a month's stay; If you arrived in Kuala Lumpur and are traveling on Sabah and Sarawak, you will need to go through immigration procedures again and another stamp will be made in your passport.

SINGAPORE

As with Malaysia, American, British and most other European citizens do not require a visa. A fourteen-day stay will be automatically granted, although if you wish to stay up to one month, this will usually be granted. Any extension should go through the Immigration Office (532-2877, but as they require a local guarantor, it is much easier to pop into Malaysia by visiting Johor Bahru for a day. On your return another fourteen-day visa will be granted.

CUSTOMS

Duty-free goods allowed in are one liter of spirits, one liter of wine, 200 cigarettes or 50 cigars. This applies to travelers arriving in Malaysia or Singapore but note that it does not apply to travels between the two countries. Getting through customs is quite straightforward for most travelers but Malaysia and Singapore are extremely alert to the problem of narcotic trafficking in this part of the world. If you arrive in Singapore by train you will notice the caged police dogs strategically placed to monitor each passenger that passes by. Be warned: the penalties for attempting to bring in illlegal drugs are, literally, fatal. Malaysia's anti-narcotics laws mandate the death penalty for anyone found guilty of drug trafficking, which is defined as possession of 14 g (half an ounce) or more of heroin or morphine, 900 g (31 oz) of opium or 180 g (six ounces) of marijuana. The execution of two Australians in 1987 is evidence that this policy is rigorously enforced. Singapore's anti-narcotic penalties are for the most part the same.

WHEN TO GO

Whatever the time of the year, Malaysia and Singapore will be hot and humid. Temperatures hover around 30°C (86°F) during the day and even at night are seldom lower than 23°C (74°F) except in Malaysia's hill stations.

The wet season makes itself felt along the East Coast of Peninsular Malaysia and Sabah and Sarawak, as well as in Singapore between October and February. Even then, the rain does not make travel impossible, although Taman Negara, the wonderful national park in Peninsular Malaysia, is closed around this time.

WHAT TO TAKE

It is difficult to think of actual items that would be either unobtainable or extravagantly priced in the cities of Malaysia or Singapore, so it is hardly appropriate to draw up a survivor's kit. Even if you are planning to spend most of the time in the jungle interior, a quick visit to one of the big shopping plazas would provide most of what you need. The cost of film and development, for example, is inexpensive compared to Europe or the United States. You certainly do not need a full wardrobe of clothes, as the climate tends to dictate a simple style of dress. A pair of shorts is a good idea and stick to light cotton clothes generally. Because of the heat, a can of powder for the relief or prevention of prickly heat can prove to be an essential item, but again this is easily purchased anywhere upon your arrival.

GETTING AROUND

BY AIR

If you are planning to travel to Sabah and Sarawak, or just hoping to see a lot of Malaysia and Singapore in a short amount of time, then air travel is essential. Malaysia Airlines has an extensive and well-established network of routes which are particularly recommended. Other airlines in Malaysia include Pelangi (now managed by MAS), AirAsia ((03) 202-7777, Transmile ((03) 243-2022 and, within Sarawak and Sabah, Seaga ((088) 233-000. Although their routes are currently limited, these smaller airlines are likely to expand and it's worth checking their prices. SilkAir ((65) 322-6888, SIA's regional airline runs a twice-daily service to Tioman island and to Kuantan in Malaysia, as well as flying from Singapore to twenty other Asian destinations. AirAsia currently flies from Kuala Lumpur to Penang, Langkawi and Kota Kinabalu in Sabah six times a week (and is cheaper than MAS), and Transmile flies from Kuala Lumpur to Kota Kinabalu four times a week.

OPPOSITE: A dancer in traditional dress, Portuguese settlement, Melaka.

If you are planning to travel from Singapore to Sabah or Sarawak and want to save at least 25 percent of the fare, consider taking a Malaysia Airlines flight from Johor Bahru instead of one from Singapore itself. Malaysia Airlines runs its own buses shuttle service that departs from the Novotel Orchid Inn in Singapore and goes straight to the airport northwest of Johor Bahru. Malaysia Airlines also operates special advance booking fares if you can commit yourself to a fixed schedule and can provide fourteen days' notice.

BY TRAIN

There are few advantages to traveling by rail in Malaysia: although the trains are fairly reliable and comfortable, they are much slower than the bus, more expensive and there are only two main lines (other than a small one in Sabah). One line, which runs from Singapore through to Thailand via Kuala Lumpur and Butterworth is the most popular, partly because of its international connections and also because it passes through the main population centers. The other main line is a branch-off from the first one at the town of Gemas, and from there, a line runs through to the state of Kelantan in the northeastern corner of Malaysia and onto Thailand.

Reservations are a very good idea, especially for the Singapore-Bangkok route, and they can be easily arranged at the main line stations. At certain times of the year, Chinese New Year, the Muslim Hari Raya festival and the Christmas period particularly, reservations are essential. The difference between third class fares and first or second class makes it well worth paying the extra. Third class is more crowded, more uncomfortable and less airy. Second class and first class are indistinguishable for daytime travel, but the night sleepers in first class have air conditioning and private twin bed compartments, though the second-class sleepers are, by no means, uncomfortable. The food on the trains is barely okay, so for a long journey it is better to bring along a picnic.

There is also a rail pass valid for foreign tourists that allows unlimited travel by any train on Malayan Railway (KTM), including Singapore. However, for reasons already given, unless you happen to be a train freak these are not recommended. If you want further details on the rail pass, contact the Director of Passenger Services, KTM, Jalan Sultan Hishamuddin, 50621 Kuala Lumpur ((03) 274-9422 FAX (03) 274-9424

If you are in Singapore or Johor Bahru, there is a shuttle train service between the two countries. See the Johor Bahru section for details. Finally, within Singapore, the Mass Rapid Transit (MRT) system is a fast way to get around. It's worth buying a prepaid ticket, the TransitLink Farecard, (S$10 plus S$2 deposit) which you can use on both the trains and buses; the fare is deducted from the card electronically, and if you've used up the entire value before your trip is over, you can add another S$10. It saves you fumbling for change and queuing at the ticket dispensers each time you want to take the MRT.

BY BUS

Malaysia has an excellent network of bus lines connecting all the towns and cities. For certain routes, like traveling down the East Coast of the peninsula, they are indispensable because there is no train alternative and flying is nonstop and relatively expensive.

In Singapore, the local buses (most of which are air-conditioned, will take you everywhere; there is also a bus running to and from Johor Bahru in Malaysia. Driver conductors do not dispense change, so keep some coins handy. There is also an Explorer's Ticket, available from hotels and tour agents, that allows unlimited travel for one or three days and comes complete with a map detailing the major attractions. Better still is the TransitLink Farecard, valid on both the bus and the MRT (see above).

BY CAR

In Malaysia, the roads are in good condition and are well signposted. Petrol stations are never a problem to locate, though on long car journeys it makes sense to fill the tank when reaching a town. While the roads are safe to drive on, other drivers are best treated with a wary respect. Taxi drivers in particular seem to possess distinct suicidal tendencies when it comes to passing on a curve, and though it is tempting to try and emulate them when stuck behind some interminably slow truck, the fact that horrific crashes are not uncommon should give you pause for patience.

In the towns and cities there is little concept of lane discipline and giving way to other vehicles is not really understood. Westerners may also find the constant use of the horn a little irritating but this should not be taken personally.

There is no free parking in Singapore and unless you are using a private car park, you will need to purchase booklets of parking coupons that are used in most public car parks. The coupons are available at 7-Eleven stores, gas stations, newsagents and other small stores. Driving around the city center, you will notice the metal girders that straddle certain roads with signs reading Restricted Area. Vehicles wishing to enter the Central Business District (CBD) between 7:30 AM and 6:30 PM on Monday to Friday, and 7:30 AM to 2 PM Saturday, must display a special sticker on the windscreen showing that they have purchased a license for that day or month. Each day has a different colored coupon so it's easy to spot lawbreakers. Licenses can be bought at strategically placed booths on roads leading into the city and at many gas stations.

BY TAXI

In Singapore taxis are plentiful and well regulated. If you want to go into the Central Business District during the day you will have to pay the S$3 extra for the coupon, unless it has already been paid for by a previous customer and is already pasted on the windshield. There is a peak period surcharge of S50 cents for trips commencing between 7:30 and 9:30 AM Monday to Saturday, and from 4:30 PM to 7 PM Monday to Friday and from 11:30 AM to 2 PM Saturday.

In Kuala Lumpur taxis are not as plentiful but they are cheaper, and as long as you ensure the meter is turned on, the fare is regulated. In other towns in Malaysia it is best to agree on the fare before setting off,

and often it is a good idea to just check with someone in your hotel about the current rate for a particular journey. In places like Penang the rates are well established and usually adhered to, and even if they add on a *ringgit* or two you will most likely find the rate reasonable.

For travel within Malaysia, long-distance taxis are a real bargain and should always be considered. It is simply a matter of turning up at the long distance (or, as it is known locally, "outstation *teksi"*) area, announcing that you want to go to a certain destination and then waiting until a taxi has its quota of four passengers, which does not take very long. Alternatively, you can charter a whole taxi. The drawback is not the waiting but rather the kamikaze driving that the drivers sometimes engage in.

OPPOSITE: Buses are still the principle means of transport for Singaporeans despite the new MRT system. ABOVE: Young people at the central market display their colorful sense of fashion.

By Thumb

The natural friendliness of Malaysians makes for good hitchhiking prospects. If you are contemplating a long journey it is often a good idea to wait around a petrol station on the outskirts of town and approach a friendly face. Looking like an obvious tourist makes all the difference because hitchhiking by anyone else would be unheard of. Tourist or not, women should exercise discretion when hitching alone. If you are wondering about the hitchhiking possibilities in Singapore, forget it. The island is just too small and too fast and too busy to accommodate the very notion of thumbing a ride.

EMBASSIES AND CONSULATES

Malaysia

American Embassy ((03) 248-9011, N° 376 Jalan Tun Razak, 50400, Kuala Lumpur.
Australian High Commission ((03) 242-3122, N° 6 Jalan Kwan Seng, 50450 Kuala Lumpur.
British High Commission ((03) 248-2122, N° 185 Jalan Ampang, 50450, Kuala Lumpur.
German Embassy ((03) 242-9666, N° 3 Jalan U Thant, 50450, Kuala Lumpur.

Singapore

American Embassy; 27 Napier Road, Singapore 258508 ((65) 476-9100.
Australian High Commission; 25 Napier Road, Singapore 258507 ((65) 737-9311.
British High Commission; Tanglin Road, Singapore 247919 ((65) 473-9333.
German Embassy; 545, Orchard Road, N° 14-01 Far East Shopping Centre 238882 ((65) 737-1355.

HEALTH

Compared to most other Asian countries, Malasyia and Singapore present the least problem to visitors concerned about matters of health. No special vaccination certificates are required unless coming in from certain African or South American countries. Consult your doctor if in doubt because sometimes a few jabs make you feel better. Travel

insurance is a far better idea and is highly recommended. For any emergency you should go to the local hospital. AIDS is not as big a problem in Malaysia or Singapore as it is in neighboring countries, and there is no need to bring your own disposable syringes. If you are spending some time in the interior in Sarawak, malaria tablets might be a good idea. Again, consult your doctor if in doubt.

MONEY

Dollar prices in this book are in United States dollars unless shown otherwise as Malaysian ringgit or RM or Singapore dollars, S$. At the time of going to press, exchange rates to the US dollar were RM2.5 to US$1 and S$1.43 to US$1.

In both countries the most common coins are 10¢, 20¢ and 50¢ and $1 or RM1, while notes come in denominations of two, five, 10, 20, 50, 100, 500 and 1,000. The Brunei dollar is on a par with the Singapore dollar and occasionally you will be given a Brunei note in your change. This is quite acceptable and can be used anywhere in Singapore.

Exchanging money is rarely a problem in Singapore or Malaysia unless you are spending some time in rural areas, like the national parks, when you need to bring sufficient cash with you. Generally, hotels and the large department stores should only be used as a last resort because their rates will be slightly less than those obtainable in banks or from money changers. In the states of Kedah, Perlis, Kelantan and Terengganu, banks will be closed on Fridays and open from 9:30 AM to 3 PM on Saturdays through to Wednesdays and from 9:30 AM to 11:30 on Thursdays. Elsewhere in Malaysia banks are open from 9:30 AM to 3 PM on weekdays, although in some areas they operate from 10 AM until 4 PM; Saturday opening is from 9:30 AM to 11:30 AM, closed on Sundays.

In Singapore banking hours are flexible, with some banks being opened from 8:30 AM until 5 PM; the general rule is 10 AM to 3 PM on weekdays and from 9:30 AM to 11:30 AM on Saturdays. Automatic teller machines (ATMs) which dispense cash for major international credit cards and local bank cards are virtually everywhere in Singapore.

ACCOMMODATION

Both Malaysia and Singapore are well geared to meet the accommodation needs of most visitors an Malaysia is better than Singapore in providing for all budgets. The general standard is very good, and unpleasant events like thefts or sudden electricity cuts are a rarity. Nearly all the hotels referred to in the WHERE TO STAY sections provide air conditioning, hot and cold water and a private bathroom. Exceptions are some of the beach areas

to charge 10 percent for service, three percent GST and another one percent that goes towards the STPB. The cheaper hotels often quote a net price, but most others will add the 15 percent to the quoted price. In Malaysia, the taxes add another 15 percent to the bill.

SHOPPING

Shopping hours are invariably longer in Malaysia and Singapore than those in Europe, the United States or Australia. As a generalization, the corner store type of shop

on the East Coast and inexpensive homestay-type accommodation on some of the islands off the East Coast of Peninsular Malaysia or in remote areas in Sabah and Sarawak.

As a general rule it is worth looking at a hotel room before committing yourself. Intense competition in the hotel industry in Singapore and in most places in Malaysia means that you can almost always get a better price than that quoted. Ask for their "promotional" price and you may get up to 30 percent off. The rates quoted in this book all refer to a standard double and, in the case of the international hotels, these published room rates can often be reduced if you go through a travel agent in Kuala Lumpur or Singapore. Be aware that hotels in Singapore are obliged

(and 7-Eleven supermarkets) will open early and will close very late. Department stores and chain supermarkets will open around 9:30–10 AM and will close after 9 PM; some supermarkets stay open as late as 10 PM.

Shops in Singapore are usually open seven days a week though a few — those in less busy areas or those owned by Christians — will close on Sunday. In Malaysia, some shops, especially those on the East Coast or in Langkawi close on the Muslim day of rest, Friday. Many shops however will be open for business every day of the year, even on national holidays, though Chinese-owned businesses (and in

---

The beautifully ornate façade of one of Melaka's town houses.

Singapore that is the majority) will close for two days during Chinese New Year, Muslim-owned concerns (the majority in Malaysia) will close up for Hari Raya Aidilfitri and Indian-owned enterprises will take a couple of days off over Deepavali.

Bargaining is still the order of the day in most shops. Even in department stores it is worth asking if a discount is available for things that interest you. A few places advertise themselves as "fixed price stores" which is a blessing for those who shy away from bargaining. They also provide a yardstick for

comparative pricing and accept credit cards without obliging you to pay any surcharges (which some smaller places do). You might be able to buy a camera a few dollars cheaper in a smaller store, but you'll have to be prepared to bargain hard and long, and to pay in cash. Sometimes it's just not worth the effort.

Most shops take credit cards (Visa being the most commonly accepted card) but the small stores whose profit margins are minuscule, may insist on a two or three percent surcharge. Avoid that by paying cash.

For a run-down of the best buys in Malaysia and Singapore turn to SHOP TILL YOU DROP on page 47. Information on shopping is also found under the major city headings.

ETIQUETTE

Politeness is appreciated everywhere in Malaysia and Singapore and you shouldn't allow the occasional encounter with a rude person to blunt your sensibilities. Really losing your temper and blasting away at someone is unlikely to produce an instant

solution although it will always produce an instant crowd of curious onlookers. Generally speaking visitors are treated with respect and forbearance and it is good manners to try and do the same when dealing with Malaysians and Singaporeans. When you are concerned about trying to make a point, a controlled manner will be far more effective than actually exploding into a rage.

If you are invited into someone's home, remove your footwear at the door. A special point of etiquette applies only to conservative Malay women, who are forbidden to have any physical contact with males past puberty who are not members of the family. This extends to the shaking of hands, and even in sophisticated Singapore many Malay women would prefer a smile and a nod.

A final word about dressing in the more traditional parts of Malaysia. As Malaysia is a predominantly Muslim country, women should dress modestly as is the custom here. One should try to respect the cultural values of the country in which one is a visitor.

MAIL

Poste restante is available in Singapore and Kuala Lumpur at the main post offices. Chinese, Malay and Indians place their family names first, so be sure to check under your first name as well.

TELEPHONES

Singapore has no internal area codes. To phone Singapore from overseas, dial the country prefix (65) followed by the telephone number; when calling Singapore from Malaysia, dial 02 before the number. To call Malaysia from overseas, dial the country code (63) followed by the internal area code, dropping the 0; when calling Malaysia from Singapore, dial the internal area code, the number, omitting the country prefix. Throughout the guide, you will find Singapore phone numbers preceeded by the country code, while Malaysia phone numbers are preceeded by area codes.

Making local or international calls within Maylaysia and Singapore usually presents

ABOVE: A young girl in the traditional dress of Sarawak. OPPOSITE: At the Festival of the Hungry Ghosts, in Penang, there is always a colorful display.

no problems. Although you can make calls through your hotel, they'll generally charge a heavy fee. Better to use your credit card in the few public phones accepting these (generally in major cities), or use a telephone with an IDD sign above it. In Malaysian towns and in Singapore, public phones operating on a card system are common. The phone cards can be purchased in stores which display the sign. Be warned that Malaysia has three systems, Telekom, Uniphone and, in a few towns and cities in the peninsula, Citifon. They all require different phone cards. If you expect to be using the telephone much, buy both the Telekom and Uniphone cards because sod's law ensures that when you arrive in a remote place where the only phone takes Uniphone card, you'll have a Telekom card in your wallet.

HELPFUL NUMBERS

Malaysia
Police/Emergency Services (1999
Directory Assistance (103
International Directory Assistance (108
Kuala Lumpur Airport (Subang)((03) 746-1014/1235
Malaysia Airlines((03) 261-0555 RESERVATIONS ((03) 746-3000, Jalan Sultan Ismail, Kuala Lumpur.

Singapore
Police (999.
Ambulance and Fire Brigade (995.
Directory Assistance (103 (local); (104 (international); (109 (Malaysia).
Taxi Service ((65) 452-5555 and 250-0700 (24 hours).
Changi Airport ((65) 542-4422 (recorded information on arrivals and departures only).
Malaysia Airlines ((65) 336-6777.
Singapore Airlines((65) 229-7270, SIA Building, 77 Robinson Road; and Ground Floor, Mandarin Hotel, Orchard Road.

BASICS

Both Malaysia and Singapore are eight hours ahead of GMT (London), 13 and 16 hours ahead of American Eastern and Western Standard Time respectively, and two hours behind Australian Eastern Standard Time.

Malaysian and Singaporean current is 220–240 volts, 50 cycles, and most of the electrical goods for sale will also run on 220 volts.

Water is safe to drink throughout Peninsular Malaysia, Singapore and in the main towns in Sarawak and Sabah. If traveling in the interior in Borneo, bottled water is recommended.

The metric system is used throughout Malaysia and Singapore.

NEWSPAPERS AND MAGAZINES

Daily English language newspapers are published in Singapore and Malaysia. The established papers are the *Straits Times* and *New Straits Times*. Both are government controlled.

Malaysia's *Star* used to be more critical and open-minded but practices self-censorship in order to avoid being closed down. Another English language daily is the *Sun*. Singapore's basic *New Paper* appears in the afternoon.

Foreign newspapers are easy to find in Kuala Lumpur or Singapore, but costly. Weekly magazines such as *Newsweek* and *Time* are easily available and reasonably priced.

OPPOSITE and ABOVE: A kaleidoscope of ethnic dress.

The *Asian Wall Street Journal* and the *Far East Economic Review* fell afoul of the Singapore authorities and are virtually unobtainable.

WOMEN ALONE

Women can feel safer traveling alone in Malaysia and Singapore than most other countries in Europe or Asia. Stories of women being subjected to assault or rape are extremely rare and the only problem area is in the more traditional parts of Peninsular Malaysia. Here Muslim men sometimes

mistakenly equate some forms of western female dress with a degree of amorality.

TIPPING

In both countries, generally speaking, tipping is not expected, and certainly not in restaurants when the menu specifies the addition of ten percent to the bill. In Singapore tipping is officially discouraged and taxi drivers, for instance, do not expect anything above the stated fare (but never object if offered).

LANGUAGE BASICS

English is the language of education and commerce in Singapore and it is difficult to

imagine situations when you would need an English-Chinese/Malay/Tamil dictionary. Malaysia is a different story — despite its historical and cultural links with Britain — because of its decision to promote Malay as the official language. The result is that young Malaysians are increasingly unfamiliar with English; a few language basics can be useful.

Unlike Chinese, the Malay language is not a tonal one and is not nearly so difficult to master. There are no articles or complicated tenses. The plural is usually formed

by just doubling the noun. A is pronounced as in *far*; c as in *chip*; sy as in *shut*; g as in *girl*.

DAYS OF THE WEEK

Monday   *hari senen*
Tuesday   *hari selasa*
Wednesday   *hari rabu*
Thursday   *hari kamis*
Friday   *hari jumat*
Saturday   *hari sabtu*
Sunday   *hari minggu*

GREETINGS

how do you do?   *apa khabar?*
good morning   *selamat pagi*

good afternoon   *selamat petang*
good night   *selamat malam*
good bye   *selamat tinggal*
bon voyage   *selamat jalan*

FOOD AND DRINK

bread   *roti*
tea   *teh*
coffee   *kopi*
fried rice   *nasi goreng*
fried noodles   *mee goreng*

fish   *ikan*
chicken   *ayam*
prawns   *udang*
vegetables   *sayur*
egg   *telur*
sugar   *gula*
meat   *daging*
to eat   *makan*
to drink   *minum*
water   *air*
ice   *air batu*

NUMBERS

1   *satu*
2   *dua*
3   *tiga*
4   *empat*
5   *lima*
6   *enam*
7   *tujuh*
8   *lapan*

9   *sembilan*
10   *sepuluh*
11   *sebelas*
12   *dua belas*
13   *tiga belas*
20   *dua puluh*
21   *dua puluh satu*
30   *tiga puluh*
55   *lima puluh lima*
100   *seratus*
1000   *seribu*

USEFUL WORDS AND EXPRESSIONS

east   *timor*
west   *barat*
south   *selatan*
north   *utara*
market   *pasar*
river   *sungei*
toilet   *tandas*
post office   *pejabat pos*
How much does this cost?   *berapa harga?*
today   *hari ini*
tomorrow   *esok*
I   *saya*
a little   *sedikit*
a lot   *banyak*
beach   *pantai*
do not have   *tidak ada*   or   *tiada*
excuse me   *maafkan saya*
I am sorry   *saya minta maaf*
how far?   *berapa jauh*
when   *bila*
where   *di mana*
why   *kenapa*
thank you   *terima kasih*

A penitent at the Thaipusam Festival seeks an indulgence.

Recommended Reading

History and General Background Reading

ANDAYA, BARBARA WATSON AND LEONARD. *A History of Malaysia. St. Martin's Press*, New York, 1982. An authoritative if somewhat dry history.

FOLLOWS, ROY WITH POPHAM, HUGH. *The Jungle Beat*. Cassell, London, 1990. A young Englishman joins the Malayan Police in 1952 seeking adventure and action. He tells his naive but honest account of the war against the Communist guerrillas in the jungle.

GEORGE, T.J.S. *Lee Kuan Yew's Singapore*. Andre Deutsch, London, 1977. Alex Josey's biography of Singapore's political leader is the standard work but it is far too uncritical; this is the best work on the subject. For a while it was banned in Singapore.

INSAN. *Where the Monsoons Meet: A People's History of Malaya. Institute of Social Analysis*. 11 Lorong 11/4E. 46200 Petaling Jaya, Malaysia, 1987. (An appealing alternative to the academic histories; a convincing radical view told in comic book/documentary style.

HARRISON, TOM. *World Within. A Borneo Story*. Oxford University Press, 1984. First published in 1959, this book tells the story of Harrison's parachute descent, toward the end of the Second World War, into an unknown part of Borneo. His official mission was to organize resistance; his unstated one a desire to boldly go where no (white) person had gone before. If you visit the highlands of Bareo in Sarawak, this book is indispensable.

HALL, TIMOTHY. *The Fall of Singapore*. Octopus Publishing, Mandarin Australia, 1990. A journalistic and unsentimental account of the ignominious fall of Singapore to the Japanese in the Second World War.

LAT. *With a Little Bit of Lat*. Berita Publishing, Kuala Lumpur, 1990. This is the title of just one collection of Lat's cartoons, first published in 1980 and reprinted regularly. The longer you stay in the country the more they grow on you; Malaysia seen and commented on from the inside. The Coliseum in Kuala Lumpur has an original on the wall.

MAHATHIR, BIN MOHAMMED. *The Malay Dilemma. Federal Publications*, Kuala Lumpur, 1982. First published in 1970 this book, by the Prime Minister of Malaysia, is still an astonishing read. Set in stark racial terms Mahathir sets out to explain the case for positive discrimination to favor the Malays. The sort of book you could never imagine your own prime minister ever writing.

PAYNE, ROBERT. *The White Rajahs of Sarawak*. Oxford, 1986. The history of the Brooke family, from James to Vyner, and their tropical kingdom.

TURNBULL, MARY. *History of Malaysia, Singapore and Brunei*. Allen & Unwin, 1989. A readable and reliable historical account.

Natural History

CUBITT, GERALD AND PAYNE, JUNAIDI. *Wild Malaysia*, London, New Holland. Superb photographs and a highly readable text on all aspects of Malaysia's flora and fauna by the head of WWF in Sabah & Sarawak. A heavy, large format book but highly recommended.

The Battle for Sarawak's Forests. World Rainforest Movement, 87, Cantonment Road, 10250 Penang, Malaysia, 1989. Essential reading if you are traveling into Sarawak's interior, a collection of documents and articles about the plight of the natives in Sarawak and their struggle against the logging.

K M WONG AND C L CHAN. *Mount Kinabalu: Borneo's Magic Mountain*. Natural History Publications, Kota Kinabalu 1997. Every visitor to the regions highest mountain needs a copy of this excellent little book which introduces the natural history of the mountain; full of photographs to help in identification.

Guide Books

BRIGGS, JOHN. *Parks of Malaysia. Longman Malaysia*, Kuala Lumpur, 1991. (If you are intending to selectively visit both East and West Malaysia primarily for its wildlife and jungles then this book is invaluable. Practical and informative, written by an "amateur" enthusiast. Recommended.)

BRIGGS, JOHN. *Mountains of Malaysia*. Longman Malaysia, Kuala Lumpur, 1988. Another specialist guide book, worth every penny if mountaineering is your motive in visiting Malaysia.

MOORE, WENDY ET AL. *Travel Guide to Peninsular Malaysia and Singapore*, Periplus, Singapore, second edition 1997. A thoroughly researched and well written guide, full of interesting cultural as well as practical information.

HUTTON, WENDY ET AL. Travel Guide to Sabah, Sarawak and Brunei, Periplus, Singapore, second edition 1997. Edited and largely written by a writer who has lived in Borneo for a number of years, this book gives an insight into all aspects of the Malaysian Borneo states.

HUTTON, WENDY ET AL. *Insight Pocket Guide Sabah*. APA Publications, Singapore, second edition 1997. A highly personalized guide to this Malaysian state in the north of Borneo, with suggested itineraries and detailed maps.

Travel Books

BARCLAY, JAMES. A *Stroll Through Borneo*. Hodder & Stoughton, London, 1980, and January Books, Wellington, 1988. The title is an amusing understatement typical of the delightful style that characterizes this unpretentious and funny account of travel deep into the interior.

O'HANLON, REDMOND. *Into the Heart of Borneo*. London, 1986. An account of a journey made to the mountains of Batu Tiban with James Fenton. Funny and serious and a great book to take with you to read while traveling in Sarawak.

STIER, WAYNE. *Time Travel in the Malay Crescent*. Meru Publishing, Hawaii, 1985. At first the style may disconcert because the whole book is written in the second person singular but the anecdotal manner can grow on you as some of the stories prove interesting.

WALLS, DENIS, AND MARTIN, STELLA. *In Malaysia*. Brandt Publications, 1986. Two English teachers tell their tale of living in Peninsular Malaysia. A perceptive, well-written and reliable account of what everyday life in Malaysia is all about.

WELLS, CARVETH. *Six Years in the Malay Jungle*. Oxford University Press, 1988. Tale told by a civil engineer who came to Malaya in 1913. Pleasantly unscholarly yet full of interesting observations.

Fiction

BURGESS, ANTHONY. *The Malayan Trilogy*. Penguin Books, 1972. Written after Burgess was an Education Officer in Malaya in the 1950s, prior to Independence. Typical Burgess.

FAUCONNIER, HENRI. *The Soul of Malaya*. Oxford, 1985. First published in 1931, this autobiographical novel by a French rubber planter is one of the better literary excursions into colonial Malaya.

MAUGHAM, W. SOMERSET. *Collected Short Stories*. Pan, 1986 and The Casurina Tree. Oxford, 1985. Authentic tales of the decadent colonials who once ruled Malaysia and Singapore.

THEROUX, PAUL. *Saint Jack* and *The Consul's File*. Penguin Books, 1973 and 1977. Paul Theroux taught at the university in Singapore so this novel and collection of short stories, respectively, have their basis in a firsthand experience of postcolonial Malaya. He also wrote a brilliantly scathing essay on Singapore which is reprinted in his collection of autobiographical pieces, *Sunrise with Seamonsters* (1985).

Photo Credits

All photos are by Alain Evrard with the exception of those listed below:

Jill Gocher: pages 10, 14, 15, 16, 17, 19, 20 23 (top and bottom), 24, 25, 26, 29, 30, 31, 32 (top and bottom), 33, 34, 35, 36, 37, 38, 39, 40, 41, 44, 46, 47, 48 (top and bottom), 50 (top), 51, 54, 55, 85, 89, 91, 94, 95, 122, 125, 147, 148, 149, 159, 161, 170, 171, 173, 174, 179, 180, 189, 198, 212, 214, 225, 241.

Fiona Nichols: pages 13, 18, 21, 27, 42 (top and bottom), 43, 45, 49, 50 (bottom), 53, 57 (top and bottom), 68, 99, 120, 206, 213, 215, 230.

Quick Reference A–Z Guide
to Places and Topics of Interest with Listed Accommodation, Restaurants and Useful Telephone Numbers